Praise for *Organize &*

"Justin Klosky has cracked the code on teaching organizational skills to everyone. His book is not only the perfect reference guide for people who need assistance getting organized, but also has plenty of useful tips for those who consider themselves organized. His approach works because he starts with honesty and compassion, sharing his own personal story. . . . This book is a great reference guide for professional organizers and a great gift for your clients." —*NAPO (NATIONAL ASSOCIATION FOR PROFESSIONAL ORGANIZERS) NEWS*

"If there was ever a 'go-to guide' for organization, this would be it. . . . The advice is fabulous, but it's laid out in a way that is so easy for reference. . . . It's an 'as needed' book, always there and promising to help when you need it the most, whenever that is." —*THE SPENCER DAILY NEWS*

"*Organize & Create Discipline* is a great blueprint for getting your home and your life order. From A to Z, Justin has nailed it!"

—**PETER WALSH,** CLUTTER EXPERT AND BESTSELLING AUTHOR OF
LIGHTEN UP: LOVE WHAT YOU HAVE, HAVE WHAT YOU NEED, BE HAPPIER WITH LESS

"As an expert on the potential clutter of a makeup drawer, I can confirm Justin's book knows how to effectively handle that chaos as well as many other organizational danger zones. What I love most about the O.C.D. system is that it not only tells you how to organize, but also how to avoid the mess in the first place. Genius!" —**HAYLEY BARNA,** CO-FOUNDER, BIRCHBOX

"Justin organized my life, so it's a thrill to find out just how he organized his own. He knows of what he speaks. Listen to this man!"

—**PAUL FEIG,** WRITER, PRODUCER, DIRECTOR OF
BRIDESMAIDS, AND CREATOR OF *FREAKS AND GEEKS*

"Justin is an organization expert with a passion for helping people live clutter free. Organize, Create, Discipline, now that's my style! I'm a Packer, not a 'pack rat!'" —**RYAN PICKETT,** NOSE TACKLE, GREEN BAY PACKERS

"O.C.D. is a friendly, personal service that really helps you get settled into a new town. Thank you O.C.D."
—**ED WESTWICK**, ACTOR

"Justin has trained me not only to happily live with less, but how to live an organized lifestyle."
—**SUZANNE JOHNSON**, SENIOR EXECUTIVE VICE PRESIDENT, SAKS FIFTH AVENUE

"Justin's talent and passion for organizing is unparalleled. He literally makes life easier for you! He was born to help us organize!"
—**JULIE CHEN**, TV PERSONALITY, NEWS ANCHOR, AND PRODUCER

"Thank GOD all his nonsense growing up turned into something useful."
—**ABBIE KLOSKY**, JUSTIN'S MOM

"*O.C.D.* is the most comprehensive, easy-to-navigate self-help book you'll find."
—**JESSICA RADLOFF**, ENTERTAINMENT JOURNALIST

"Justin's incredible story is compelling and unique. He's turned a deficit into a strength and has become an invaluable asset at Apartment Therapy. Run, don't walk, to read this book."
—**MAXWELL RYAN**, FOUNDER, APARTMENT THERAPY

"This book is hard to read—because every page will inspire you to set it down and go fix up another part of your life."
—**JASON FEIFER**, SENIOR EDITOR, *FAST COMPANY*

"It's choose-your-own-adventure for organization."
—**ASHLEY PARRISH**, EDITOR-IN-CHIEF, DAILYCANDY

ORGANIZE

&

CREATE

DISCIPLINE

ORGANIZE

&

CREATE

DISCIPLINE

JUSTIN KLOSKY

AVERY
A member of Penguin Group (USA)
New York

Published by the Penguin Group
Penguin Group (USA) LLC
375 Hudson Street
New York, New York 10014

USA · Canada · UK · Ireland · Australia
New Zealand · India · South Africa · China

penguin.com
A Penguin Random House Company

First trade paperback edition 2014
Copyright © 2013 by Justin Klosky

Most Avery books are available at special quantity discounts for bulk purchase for sales promotions,
premiums, fund-raising, and educational needs. Special books or book excerpts also can be
created to fit specific needs. For details, write: Special.Markets@us.penguingroup.com.

The Library of Congress has catalogued the hardcover edition as follows:

Klosky, Justin.
Organize & create discipline : an A-to-Z guide to an organized existence / Justin Klosky.
p.   cm.
ISBN 978-1-58333-529-1
1. Storage in the home.   2. Organization.   3. Orderliness.   4. Obsessive-compulsive disorder.
I. Title.
TX309.K56   2013   2013029137
648'. 8—dc23

ISBN 978-1-58333-552-9 (paperback)

Printed in the United States of America
1   3   5   7   9   10   8   6   4   2

BOOK DESIGN BY TANYA MAIBORODA

CONTENTS

AN A-TO-Z GUIDE TO
AN ORGANIZED EXISTENCE

FOREWORD

by Bryce Dallas Howard

AS FAR BACK AS I CAN REMEMBER, I HAVE ALWAYS HAD A DESIRE to be organized, which does not mean that I actually *was* organized. I was pretty structured in my schoolwork and professional life, never quite what I would aspire to, but I was at least maintaining some semblance of order. However, in my personal life and at home, it was a completely different story. I was a disaster! My bed and floors were covered with all the things I needed to do, put away, return, read, work on, add to my hobby list, or sort through, all in the form of piles I convinced myself were an "organized chaos." I won't even describe what my car looked like!

In my preteen years, the chaos of my room was a constant source of friction between my parents and me. Finally, as a punishment, they took EVERYTHING out of my room other than my books and furniture. It was a massive relief (not the response my parents expected), and for a time I lived monastically: reading, writing, and feeling the freedom of my space without suffocating underneath the heaps of my own clutter. My parents eventually brought my items back from storage, hoping I had learned my lesson, but what I actually learned was that I needed to figure out how to manage all the stuff in my life, and I genuinely didn't know how.

I became obsessed with learning about organization. I would read books about it. I would pick up magazines that promised to reveal the latest tips and techniques. I would regularly visit the Container Store and Staples, simply browsing the newest appliances and shelving units and systems for filing. Unfortunately, this desire to learn about organization didn't translate into any discipline I could sustain. Like a chronic dieter who would try the newest fad and then promptly gain all of the weight back and more, I would binge and purge with organization. I would passionately apply the techniques I read about, giving 100 percent of my focus to organizing everything around me according to the prescribed set of rules. At first, my space would look fantastic and I would be so excited about the new leaf I had turned over. But then a day, two days, a week would go by and things would eventually fall apart again. I would inevitably feel more discouraged than when I started. I was a habitual yo-yo organizer.

As one can imagine, this behavior was a source of subtle and ongoing stress. I had the desire to change, I thought I was applying the techniques necessary to change, and yet things weren't changing. Inevitably, twenty-four hours after any exhaustive overhaul I completed, I would get caught up in life again. My environment would begin to reflect an ongoing internal disconnect that I was never fully aware of. I had not yet made the connection that none of the pretty organizational containers, lists, or rules would make a dent in my disorganized life if I didn't do the work of figuring out WHY I was so disorganized in the first place.

This yo-yo pattern continued until a few years ago, when I finally asked the right person for help. Justin Klosky, a dear and longtime friend from NYU, offered to help me set up a nursery for my son. What I initially thought was going to be typical "guy friend" support, with assembling shelves and hauling heavy trash outside, became the most precise and incredible display of organizational mastery I had ever witnessed. What was most remarkable was that it stuck! While the rest of the house would ebb and flow between impeccable and disaster, the nursery remained constant. Somehow Justin tapped into my psychology and created an easy-to-follow system that I could—shocker—maintain! I was hooked, but there was one problem: Justin wasn't yet a professional organizer, and I didn't want to strain our relationship by harassing him for advice every time my environment spiraled out of control. So when I heard that Justin had taken steps to launch a company focused on offering professional organizational support to individual clients, I was elated.

Awesomely, Justin started his business around the same time I was about to move to a new home. Neither my husband nor I could be present for the move, as I was shooting *The Help* in Mississippi and he was shooting a TV series in Canada. I knew that Justin could handle everything with ease, but there was one catch: we were moving into a home that was less than half the size of our current one and we had a lot of stuff. And I mean A LOT. We were downsizing drastically, and I was essentially unavailable to decide what should stay and what should go. This meant the task fell to Justin. Part of me felt awful for dumping that kind of responsibility on my friend, but I also remembered the peace I felt during that period in my childhood when my parents had removed everything from my room. While I did not yet have the confidence that I could maintain it, I was excited by the notion of moving into a house completely set up by Justin. Knowing him so well, I had high expectations, but I could never have predicted what happened next.

I call what he did "the greatest hits." Justin intuited what should stay and what should go based on knowing not only my family's tendencies but also human nature. What resulted was a space that represented the best version of myself and my family, organized in a way that we uniquely understood. He figured out the complexities of our family and all the aspects of our lives, and applied this wisdom to how he designed our newly organized space.

When I was finally done with shooting, Justin spent quite a bit of time with us, empowering each of us to take charge of our home so that we could maintain the structure he had created for us. He helped us get in touch with why we wanted to be organized in the first place. Realizations began to dawn on me as to why certain things had worked for me in the past and others hadn't. He taught me to be honest with myself by acknowledging my habits and my tendencies, embracing them all. There was tremendous self-discovery in this process, and from there, true, honest, and lasting structure finally emerged.

Because we were downsizing, Justin helped us realistically decide what was an asset and what was a liability. And when I say "liability," I'm referring to the objects, habits, and systems that were roadblocks in the path toward organization. He created simple systems that I could maintain myself, systems that I could make a daily routine of.

But the most beautiful thing he did was take it upon himself to come over to our house several times in order to spend time with our son, Theo (who was three years old at the time). Justin patiently taught him how to maintain his own room and play area, engaged him in learning how to put away his own toys, and inspired him to keep order and cleanliness in his life. To this day, Theo (who is almost six now) offers to help clean up when things get disorderly and makes sure that things are put back in their place after being used. He actually gets excited about keeping our house organized! I am so grateful that my son learned in just a handful of sessions what took me twenty-some years to figure out.

When we become aware of the fact that the space around us directly reflects what we experience inside ourselves, we realize the opportunity we have to transform ourselves by transforming the environment around us.

Organization is truly a lifestyle choice. It is something that can begin at any age and any stage in life. It does not hold your past against you and does not care about what organizational tools you can afford or how pretty or stylish they are. It only asks you to be honest with yourself and consistent with your purpose.

As you read this book, I encourage you to look deep within yourself and connect to your desire to make lasting changes to create an environment that reflects and represents your innermost strengths and values. Embrace the things that work for you, be honest about the things that don't, and be open to finding new ways of approaching tasks or problems.

I hope that just as Justin guided me, this book will guide you toward the discipline to organize, so that you can create . . . create whatever you imagine to be possible and manifest it into your reality. Happy organizing!

A NOTE FROM
ARTHUR GRADSTEIN

■ ■ ■

I AM NOT A PROFESSIONAL ORGANIZER. FAR FROM IT. IN FACT, BEFORE helping my good friend Justin write this book, I knew nothing about organization and my life reflected it. I used the "pile it up" system on my desk. I used the "just stick it in the garage" system for storing stuff I didn't want to deal with. When I would open my tool cabinet, random hardware would come snowballing out because I had just carelessly tossed it in there. For events and appointments, I just assumed that I'd remember them all in my head. My wife can tell you how effective that was.

I am a writer, and my job was to help Justin capture his real-life voice and in-person enthusiasm in the pages of this book. We wanted to present his information in a way that would be simple, fun to read, inspiring, and empowering, with truth and heart. Those aren't the adjectives one would normally use to describe a book about organization, so I wasn't sure we'd succeed. I'll be honest: when we started writing, I had no intention of making any changes to my life. I was resistant to Justin's organizational advice. Skeptical even.

I know this book will change your life because I am a walking testimonial.

Organization is addictive. For me, it infiltrated my home by way of my tool cabinet. Fed up that I could never find the right screwdriver or tape measure when I needed it, I finally decided to follow the advice Justin and I had just written in the Tools entry of the book. I marveled when I looked at my newly organized tool cabinet. Never again would I feel the anxiety of needing a tool and knowing I'd have to deal with the chaotic experience of finding it. The sense of lightness was so refreshing that I couldn't stop. From there, I applied the O.C.D. system in my office, my closet, my garage, my car, and my calendar. Suddenly I could see my desk, know what clothes I had, park in my garage, put an actual cup in my car's cup holder, and not forget important dates with my wife! And I've been able to maintain those systems to this day.

Organize & Create Discipline doesn't just offer a way to deal with the clutter in your home or office. It's a way for you to make peace and find balance with your belongings, to have a healthy relationship with your space, to become the master of your time, and to live and work in an environment that is calming, inspiring, and free from chaos. You won't believe how much embracing the O.C.D. Way will change your sense of well-being until you dive in. I'm glad I did.

ORGANIZE

&

CREATE

DISCIPLINE

INTRODUCTION

■ ▪ ▪ ■

ONE DAY, WHEN I WAS SEVEN, I WAS SITTING BY MYSELF IN OUR screened-in patio. Suddenly, I became fixated on the screen door, unable to look away. I was hypnotized by the tiny mesh holes that gave the screen door its balance and functionality. I began to count methodically as time slowed down around me. Not satisfied by the door alone, I moved on to the next mesh panel, and then the next, counting every tiny hole around the entire patio. Following patterns, seeing shapes and depth, I couldn't stop until my task was complete, propelled by some unexplainable urge. And the weird thing—I was having a blast. I was in flow. It wasn't until I shared my great new activity with friends (much to my ridicule) that I realized I was different, that I suffered from obsessive-compulsive disorder, or OCD, and attention deficit/ hyperactivity disorder, or ADHD.

I wish I had known at the time that my condition would eventually lead not just to a career but to a philosophy and mind-set. Being unusual and different is a scarlet letter in the world of child social politics, so perhaps knowing where it would lead me would have offered some solace. Nerds never have it easy growing up, and being unique only becomes cool when you get older. What I did know then was that I had to make a choice: be taken over by my obsessions and compulsions or embrace them and take control.

To this day, I am still constantly assessing patterns, habits, systems, flaws, and the functionality of everything around me. But now I do it for a very intentional purpose: to help others create organization and efficiency. I've channeled my eccentricities into a system that not only helps me maintain control and balance of my own life, but has helped individuals and multinational corporations alike take back control from the growing mass of goods and information that has become a part of our everyday lives. I'm transforming the stigma associated with OCD and creating a new acronym for it: Organize & Create Discipline.

Thus, my company, the O.C.D. Experience, was born, changing the way people think about organization one space at a time. From friends such as Bryce Dallas Howard, Julie Chen, Topher Grace, and Sharon and Jack Osbourne; companies like Saks Fifth Avenue, Pfizer Pharmaceuticals, NBC, and PricewaterhouseCoopers; to schoolteachers, store owners, athletes, and families, the O.C.D. Experience is streamlining and improving people's lives and the lives of those around them.

Now, your entire life is about to get organized. Seriously. In the pages that follow, all your organizational doubts, worries, and stress will disappear, and you will realize the profound effects that organization has not only on your outlook but in every aspect of your life. You'll have a newfound power in knowing when and where everything is the moment you need it. That is what O.C.D. brings to you: the ability to simplify so you can function at your best.

PART I: THE EVOLUTION OF O.C.D.

Life isn't easy. That's why it's so important that the things you surround yourself with help you in the tough times instead of exacerbating them. Imagine if you were in a sinking ship. You look around and see thousands of items floating in the water. How can you possibly find those things that will save you? You'd only want to see the most important things that could truly help you at that moment and nothing else. So too should be the items in your life, all the time. Get rid of the chaos and bring clarity to life. That is what I want to show you how to accomplish: clarity as I discovered it through my OCD filter, streamlined in the O.C.D. Way.

If you scrutinize everything and everyone, like I do, you might be asking yourself, "Why Justin Klosky and O.C.D.? I saw some other organization guy on *Dr. Phil* who told me to put my socks in a wicker basket." Well, we'll get to where to put your socks later, and a lot more. But first, if you understand my background and the evolution of O.C.D., you'll understand the superiority of the O.C.D. Experience and how, because of my neurosis and obsessions, it's the most efficient, effective, and evergreen system out there for transforming your life.

Obsessive-Compulsive Disorder

Before I get into my experience with OCD, I want to make something clear: this is a book about organizing your life. It's not a book about obsessive-compulsive disorder, nor am I making a statement about how to treat OCD. OCD can be a debilitating condition and can manifest itself in many different ways. Thus, everyone's experience with OCD and its severity is different. My OCD manifests as a compulsion to organize, arrange, and count, which I've been lucky enough to be able to direct and focus into a positive. Not everyone is so fortunate. OCD can also prompt compulsions to carry out repetitive tasks, hoarding, obsessive washing and cleaning for fear of contamination, checking things repeatedly out of fear of them doing harm, or not being able to control unwanted and disturbing thoughts. If you or someone you know has OCD and is suffering, please get help. I would like my story to serve as inspiration that OCD can be conquered, but it is a very complicated condition and most often requires professional help. Even I seek therapy on a consistent basis to manage some of the more difficult challenges.

A Wild Childhood

Discovering the O.C.D. Way wasn't easy. Growing up, my OCD constantly had me distracted, upset, and feeling alone. I couldn't resist analyzing and categorizing everything around me, but at the same time it was overwhelmingly embarrassing—an inescapable burden. It started early because I had to deal with a situation no child should have to deal with. I was abused, a similarity among many sufferers of obsessive-compulsive disorder.

I enjoyed performing at an early age and even won second place in a kindergarten talent show, singing "Chim-Chim-Cher-ee" from *Mary Poppins*. A year later, I started acting and singing professionally, starting with the role of Tiny Tim in *A Christmas Carol* at Burt Reynolds's Jupiter Theatre. To improve my craft, I remember begging my mom to buy me a guitar and to sign me up for guitar lessons. We went out, bought an awesome black electric guitar, and found a school to teach me how to play it. Around my third or fourth lesson, my teacher asked me if he could help show me the right way to hold my guitar. He sat down next to me. Before I knew it, his hands were slowly moving toward my groin. I remember not knowing what to do or how to react. After the lesson, I told my mother, who immediately told the manager. The instructor was fired, but the guitar was ruined for me. Every time I picked it up, it was a reminder of what had happened.

Having a supportive, loving, and incredible family was a great help, but we all have our path and mine was greatly and permanently disrupted. My OCD became inflamed, perhaps in an attempt to take control wherever I could get it. And so I organized anything and everything. Unfortunately, it seemed that I was a magnet for abuse.

When I was ten, I landed my first acting manager. He, my mom, and I all flew out to Los Angeles to audition for movies. I booked a part at my very first audition for the film *All I Want for Christmas*. We all celebrated, but unfortunately the celebration was very short-lived. My mother, a schoolteacher, had to return to Florida for the start of the school year, while my manager and I stayed in Los Angeles at his sister's house to shoot the film and continue auditioning. One night, he called me into his room where I found him sitting naked. He decided to take it upon himself to teach me how to masturbate. The experience was so disturbing that I repressed the memory. It wasn't until one night years later, while attending NYU, that I had a few too many drinks and suddenly the memory came flooding back. In hindsight, I realize the experience sent my OCD further into a tailspin and also started my years-long battle with sex addiction, another obstacle many people with OCD face. Immediately after wrapping the film and returning to Florida, and for years to follow, I aggressively pursued any and every girl I came across, embarrassing myself and emotionally hurting many of them in the process.

I'm sharing these experiences for two reasons: First, I want those who have been abused and/or have OCD to know they are not alone and don't have to suffer silently. Second, I want to stress that if the O.C.D. system can help me find peace and clarity in my life, it can help you find it in yours. It helped me regain control of my destructive habits. I know it's hard to think of organizing as being destructive, but when you let it grow into an obsession and distraction, which is what happened to me as a child and adolescent, that's exactly what it becomes.

I organized my stuffed animal collection by height, from tallest to shortest, and if someone moved them, I'd get very upset. Every night, I would set out the next day's clothes, which absolutely had to be Z. Cavaricci pants and a matching T-shirt, in the shape of a body on the floor, as if someone had laid down, then vanished, leaving their outfit behind. I would meticulously pack my backpack with color-coded folders; English was always purple thanks to a suggestion from a teacher who may have had OCD herself. When I began prepping for my acting work, I would highlight every one of my lines perfectly—flawless blocks of yellow that were even, level, and centered. If I did make an error, I'd ask if my mom could replace that page for me so I could rehighlight it correctly. I vacuumed every weekend and made sure that the lines in my carpet were evenly spaced and perfectly parallel. I would even WD-40 my Formica furniture because it shone so nicely. And these are just a few examples of what life was like for me in my youth. With no therapy or medication, I had almost no control over my compulsions. For the longest time, I thought nothing good could come of my affliction. But when I was ten years old, I had an experience that would plant the seed that my OCD could actually be helpful.

My parents were far from organized people. Though they loved each other deeply, and still do, like most couples they frequently fought with each other over disorganization. My mom would constantly misplace her jewelry and blame my dad for moving it. Or my dad would forget where he put his bills and claim my mom had them last. The end result was always an unnecessary yelling match. So when my parents left me and my brother at home to go on a vacation to Egypt, I did what every kid would do: I cleaned and organized the entire house. I picked apart cabinets, closets, bathrooms, the garage, and even my parents' bedroom, moving every item to the most appropriate place based on my observations of how the family actually used them.

My grandmother, who was babysitting, cheered me on. Years later, we dubbed it the "What the Fu*k Did You Let Him Do" project, and she gets executive producer credit for letting a ten-year-old indulge his organizational instincts and ransack the house. I assure you, going through my parents' belongings quickly taught me that we all have things we hide and not to judge. I learned that I shouldn't have decided to prematurely "inherit" my father's coin collection and baseball cards, a decision he wouldn't be happy about later on. I also learned that I shouldn't have tested the mace I found in my father's sock drawer on my younger brother. I had to do a sympathy spray in my own face to make him feel better.

But as we sat there on the floor of my parents' room crying, I surveyed the newly organized room. Despite my searing face pain, and my guilt over harming my brother, I was giddy with the idea that my parents would return home delighted with me and wouldn't fight anymore. In that mace-induced moment of clarity, I realized that perhaps some of my OCD tendencies could actually be useful. Although my parents were initially pretty pissed off to find all of their belongings relocated and reorganized upon their return, their anger quickly gave way to pleasant surprise when they found that everything had been staged intuitively and effectively. If they couldn't find something, they knew to ask me instead of badgering each other. I, of course, always knew exactly where everything was. I can't say my parents never fought again, as all parents argue about things from time to time, but they did stop fighting about jewelry and bills, and that was enough for me to realize my newfound potential. It also taught me the value of feeling in control of my environment and the possessions in my environment.

I knew I couldn't suppress my urges, but that was the first time I realized I could transform them to be socially acceptable and actually helpful. I was still far from in control, though. In middle school and high school, I would get angry at my teachers when they didn't write neatly on my homework or report cards. I acted out compulsively, so I often found myself in trouble and would get thrown out of class. Luckily, my teachers still liked me because of my good grades and couldn't help but respect my strength and determination, but they still had to maintain their own control of the classroom. But it was from that point on that I began a years-long process of trial and error and social feedback to be able to separate my OCD urges into two categories: productive and positive versus arbitrary and negative.

Counting all the holes in my patio screens was arbitrary and negative. It helped no one and achieved nothing other than satisfying my unhealthy desire to accomplish the task. But reorganizing my parents' house was positive and productive. It made their lives better. Instead of incredulous stares and ridicule, I was met with gratitude. So I started acting on the positive urges and suppressing the negative ones as much as I could. I began to take control of my OCD and, instead of burdening myself and others with my affliction, I tried to give back something useful.

The College Years

I was forced to further hone my skills when I moved to New York to attend NYU. I was assigned to live in a dorm room with two other people. Imagine it: an OCD loon sharing a tiny room with two normal, messy college students. At first, it was a disaster. Without permission, while my roommates were in class, I would reorganize their desks, mop the floors, and clean the bathroom. I satisfied my needs without considering theirs. They were pretty upset that I had violated their space. I learned that I'd have to work with people to organize their space, understand their habits, and, most important, get them to understand their own processes instead of simply ambush-organizing their possessions. After I learned to respect my roommates' boundaries and they learned to respect my need for order, we reached an agreement where I'd keep their spaces clean and organized, but in the way they needed.

It became a win-win situation. I satisfied my urges, and my roommates had a free maid. I learned that everyone is different and that although my instincts made sense to me, organization needed to be specific to the person. I also realized that it isn't always easy for people to change their habits. At the age of eighteen, I was beginning to understand how important it was to involve people in the reorganization of their belongings with patience, understanding, and compassion, and that they needed to be taught strong organizational discipline. I began to understand people's psychology when it came to their possessions, which helped me gain greater control of my own psychology. At the very core, our relationship with our belongings is about security. People experience a sense of power and control of their lives in keeping possessions, and anxiety in getting rid of them, just like I experienced power and control by compulsively organizing and cleaning. But those feelings are just an illusion that must be shattered with healthy balance. That is true security. To this day, I am still best friends with my college roommates, and we still laugh over some of the stories from our time living together.

While at NYU, I was studying to become an actor. So to further that goal, I took an internship at a prestigious New York talent agency (which translates to working in the mailroom). I made it my job to transform that poor excuse of a mailroom into something organized and beautiful. Everyone at the agency took notice and put me to work reorganizing their offices. My efforts even won me a job, as I jumped from mailroom to office manager and then eventually serving as the assistant to the president of the agency. The owner even offered me a position as an agent, but that wasn't the path I wanted to take. Before I knew it, I not only had representation as an actor and helped my friends get representation, but I earned massive respect from the entire agency for my organizational skills.

I created a methodology for everything in the office: systems for incoming scripts, updating of résumés, client files, and ordering supplies, among other tasks. I also made sure to teach everyone how it all worked so it would be maintained when I was away on auditions or at class. I created manuals and one-sheets for people to follow when I was at school and procedures for when the phone system or computers went down so there wouldn't be a panic. Several agents suggested that I do this for a living once they saw the results of my work. Without realizing it, my OCD was morphing into its new moniker, O.C.D.: Organize & Create Discipline. But I didn't have a chance to take their suggestions seriously because soon after graduating NYU, I landed a role on CBS's daytime drama *Guiding Light*.

Though my O.C.D. career was on hold before it ever began, I continued to help the people around me and I managed to tackle my most challenging transformation yet. While shooting *Guiding Light*, I was sharing an incredibly beautiful penthouse apartment near Wall Street with one of my best female friends. The only problem was that she had grown up with a mother who was a hoarder, and unfortunately, she had inherited some of those characteristics. But she was respectful enough to keep the mess to her room, behind closed doors. When I say "mess," I mean piles of stuff everywhere, five layers deep, with not a thing in order or an inch of floor visible. She called it organized chaos. I just called it chaos.

Up to this point, I had only helped the average, disorganized person. But she was on a whole other level. When we finally organized her room, she broke down crying, not because her stuff was gone, but because by taking the mess she was hiding behind and organizing it, I made her face herself and her issues. We learned powerful things throughout the process together: never underestimate the power of a pile or getting rid of it. Most people create piles for specific reasons that need to be addressed before those piles can disappear. We also learned that in order for change to occur, someone must want it to. We were both forever changed and I realized that organization could be a liberating psychological tool. By going through your physical stuff, you are often forced to deal with your emotional stuff. Organization doesn't just rehabilitate a space; it can also be powerful therapy for rehabilitating your mind.

OCD Becomes O.C.D.

After *Guiding Light* came to an end for me, I decided to take some time away from acting and move to Los Angeles. I needed a job, so I applied to be Benny Medina's executive assistant at Handprint Entertainment and was hired. Once again doing my thing, I quickly and efficiently organized Benny's work life according to his needs and habits. I consolidated e-mails, scanned papers, and turned the office into a well-oiled machine. Months after I left, some of his assistants called me to ask about my process and how to keep it organized.

Word spread of my abilities, and I eventually starting getting work as an organizer to friends and their families. My dear friends Bryce Dallas Howard and her husband, Seth Gabel, gave me my first real project as a professional organizer. They asked me to get their home organized for the addition of their newborn son, Theo. I helped them overhaul their entire house—allocating spaces, organizing, and simplifying—so they could devote all their attention to their son and not to their stuff. They were so impressed with my work, they referred me to their friend Topher Grace.

I got a call from Topher to work on a private project on the East Coast. I began realizing how important trust and discretion were when working with people who valued their privacy. I wasn't just being hired for my organizational skills but also for my ability to be discreet and nonjudgmental while creating solid systems for organization and teaching the discipline to maintain it. My work helped my clients and their families find structure in their lives, allowing them to focus on their careers instead of the minutiae that had previously bogged them down.

With the momentum I had growing, it was the obvious time to turn my abilities into a full-time career—to take everything that I had learned, developed, and structured in my life and make a business out of it for others. It was time to launch O.C.D.—Organize & Create Discipline. There was just one problem: I knew nothing about starting a business.

The Early Stages of O.C.D.

I had a vision—and luckily some very supportive friends who believed in me. They helped me launch a Web site and lent me their creative expertise, legal know-how, and business savvy. I sat down with my friend Jordan Roth to evaluate my proposed Web site and business plan. He took his time to give me suggestions and corrections, and he pointed me in the right direction to get my business off the ground. Another close friend, Alex Lorenz, created the O.C.D. logo in exchange for letting him stay with me in L.A. for a few weeks. Thank God he did because my original logo would have been laughed at. I'm an organizer, not an artist, although organization is its own art form. But I could never have imagined how quickly O.C.D. would grow.

I knew that very few people had ever heard of professional organization. Nevertheless, O.C.D. took off in Los Angeles, and it wasn't long before O.C.D. was even bicoastal! When my cousin Andrea Saper back in New York heard I had finally started a business, she demanded that I offer my services to her inner circle of friends and family who helped spread the word. I began working with Fortune 500 companies and very influential New Yorkers. I was an organizational jet-setter, trotting back and forth between New York and Los Angeles. It was hectic but rewarding. And the opportunities kept coming: I searched out Oprah Winfrey's organizer, Peter Walsh, and after a little persistence he offered me a job. I helped him and his team and was also part of his television show on OWN. As wonderful as professional success is, it's nothing compared to the satisfaction that I get sharing Organize & Create Discipline and helping people change their lives.

O.C.D. Today and in the Future

At the time of this writing, O.C.D. has been helping people organize and better their lives for six years. We have O.C.D. Team Members in New York, Los Angeles, and Miami helping to spread the O.C.D. Experience. And the brand keeps growing. We recently launched O.C.D. Events (Original & Creatively Designed Events) and are developing other arms of the O.C.D. Experience. We've branded an exciting deal with Saks Fifth Avenue, partnered with the Container Store, been featured on *Anderson Cooper,* served as the organizational expert on *The Talk*, and have worked with various production companies, including Nigel Lythgoe Productions (*American Idol*, *So You Think You Can Dance*, *Opening Act* on E!) and Kelly Ripa and Mark Consuelos's Milojo Productions, to develop new original television projects.

For me, the O.C.D. Experience is a journey, the conquest of an illness, and a transformation into something meaningful. It also represents me taking back power and control from those who tried to rob me of it in my past. I never dreamed that counting holes in a patio screen would eventually lead me to a career, and with it the power to show people that everything can be made a little easier with thoughtful organization.

PART II: ORGANIZE & CREATE DISCIPLINE

The Benefits of an Organized Life

Life is one big set of attachments. Some of them are meaningful. Most are not. But these meaningless or misplaced attachments are just distractions. If you can purge your life of these, not only will you have more time, energy, and space to focus on and feature what truly matters, you'll also feel a sense of clarity and freedom. Imagine the power you'll have in knowing when and where everything is in a split second.

That is the ultimate task of O.C.D.: getting clients open to the idea of letting things go that are holding them back from operating at their best. We help clients filter out what they really need in order to be more productive and bring fresh energy into their lives, making space for new opportunities, both spatially and on the calendar.

There are other professional organizers out there, but they don't have my unique background. I know that there is no quick fix and no easy answer to getting organized. Anyone who says otherwise is a salesman. I understand organization from life experience, and I know that every individual needs his or her own solution. So don't put your socks in that wicker basket just yet.

I've guided dozens of companies and hundreds of individuals through the O.C.D. Experience. I know what works and what doesn't, what's sustainable and what isn't, and how to get the most out of new technologies. My clients can rest assured that the organization I create will improve their quality of life, profitability, and success for the long term *if* they have the discipline to maintain it and live it the O.C.D. Way.

The problem is that human cloning is still illegal and there isn't enough of me to go around. That's where this book comes in. In it, I teach you the hard questions to ask in order to determine what will work for you. From there, you can design an organizational system custom-tailored to your life, based on my expertise.

I also teach you how to maintain that system. Unlike other professional organization companies and books, we don't just show up, make things look nice, or tell you where to put things, then leave you to admire the pretty picture until the tornado of life hits.

Organization is nothing without discipline, so we show you the tricks to maintain your newly organized life. If discipline were easy, I wouldn't have a growing business. Thanks to the increasingly noisy landscape, our everyday lives are overwhelmingly cluttered. Now we even need to organize our digital selves with the growing number of social media sites out there! People need help. O.C.D. is here for you.

The O.C.D. Way

You know how it evolved. You know what it can do. So what is the O.C.D. Way?

Think about the difference between going to the gym with a personal trainer and going on your own. Creating your exercise routine and staying on top of it would be much harder without that extra support. Think of the O.C.D. Way as your personal trainer for organization.

First, I help you tackle the hard questions: How is this attachment best used? Where should it be stored? How often will it be accessed? What determines a necessity? What adds functionality to your life or business? What distracts you from being productive? How can I take control of this space?

Simply put, the O.C.D. system is a set of field-tested questions that assist you in making choices when reclaiming a disorganized space. I help you determine the appropriate action to take once those choices have been made, I show you how to create organized systems that work for you, and, finally, I share the tools to help you to maintain your accomplishments. That is the greatest difference between the O.C.D. Way and other professional organizers' systems. I don't just tell you where to put things. I teach you the philosophy and process behind my organizational techniques and the discipline to maintain your organization, which means that you can apply it to any area in your life in a way that works for you.

Although comprehensive, this book can't possibly cover it all, but you'll know how to organize what it doesn't cover. The O.C.D. Way is an evergreen process: as technology changes, spaces grow or shrink, new products are available for sale, and trends change, you'll still be able to use the O.C.D. Way to stay organized while other systems will become obsolete. Organize & Create Discipline isn't just another professional organizational service but a way of life.

The O.C.D. Way can be broken down into a three-step process that can be applied to any space:

O—ORGANIZE

OBSERVE YOUR ATTACHMENTS

Organization the O.C.D. Way, as presented in the A-to-Z Guide, isn't just physically organizing your belongings and attachments, it's identifying what you truly need in your life to make you more productive. Whether electronically, physically, or emotionally, take the time to go through your entire life, one room, drawer, closet, or electronic document at a time and assess the contents that surround and affect you. Ask yourself: Why do I have this? What purpose does this serve in my life? What opportunities am I sacrificing by keeping it? Is there a better place for it? What should this space really be used for? There are no wrong answers! Once you determine the value of each attachment and space, you can begin to prioritize, and then organize.

In real terms, this is the step in which you'll pull everything out of a space you are trying to organize. Once you've laid everything out in front of you, it's easy to see what you have. A puzzle is completed faster when you can see all the pieces you have to work with. It is the same thing when it comes to organizing. Get rid of the obvious trash and anything you don't need or use in your life now. You'll begin to sort and group similar items and get rid of anything you have an excess of. Now, based on what you have left, you'll define a purpose for the space and only return the items to that space that fit that purpose. Anything else has to find a new home.

C—CREATE

CREATE ORGANIZED SYSTEMS

You've already determined that you need certain belongings. Now it's time to create systems to store and process them, systems that can effectively and efficiently be a part of your life or business and daily routine. Ask yourself how you can best use this space for its newly defined purpose. This may mean investing in new hardware, equipment, bins, furniture, or whatever else is necessary to provide you with the framework to keep your newly sorted possessions and systems in an organized, efficient, and accessible way. It may mean repurposing and modifying other existing spaces. It may mean going digital. The A-to-Z Guide helps you make these choices and embrace the newest digital technologies, and gives you step-by-step instructions, item by item, topic by topic, in an easy-to-read format.

D—DISCIPLINE

DEDICATION THROUGH DISCIPLINE

Now you've purged yourself of superfluous possessions. And you've created organized systems for what you've kept. But how will you maintain that organization? Discipline. Discipline is a practice, and practicing the methods in the A-to-Z Guide will lead you to a clearer mind and a better life. What good is getting organized if you don't stay organized? Without discipline, you can't form habits, and forming solid habits is the key to maintaining organization. The A-to-Z Guide provides instructions on how to maintain your organization and offers real-life examples, inviting readers to draw conclusions from their own lives.

A Note on Going Digital

You'll notice throughout the book that many of my organizational solutions are digital in nature. I make these recommendations unapologetically. Part of the O.C.D. Way is embracing the newest technologies, and you must get with the times. I know it can be scary, but I can't in good conscience suggest methods that are antiquated and obsolete, because they won't be the most efficient. That does you a disservice and already starts you a step behind. That being said, let's get you up to speed on some of the more important basic terminology.

Scanner: It's just like a copy machine, but instead of printing out a copy, it saves it to your computer as a digital file. Your scanner will become your best friend. You'll use it often and it will virtually eliminate paper from your life. Once you have something scanned, saved, and organized digitally, you can ditch the hard copy because you'll always be able to reference the digital file if you need it, or even print it out. Don't worry: you'll still get to keep some important paper, but you'll come close to being completely paperless! My personal favorite scanner is the Fujitsu ScanSnap coupled with the Adobe Acrobat scanning program.

PDF: PDF stands for "portable document format." When you scan documents with your scanner, this is the format you should save them as, unless they are photographs, in which case they should be JPEG. I recommend PDF because it's the most universally accepted file format. Anyone on any computer, device, or program should be able to view a PDF file. That way, you'll never run into compatibility issues down the road. PDFs can be a single page or multiple pages and are easy to edit, combine, and share. They can also be password protected if the information is sensitive. Their versatility makes them O.C.D. preferred.

OCR: OCR is an option you can select when you scan documents. It stands for "optical character recognition," which is a fancy way of saying the scanner recognizes the text. Instead of just seeing your document as an image, the scanner will recognize the text and store that information so you can edit, copy, and search the text later on. OCR scanning will give you greater power over your digitally saved documents.

JPEG: Just as the PDF file format is the best for documents because it's universally accepted on any computer and device, JPEG is the best for photographs. It stands for "Joint Photographic Experts Group." Even though the name sounds like a self-help group for photographers, JPEG is the simplest format for storing, sharing, uploading, and editing your digital photos.

Digital Folders: Creating folders and subfolders on your computer is the key to keeping your digital life organized. Throughout the book, I'll make recommendations as to what folders to create and where to keep certain types of files that you save or scan. To make it easy, I've written it like this:

FOLDER → SUBFOLDER → FILE NAME. That tells you exactly what folders to create on your computer, where to put them, and what to name them. For example, if you scan a tax document for 2013, I might suggest you save it in DOCUMENTS → FINANCES → TAXES 2013 → MY EMPLOYER's W2. This means that in your documents folder, you'll have or create a folder called "FINANCES." Within that folder you'll create a folder called "TAXES 2013." You'll scan your W2, name the file "My Employer's W2," and save it in this folder. Don't save files or create folders using all capital letters—we're just using them to demonstrate how to create directories. The point is to make your system self-explanatory, so you always know exactly where to find anything you are looking for.

Backing Up: What good is getting digitally organized if you risk losing all your information? Your digital information is stored on a hard drive. Sometimes hard drives can crash. So you must continually back up, which means making a copy of all your data to a second hard drive, or even uploading it to the cloud. You should install software on your computer that will back everything up for you automatically. Technology might seem complicated if you've never heard of my suggestions, but I assure you that if my mother can manage it, so can YOU!

The Cloud: The cloud is a vague term for any information that you save and store in cyberspace instead of on your local hard drive. The best part about the cloud is that it is constantly connected to the Internet and accessible anywhere with an Internet connection. For example, Apple allows you to keep your music in the cloud, which means your music is actually stored in some giant warehouse somewhere filled with hard drives that you can access anywhere you are connected to the Internet.

Synching: These days, people own multiple computers and devices and want to access their files from all of them. Synching simply means choosing the data you wish to share among your devices and making sure that the latest versions and files exist on each device.

PART III: HOW TO USE THIS BOOK

Navigating through the Guide

Whatever it is you wish to organize, simply look up that topic alphabetically. But a single room in your home may require a vast array of organizational techniques. For example, your kitchen contains cabinets, a pantry, a refrigerator, and a freezer, at the very least. In your cabinets, you'll have pots and pans, dishware, plastic storage containers, and so on. I have suggestions on organizing all of these items, but to try to cover all of these areas and sub-areas in detail under a single topic would be overwhelming and boring! Thus, I've set up this book as a "choose your own adventure" of organization. You'll notice in various entries that certain words are **BOLDED**. That means that a separate entry exists for that specific topic and goes into further detail. So if you are reading about organizing your laundry room, and you see that **CLEANING SUPPLIES** is bolded, you can jump to that section for further advice on organizing and maintaining your cleaning supplies. If you are reading about organizing your living room and see **COFFEE TABLE**, you'll know you can jump to that section for information on keeping your coffee table organized. Instead of always having to actively search for a topic, you can start anywhere and let the book guide you as you improve your general organizational knowledge. Changing your life is an adventure, not a chore, so have fun!

What Are Those Gray Boxes?

After each entry, you may see one of a few different gray boxes. These gray boxes are meant to provide you with additional information, support, or inspiration.

O.C.D. Approved Technology: This gray box will feature a specific product that is an O.C.D. favorite for simplifying and streamlining organization. Usually there are many solutions for a given problem, but we provide you with a tried-and-true product or service that has been used by myself, my friends, my clients, and my team members.

An O.C.D. Success Story: It's nice to share stories that have inspired me to work harder to share solutions that really work. Aside from being inspirational, sometimes it just helps to know how a technique is going to help you in the real world. Having worked with as many clients as I have, I like to share how adopting an O.C.D. technique has actually helped someone change their life for the better, so you know that it can work for you too!

An O.C.D. Summary: Sometimes I have to go into great detail to give you all the specifics for organizing a certain area or your life or home. It's easy to get overwhelmed! So I provide you with a simple summary to motivate you to jump right into the process, broken down into Organize, Create, and Discipline.

O.C.D. Extreme: I always practice what I preach. But I don't always preach everything I practice. That is because I have OCD and I've spent my life separating what's appropriate for me and what's appropriate for everybody else. Nevertheless, if you want to take organization to the O.C.D. Extreme, I provide you with some of my more eccentric organizational habits.

Now turn the page and start improving your life through organizational discipline, the O.C.D. Way!

AN

A-TO-Z GUIDE

TO AN

ORGANIZED

EXISTENCE

Vitamins

Voice Mails

W Walk-In Closets

Wallet

Wardrobe

Watches

Web Site

Wires

Wine

Wives

Working Out

Wrapping

X X-Rays

Y Yard Sale

Yarn

Yoga Equipment

Z Ziplock Bags

A

ACADEMIC PAPERWORK reminds us of the hard work and countless hours we spent improving our minds. If you look back on these **ASSIGN-MENTS** with the same feeling of dread in the pit of your stomach that you had while working on them, trash them! If you are proud of your work and find it meaningful and sentimental, it's fun to save your old essays, report cards, and projects, or your child's, to look back on them. Seeing a teacher's positive comments can be rewarding, inspiring, and reassuring years later when your overly critical boss sends you to the **BATHROOM** crying. But there's no reason to save them all. Choose to save those that have special meaning or that you are most proud of. Scan your work as a PDF, which is viewable by virtually any device in existence, and save it. DOCUMENTS → MEMORABILIA → ACADEMIC PAPERWORK. We'll be using this **MEMORA-BILIA** folder a lot. If you are nostalgic and choose to keep your work the old-fashioned way, which I do *not* recommend, store the paperwork in an airtight and waterproof **BIN** where time and the elements won't ruin your precious memories. Go through the bin once a year to reminisce and to purge paperwork that has lost its significance, so you don't get an overwhelming stack.

O.C.D. APPROVED TECHNOLOGY

You'll notice very quickly as you read through this book that I tell you to *scan almost everything.* If it gets annoying . . . good! Digitization is a cornerstone of Organize & Create Discipline. So when you go out and buy your scanner, look for one that is small, compact, and fast. It should fit on your desk without taking up much space. More important, it must be able to do double-sided scans on a single pass-through and offer batch feeding, meaning that you can load many documents at once and it will automatically go through them. It should be able to save your scans as any format and work with most programs. Don't let your office supply guy talk you into some all-in-one beast machine you don't need. Get what you need. My personal favorite is the Fujitsu ScanSnap coupled with the Adobe Acrobat scanning program.

ACCOUNTING (see FINANCES)

ACCOUNTS are tough to keep track of. Everything you do these days requires an account: banking, frequent flyer programs, utilities, **SOCIAL NETWORKING, CREDIT CARDS,** loan payments, grocery shopping, department stores, zoo rewards membership . . . you get the point. You always seem to need account numbers and **PASSWORDS** when you least expect it, like those surprise trips to the zoo. That's why you need a complete list of every account you have, and all associated information, with you at all times. Make sure this list is constantly updated. I know that seems like an over-whelming task, but it doesn't have to be. Aside from solutions you can craft on your own, like creating a password-protected spreadsheet with columns for account name, number, password, and log-on URL, there are now many great **APPS** that store this information and make it instantly accessible on your phone or tablet. I like the Keeper app, but whatever you choose, look for apps that already have the fields mapped out for you. Then, every time you open a new account, or change your credentials, take that extra minute to input the information. This will save you time and energy later, as you will never have to search for account numbers or reset usernames and pass-words. According to the Gartner Group, the world's leading information technology research and advisory company, 20 to 50 percent of *all* tech sup-port calls are for password resets, so obviously people need a better system! If you have your information saved and available, you'll give that guy work-ing at the zoo a break because he won't have to look it up for you, and you can be sure you'll receive your free churro voucher in the **MAIL**. Having complete control over and access to all of your important information will eliminate the stress of ever having to find it.

■ ■ ■ ■
AN O.C.D. SUCCESS STORY

We've all been there—staring at a log-on screen trying to guess our password with only one attempt left before we get locked out. Oh, the pressure! Well, I've never been there because I keep organized, but I know you have. I had a client who was resetting a password ba-sically every time she logged in. Because many sites don't let you use a password you've already used, she had to pick more and more ob-scure passwords and of course couldn't remember them. After she implemented the O.C.D. Way of keeping a password-protected document with all her accounts and log-on info, she never had to reset a password again. Now she can log on to her bank account without having a nervous breakdown!

■ ■ ■

ADDRESS BOOKS need to be maintained uniformly. If someone's contact is important enough to ask for, then it should be important enough to maintain. If not, delete it. The more detailed and uniform your contacts are kept, the more uniform they will be on your **COMPUTER** and in your life. And you won't have to scroll past the contact information for that insurance salesman you drunkenly met at a **HALLOWEEN** party every time you open your contacts.

First pick certain fields in a contact that you will always want to have. The most important would be full name, e-mail address, mobile number, and business number.

Use the notes sections of your contact card if you might have trouble remembering how you met this particular contact. You will be the only one looking at these contacts, so don't be afraid to take notes on anything you like, such as a unibrow or extra breast. (We've all seen *Total Recall.*) When you share a contact, the notes section does not get shared, so don't worry about the information you add to this field. These notes will also aid you in eliminating a contact in the future because you'll remember how and why you met that person and be able to decide if he or she is still relevant to your life.

BIRTHDAYS are always important, so if you like particular people, ask them their birth date. It's important to add contact information for children and spouse names also, even if you have this memorized. You can keep this information in the notes section of a contact. That way, you can call them on their birthday and remember important people in their lives at the same time.

Using categories and specific labeling of your contacts makes culling simple and effortless. Anytime you receive a card and make a choice to enter the information into your **ADDRESS BOOK**, you should get into the habit of adding the category where the person best fits into your life. It is always a good habit to make a note about the person and how you met. For the most part, you know the basic categories in your life, so you know what categories to create. For example, if I were Bill Gates, my categories might be Microsoft (for my employees who worked there), Friends, Family, Restaurants, Travel, New York, and Gates Foundation (for everyone associated with the foundation). You can adjust your categories, but only when you have a significant reason to add or amend a category.

Cutting people from your contacts should happen every couple of years, but basic maintenance should be happening constantly. Go through your contacts and get rid of everyone you don't know. They probably don't know you either. Right off the bat, you will eliminate a large amount of people who are distracting, take up space on your phone and **COMPUTER**, and make searching for specific contacts take longer than necessary. If properly labeling your contacts is an issue, then start doing it right now! Cutting people from your life can be a relief as well. You will gain a perspective as to who is in your life and whom you want to communicate with in your life, and doing so will make you think twice when adding someone new.

Be disciplined and know that if someone is important enough to add to your contact list, then that person should be important enough to be maintained properly.

■ ■ ■ ■
AN O.C.D. SUMMARY

Organize: Go through all your contacts and decide which ones are worth organizing. If you find that you are missing information, immediately request that information from your contact via phone or e-mail.

Create: No matter which address book program you use, decide on or create the fields you will be filling for your contacts.

Discipline: Always input every contact uniformly so that your database is easily searchable and visually pleasing. Consistently update information as it changes.

■ ■ ■ ■
AN O.C.D. SUCCESS STORY

At summer camp, I kept a notebook that I meticulously maintained of all the friends that I made. I had everyone I cared about write his or her name, address, and phone number (e-mail wasn't even around then). It's easy, especially for a kid, to be lazy in gathering contact info from new acquaintances. Thanks to that notebook, to this day I'm still close with many of those friends from camp. (Except for my camp roommate, known as Gassy Carl. That just wasn't going to work.) Had I not had the discipline to collect and maintain their information, many of those relationships would have been lost.

∎ ▪ ▪ ∎

AIRPORT SECURITY will be a stressful experience if you are not prepared and organized before you leave for the airport. It truly amazes me how ignorant people are and how selfish they can be with other people's time. We've all been behind people who, like Mary Poppins, magically produce another metallic item from their pocket after their seventh pass through the metal detector. Time is valuable, so imagine how much more of it you could save if everyone knew how to expedite their security screening by being informed and organized prior to arriving at the airport.

When you are getting ready to leave for the airport, make sure you dress in comfortable yet functional clothing,—that is, clothing that won't set the metal detector off when you pass through it, like **JEANS** with ornate hardware. The key is to wear an outfit that won't cause delays in your **TRAVEL** schedule. Warm-up pants, sweatpants, jeans without a belt, or a cozy dress are all things that will require little hassle. Wear footwear that you can take on and off easily. Boots, flip-flops, loosely tied sneakers, something that you don't have to untie is best. If it is real, **JEWELRY** will not set off the metal detector, so no need to take it off, no matter what that TSA agent thinks. It's an easy way to lose your valuables to theft or by accidentally leaving them behind. Make sure you put items such as your cell phone, **WALLET**, and any other accessory into your bag or **PURSE** prior to your screening so you can just stick your purse or bag in a bin and be done with it. You don't want to end up with loose or forgettable items in bins, so find a compartment that's easily accessible and designate it for this purpose. This will also help you exit the security area faster. Have your laptops and **ELECTRONICS** easily accessible, as TSA might make you take them out of your bags for a security inspection. If you prepare before the security line, then you can transcend all the chaos around you and have a pleasant and calm travel experience. If you end up behind a Mary Poppins, politely suggest that he or she pick up this book from the airport bookstore.

O.C.D. EXTREME

Load your belongings into security bins in the order you want to put them back on. Send the bin through the scanner containing your zippered shoes, then your jacket, then your computer, then your backpack, and finally your carry-on containing your wallet and phone. As soon as your belongings start coming out of the scanner, you'll swiftly get dressed, get your laptop back in your bag, grab your carry-on, and be on your way. I aim to be a security checkpoint phantom—leave no trace!

O.C.D. APPROVED TECHNOLOGY

TSA Pre-Check is the most efficient and effective way to move effortlessly through airport security. It is the best thing I have done for my travel, as I can leave my shoes and jacket on and my bags packed and get in and out of the security line in minutes.

ALCOHOL (see BAR)

ANTIQUES are an asset and an investment, which is why you should keep an organized catalog of your antiques. We all keep records of our stocks, so what makes something that's just as valuable *less* important? Get out the camera and grab the **FURNITURE** polish because it's time for a sexy antique photo shoot. The simplest way to catalog your collection of antiques is to create a folder for each of the antiques you have as follows: DOCUMENTS → ANTIQUES → DESCRIPTION OF PIECE. Take and download the photos from your camera for each piece to the corresponding folder and immediately rename the photo with a description of the piece, like "Gold-handled Curio" or "Zulu Fertility Mask." Collect invoices and repair orders for each specific antique. Scan these **DOCUMENTS** and add them to the folder for that particular antique. This will make it easy to know exactly what pieces you have and their values, which will help if you want to sell your antiques later on. Once your collection has been documented, send this information to your home owner's insurance company for them to keep on record in case of loss or damage and so they can add any valuables to your policy. If the antique is beyond their standard coverage limits, consider adding it on as scheduled personal property for an additional fee. Offer to help your eldest relatives catalog their own antique collections. Perhaps they'll leave you that special curio cabinet in their will. My grandma did!

APARTMENTS can be small, large, tall, short, wide, but the size doesn't matter. It's how you use it. Whatever the size or use of your apartment, create a space that allows you to function the O.C.D. Way: everything in its place to maximize productivity and efficiency. Ask yourself what you need in your apartment and what you just keep around because you haven't addressed it. Take a day to open **DRAWERS** and take things out that you haven't used or touched in over a year. Do you even remember putting it in there? Find things to donate or to throw away, and then start thinking about where things should actually live in your apartment based on usage. This can apply to larger **FURNITURE** pieces as well. Just because you have furniture in your space doesn't mean it is functional and worthy of keeping around. Make your space more functional by knowing what you have and providing yourself easy access to it. Go through this process every three months or on a habitual basis. Remember that when you're living in a small apartment, your space is very valuable, so don't waste an inch. Don't forget to utilize wall space effectively as well. Wall space is the most common dead space, so take advantage of it. Review the relevant entries from this guide to design the best system for you and the apartment size you have to work with. If you use it wisely, no one will even notice the size. Eventually you will be living in a space that is O.C.D. approved.

O.C.D. EXTREME

Every morning, I walk around my home to see if anything is out of place. If it is, I return it to its proper place, no matter how small or insignificant. That way, each day starts off the same way, with my home just as it was the day, week, and month before. I call it the clean reset method and it ensures that my organizational responsibilities never pile up.

APPOINTMENTS need to be entered into a **CALENDAR** with reminders, because nothing ruins a reputation, friendship, or opportunity like missing or being late to an appointment. Your friend will never forgive you forgetting about his or her Rock Band party. All appointments should be entered into your calendar as soon as you set them, with specific details such as a time, address, phone number, who you're meeting with, and why. Don't leave it until later or you will inevitably forget. A cornerstone of the O.C.D. Way is that *now is always the best time.* I will repeat this often, because I can't stress it enough. Always leave yourself enough time between appointments for travel, traffic, or just to recharge your mind. This practice applies to events you might not even think of as appointments. Car or hotel reservations should be entered in with check-in times and confirmation numbers. Airline flights should be entered in with the name of the airline, confirmation number, flight number, destination, and time of departure and arrival. Set reminders for your appointments and make sure that when you are setting appointments in different time zones, you set the appointment for the right time zone. All of this information right at hand will always keep you on time, calm and composed, and the master of your own schedule. Your friend will never have to go without a skilled video game drummer for his or her parties.

AN O.C.D. SUCCESS STORY

I worked with a client who simply could not remember people. He lived in constant anxiety of wondering if he had already been introduced to someone, which led to frequent awkward encounters. He'd always say "Nice to see you" to cover himself. He needed a better method. I got him into the habit of putting his appointments in his phone and taking notes after each meeting, no matter how silly the note, and then adding it to his contacts. Not only did the act help him commit the person to memory, he could always look back through his appointments to see if he did meet someone, as well as some helpful reminders of who that person was. As a result, he embarrasses himself much less frequently.

O.C.D. EXTREME

I send appointment reminders to all my friends, even for last-minute movie plans. That way I have a record of activities from all my friendships and help those flakier friends stick to their plans. Generally, once it's in their phones, it's as good as gold!

APPS (or applications) have always been around on our computers, but now they are spilling over into other electronic devices such as our phones, tablets, video game consoles, cars, and even our **REFRIGERATORS**. It's so important to know how to manage them, or they'll end up managing you. First, know what you need an app for and then seek it out. It's fun to randomly browse, explore, and try out apps, but get rid of them once you realize that you don't need to keep an app that simulates popping bubbles or drinking a digital beer. Don't download a chaotic mess of apps and then just leave them to stare back at you and hog up your device memory and screen space. You also don't need multiple apps that have the same functionality. If you want to compare apps, do it, pick your favorite, and delete the others. And remember, even though an app might only be 99 cents, it adds up quickly if you aren't using good discipline. If you are keeping an app, create folders for like apps, which will make finding them easier. You can even alphabetize them within the folder for extra O.C.D. points. Put the apps you use the most toward the top and constantly evaluate and purge unneeded apps. Anytime you see a notification on an app, deal with it. This could include updates and important messages. Also, be smart about which apps you allow to send you "push notifications." You don't want to constantly receive alerts that are unimportant. You don't need to be in a meeting and be distracted by a notification that reads "You can buy a new hat for your FarmTown avatar!" Don't let apps drain your battery life when they are idling in the background. Quit out of them however your device specifies so your device runs faster and the battery lasts longer.

A

33

■ ■ ■ ■

O.C.D. EXTREME

I don't like to keep apps on the first page of my phone. Leaving it blank allows me to feature my company logo, which I have set as a background, and makes my phone more inviting and less distracting. Unfortunately on the iPhone, I'm forced to have a fixed app bar at the bottom, so I put one row of my most used apps at the top to balance it out. Symmetry is beauty!

ART should be organized just like antiques. If you are an art collector, please see **ANTIQUES**.

ART SUPPLIES are usually found all over people's homes. As a result, those people can never find the art supply they are looking for when they actually need it. Many potential up-and-coming Picassos have gone undiscovered because they couldn't find their supplies when inspiration struck. Designate a space for your art supplies, and then subdivide that space into sections for each type of supply: brushes, paints, crayons, markers, paper, canvas, and so on. Keep like supplies grouped together and use plastic **ZIPLOCK BAGS** or clear tote bags to store them. If you have a larger collection, you can use plastic **BINS**. If you want to keep your art supplies on display, use stainless-steel utensil holders, but always return supplies to the same place every time so that anyone who wants to use them can find them. Make sure that after you use any art supplies, you wash, dry, clean, and put away those supplies right after you're done. Also, check your supplies every now and then to make sure they haven't dried out and are still functioning. There's nothing worse than squashing inspiration because you discover your red paint is just dried crust on the inside of a bottle.

AN O.C.D. SUCCESS STORY

Oftentimes, for reasons I don't understand, creativity and disorganization seem to go hand in hand. Such was the case with one of my clients who loved to paint. She bought bins to store her supplies, but everything was just tossed in without rhyme or reason. It was dumb luck if she found the brush or color she was looking for. On top of that, she kept canvases all around the house. Sometimes she couldn't find a blank one, so she painted over an old one. What a tragedy! Imagine if da Vinci couldn't find a blank canvas and painted over the Mona Lisa? Creative works of art lost due to disorganization! We took her existing bins and divided them up with smaller bins to keep her supplies separate and accessible. We designated a space for her canvases and a system to know when to buy more. She now paints when and how she wants, and thanked me with an original work of art!

ARTICLES are usually just read and then the magazine or newspaper thrown away, but every now and then you read a very special article, or perhaps are even featured in one, that you want to save. For most people, this means saving the entire **MAGAZINE** or newspaper. Don't be a periodical pack rat, with piles of **PAPERS** precariously perched around your place. Articles you decide to save should preferably be stored digitally in DOCUMENTS → ARTICLES. If it's press for your business, you can save it in DOCUMENTS → COMPANY NAME → PRESS. For magazine articles, save your space and follow RATS! No, not the little rodent. *R*ip out the *A*rticle and magazine cover, *T*oss the magazine, and *S*can! RATS! Save the article as a PDF with the publication, name of the article, and date in the file name. For example: Real Simple—Pack Like a Pro—03-13-14. If your magazine is digital, save the article as a PDF or take a screen shot instead of making it a **BOOKMARK** so you can view it even when you can't connect to the Internet. For newspapers, follow the RATS method described on earlier for magazines. Clip out the sections of the article and scan it, along with the front page of the paper.

If you want to keep the actual printed document because it has emotional, historical, or monetary value, like a newspaper from when an icon passed, press about your business, or that compelling interview with Honey Boo Boo, then put it in an airtight **MEMORABILIA** box. Wrap each individual item in plastic or place it into hermetically sealed bags to preserve it as long as possible, but still consider scanning it to have a backup as well.

Remember, the purpose of saving an article is to be able to reference it again in the future. Having the article accessible while taking up the least amount of space in your life is the O.C.D. Way.

■ ■ ■ ■
AN O.C.D. SUCCESS STORY

When I worked for a large management company, one of the responsibilities that assistants had was to go through every new magazine looking for press and mentions about agency clients. The entire magazine was tabbed and filed in a filing cabinet under the client's name. What a waste of space and a pain in the butt to retrieve! I quickly got the entire backlog scanned and started a scanning system for any new press that came in, scanning only the relevant article and cover. We got rid of the filing cabinets and instead set up a scanning station for the entire office. It was a much better use of space and served many purposes.

ASSIGNMENTS for work or school can creep up on you and your family fast. Helping your child finish a book report on *Hatchet* by Gary Paulsen at the twenty-fifth hour is a nightmare for both of you. So it's important to maintain a visual representation of your or your children's assignments to remind you of what's coming due. This can be a whiteboard, chalkboard, corkboard, or just reminders in your digital calendar. If you are up for it, learn how to use a digital **CALENDAR** now and start incorporating it into your life. Teach your family this system as well. It will save you a lot of time down the road. When you are assigned a project, school paper, **CHORE**, or anything that requires preparation and **RESEARCH**, add it to your visual representation. This will help you make sure you allot enough time to properly organize your thoughts, creative ideas, and work in a manner that properly represents the work you want to show for yourself. Break it down into goals and mark these so that you won't wait until the last minute to start your assignment. For example, if you are assigned a paper due in three months, break it down into a month for research, a month to start organizing your ideas and outlining your paper's structure, and then the last month to complete and polish the assignment. The night before the assignment is due, reward yourself with a massage while you think about everyone else still rushing to finish his or her assignment, or take your child to any pizza place with a ball pit. Assignments are all about time allotment, creating a schedule, and maintaining the discipline to stick to that schedule. You will always be in control of your assignments and, as a result, always show your best self.

■ ■ ■ ■
AN O.C.D. SUCCESS STORY

When I was a student at NYU, I was always the kid who started his final paper at the beginning of the semester and had it finished far in advance of the due date because I broke it down into goals on a timeline. I'd quietly laugh at my friends as they ran around like chickens with their heads cut off the night before the report was due. They would ask me why I wasn't working on my paper and I would say I had finished it two months ago. Their jaws dropped in jealously. Set goals, get things done ahead of time, and you'll be dropping some jaws of your own instead of picking your own jaw up off the floor. Who knows what's been on that floor!

ASSOCIATIONS (see MEMBERSHIPS)

ATTICS are the storage purgatory for most households. "Toys in the attic" is a euphemism for insanity, and I agree that keeping things in your attic is just plain crazy. It's an unstable environment and a fire hazard. Why do we store things that we want to keep in one of the dirtiest and least visited places in our home? If you really can't find a better home for something in your attic, and you absolutely must keep it, put it in an airtight plastic **BIN** so it doesn't get destroyed by rodents and insects. Wrap it in plastic if it won't fit in a bin. Keep a digital list of everything that is in the attic so you don't forget about it. On your list, write the date that you added that item to the attic. When you realize that the sewing machine has been in your attic for six years untouched, maybe you'll finally admit that you aren't a seamstress and be able to bring yourself to donate it. Once a year, check on everything to make sure it hasn't been damaged and ask yourself if there is a better home for your possessions, what you can start using, and what you can donate. An organized life doesn't feature the attic as a storage solution, so if you've got an attic full of stuff, apply the O.C.D. Way from the introduction to create new organized spaces that are actually in your home instead of above it.

AUDIOBOOKS are becoming digital and downloadable just like **MUSIC** and **MOVIES**. If you are still buying books on CD, stop! If you are still buying books on **CASSETTE TAPES**, shame on you! **CDs** are bulky and hard to travel with, get damaged and lost, and are much more difficult to organize and keep readily available. In order to listen to a CD, you must always be near a CD player. Audiobooks, like MP3s, organize themselves by their metatags. Purchase your audiobooks online, but only buy the ones you are ready to listen to right now; otherwise you'll buy too many and never get around to them. As you collect new audiobooks, make sure that they're not taking up too much space on your computer's **HARD DRIVE**. Many people don't know that after you make a digital purchase, you can always delete and download your purchase again later at no extra charge. Once your library is organized, synchronize your **SMARTPHONE** with your **COM-PUTER** and your audiobooks will be waiting for you to listen to anywhere you have your phone. Imagine listening to this book, read by Christopher Walken, anywhere you want to!

AUDIO FILES come in the form of voice mails, voice notes, **AUDIOBOOKS**, memos, and of course, **MUSIC**. Voice mails can be sentimental, or prove your harassment case against a crazy ex in a court of law, so make sure you download the ones that are important to you before your ex steals your phone and erases them. Unfortunately, there isn't an easy way to transfer them directly from your phone to your **COMPUTER**, so a lot of people delete them, or save them until they expire. It's worth the effort to save big news or sweet messages. There have been numerous third-party software programs popping up to aid in this process, but I still think the easiest way is to play the voice mail on speakerphone on one phone and capture it on your computer or use the voice memo feature on another phone. Then you can e-mail it to yourself. Download the audio file to DOCUMENTS → VOICE MAILS → CALLER NAME AND NOTE. Put the caller and a note about the subject matter in the file name. For example: The Literary Group— O.C.D. Way Book Deal. If you use voice notes and memos to record ideas or reminders, go through them weekly to make sure you stay on top of your tasks, and get rid of anything completed or no longer relevant.

AUDIOTAPES (see **CASSETTE TAPES**)

AUTOMOBILE organization can range from the glove compartment to the **TRUNK**. You will not make a positive impression on your mother-in-law if you pick her up from the airport and can't fit her bags in your trunk because it's full of stuff. She's tough, but in this case, she's right. In general, I believe that your car is for driving you around, not for driving your stuff around. The only stuff that should be in your car is the stuff you need that day. Your trunk is not a long-term storage space. Neither is your glove compartment. Keep only the most important items in your glove compartment, such as your **BUSINESS CARDS**, a pen, a phone charger, a flashlight, and a Swiss army knife. Keep a clearly labeled envelope containing your registration, insurance, and a copy of your driver's license in the event of an accident or encounter with the law. These situations are stressful enough without searching through a pile of disorganized junk to find your important documents.

If you are a parent and have kids constantly in and out of your car, keep a bag of baby wipes accessible, as they are great to clean anything and everything from little hands and **CLOTHES** to the leather and dashboard of your car. Keeping a small **BIN** in your trunk for select **TOYS** can be an easy way to keep those little ones occupied in a last-minute trip or long ride. You won't have to turn around and shout, "We'll get there when we get there!"

If you have a center console in your car, keep this area neat and clean and don't let it become a trash can. It's for sunglasses and your **SMARTPHONE** while you are driving to stop you from texting when you're behind the wheel. If you like keeping your phone out in the open, make sure you have a set place for it to live while driving that is accessible but not distracting. **RECEIPTS** that get thrown in the center console or side armrests of the car should be disposed of regularly, or, if they are important enough, filed or scanned. Keep the side consoles of your car free of anything because objects in these spaces will roll and shift while you drive, which is very distracting. The only thing that may be convenient to keep in the side console of your car is a small cloth for wiping down windows as needed and a small umbrella in case of rain.

Besides the items of the day, the trunk of the car should have an **EMER-GENCY KIT**. This kit should contain a full change of clothes, including a pair of shoes, a twenty-dollar bill, a bottle of water, a flashlight, and a Swiss army knife. You can keep anything else in this bag that you think is appropriate, but don't let the bag become overstuffed and disorganized. Additionally, your trunk should contain a small first-aid kit, a spare tire, **TOOLS** to change a flat, and a pair of jumper cables. On a long **ROAD TRIP** you may want to have a small gasoline canister just in case you run out of gas.

Getting into a clean and organized car feels much better and calming than getting into a car packed with things and trash that do not need to be in there. Take a few minutes at the end of each day to bring in everything you brought into your car for that day. It may seem like extra work to do, but it will only get worse as you let things pile up. It's nice to see that you are staying hydrated, but do you really need seven half-empty water bottles on the floor of your backseat? The less you bring into your car, the less you have to do to clean it out!

A

■ ■ ■

O.C.D. EXTREME

Just like you'd use space dividers in drawers or cabinets to create organization, I divide the space in my glove compartment to make it work for me. I use it like a mini-mobile office, with sections for business cards, a pen, permanent marker, phone charger, and important documents. Divide your glove compartment, designate spaces, and bring organization to even the smallest of mobile spaces!

B

BABY ACCESSORIES can become overwhelming, just like the baby they accessorize. Babies require a lot of supplies, so making sure those are organized is vital. Knowing where your bottles, diapers, and creams are will save you time and stress. Before the baby is born, start planning out where you will keep all of these items. If you have to reorganize other things in your house to make room for these items, *do it now*. The last thing you want to be doing when you have a newborn baby to care for is reorganizing. Also make room to store a **DIAPER BAG** near the accessories. Having a consistent place for your supplies will help you keep them stocked and easy to access. It will also help you get rid of supplies you no longer need as your baby grows. Donate or give these items to a friend. Always return supplies to their place and don't wait for a supply to run out before you repurchase. Make sure you know how much space you have for each accessory. If you know you can fit a **QUANTITY** of sixty diapers in your **DRAWER**, you can then assess when to rebuy diapers. For example, when the drawer is half full, you'll know you need to buy thirty more diapers. This philosophy can apply to anything in your life that requires regular replenishing, but when it comes to running out of something for your baby, it can be more aggravating than you think. Reaching for a new diaper and discovering you've run out while holding an old one full of something you didn't know a little human could make is never a situation you want to be in. You want to be able to stock up on a necessary item without creating an overflow in the rest of your home. Keeping an eye on your supplies will also let you know what to ask for when it comes to gifts. Get something you actually need! Remember: if people give you gifts you don't need, don't be afraid to get rid of them!

■ ■ ■

AN O.C.D. SUCCESS STORY

One of my high-profile clients with a very busy schedule welcomed her first child into her life. While a joy, it was also disruptive because she didn't have a good system for keeping her baby supplies organized. They were all over the room, a box of baby wipes here, a bottle or two there, diapers in multiple random areas. As a result, she never knew when she was really out of a particular supply. Sometimes, she'd go out and buy more supplies when she didn't have to, wasting time and money, because she didn't know she still had some in another location. Other times, she'd assume she still had some and run out of what she needed. Sound familiar? After she hired me to help her make sense of her nursery, she knew exactly where all her supplies were, how much she had, and when she needed to reorder.

■ ■ ■ ■

BABY BAGS (see DIAPER BAG)

BABY CLOTHES are usually gifted to you when your baby is first born. You can be inundated with clothing ranging from newborn to twelve months old and beyond. Some of it will be useful. Some of it will be from people who want to see your child in ridiculous outfits. Make sure to take a picture of your baby as a punk rocker and send it to the gift giver before you donate their thoughtful gift. To stay organized, take all of the clothing that is usable for your baby's current size and organize it by pants, onesies, **T-SHIRTS**, **SOCKS**, dress-up, and nightclothes. All of the other clothing that they will grow into should be stored in an airtight container in an easy-to-access area that you will remember, but not in the way of your child's day-to-day clothing. When the baby grows and is ready to fit into the new clothes, give away the clothes that are too small and organize the new clothes just as you did the old ones. Some old outfits can be sentimental and worth keeping, but you don't need to save every one! If you do, they will lose their significance. For the precious few items you decide to keep, you can get them framed in a shadowbox, along with a photo of your child wearing the outfit, and hang it up in your house. If you don't want to display the outfit, treat it the same way, if not better, than the paper **ARTICLES** you kept from when Michael Jackson passed away. Seal the outfit in a large **ZIPLOCK BAG** and store the bag in a plastic **BIN** labeled **MEMORABILIA**. The day will come when you want to show the clothes to your grown child and they will still be in perfect condition. Just like any item in your life, designate a specific amount of space for your baby clothes. Once this space is determined, you must discipline yourself to keep it from overflowing by going through it whenever you add something new to the space. Before you know it, your little baby will be a full-grown punk rocker and you are going to be left with piles of clothes you must relocate, donate, or give to friends. Instead of it becoming an overwhelming process, take the time and make decisions daily or weekly.

BACKPACKS should be used for carrying around the things that you need on a daily basis. People tend to carry around way too much in their backpacks. My father is a chiropractor and owes a significant portion of his business to overloaded backpacks. Help convince my dad to retire by lightening your load.

To keep an orderly backpack, you should empty it out and go through it at the end of each day, unless it is a backpack for school purposes, in which case you should go through it at the end of each school week. This will help you start the next week feeling refreshed and new. Make sure that each compartment in the backpack has a purpose and that you keep it organized. Keep your backpack on a hook on the back of the coat **CLOSET** or **ENTRYWAY**. Parents: help your kids learn these skills! It will help them, and their backs, throughout their school years and also keep you aware of the work they are bringing home. Sit down with them as often as you can to go through their backpacks when they get home from school. Nothing will enlighten you (or possibly terrify you) about your child's school day more than seeing what comes out of their backpack. Also, teach your children the discipline of hanging their backpack in the same place every night and they'll soon realize how easy it is to find things when they maintain an organizational routine.

O.C.D. EXTREME

When I was a kid, I had all of my school binders color-coded. I would load them into my backpack in the order of my classes. When I was done with the class, I would put that binder in the back. By the time the day was done, I was already reloaded in the proper order for the next day. I also convinced my teachers to give me a second set of books so I could keep one set at home and one set at school without having to transport them back and forth. Teach your children these O.C.D. extreme methods to save their backs and their time!

BANK DEPOSITS (see DEPOSITS)

BAR is any place you keep your alcohol collection and head for when it's time to celebrate the kids moving out of the house. Some people like to display their alcohol and feature their most prized acquisitions. Other people like to tuck their alcohol away in a **CABINET**. Whatever your style, your bar must be organized. Go through your bar. Get rid of any alcohol or mixers that are expired or that you just don't drink. If that bottle of cinnamon schnapps hasn't been opened since 1972, toss it! Make room for the things you actually want stocked. Keep a bottle of each of the staple alcohols, which include vodka, gin, rum, tequila, and whiskey, so you can offer your **GUESTS** their preferred libation, but for the most part your bar should be a representation of you and what you like to drink. Keep like kinds of alcohol together: scotch with scotch, vodka with vodka, **WINE** with wine, liqueur with liqueur, and so on. Make the alcohols you use most frequently the most accessible, either in the front or on the easiest-to-reach **SHELF**.

If you are a self-proclaimed mixologist and have the accessories to prove it—like shakers, mixers, strainers, muddlers, and a stack of napkins with phone numbers on them—designate a **DRAWER** and keep them all together or put them all in a labeled plastic **CONTAINER** in a cabinet. Add the phone numbers to your **ADDRESS BOOK** and throw out the napkins. Clean your bar accessories after you use them and always return them to their home. If you have room for a blender in a cabinet in your bar area, you can keep an extra blender here, but otherwise your blender should live in your **KITCHEN**.

If your bar has a **REFRIGERATOR**, use it only for items related to making and serving drinks: cocktail onions, olives, mixers, fruit, however you get funky at happy hour. Keep your beer in this refrigerator, as well as a bottle of white wine and champagne. It's always nice to have a chilled bottle ready to go. Also keep a bottle of vodka in the **FREEZER**. Make sure you've got a full tray of ice stocked as well. After every party, clear out the perishable items. Every time you restock your bar's refrigerator, give it a wipe down and check for any expired items.

Keep your bar clean and your alcohol restocked and you'll always be ready to impress and intoxicate your guests with daiquiris, mojitos, a good old-fashioned martini, or a neat Johnnie Walker Blue (in which case, I'm coming over).

B

BASEMENTS come finished or unfinished. If your basement is unfinished, see **ATTIC**. If it's a finished space, which means you'd feel comfortable walking around barefoot without a flashlight, then the goal is to make it a functional part of your home. If it has good natural light, you can use it as an **OFFICE** or **FAMILY ROOM**. If there are no windows, consider using the space as a workout room, a man cave/game room, not to be confused with a **CHILD's PLAYROOM**, or **LAUNDRY ROOM**. You can use a small portion of your basement to store seasonal items, like **HOLIDAY DECORATIONS**, but keep it limited; otherwise you'll start using your basement as a storage graveyard and give up valuable square footage of your home. If your basement contains appliances, like a water heater, enclose them in a simple covering and leave adequate space around them so that they can be accessed and serviced when necessary. To deal with an already cluttered basement, apply the O.C.D. Way from the introduction to find a better place for your items in your home, instead of beneath it.

BATHING SUITS are easy for guys: roll them in a **DRAWER** or fold them neatly with your shorts, but separate. Unless you are a professional surfer or bathing suit model, you only need to keep a few attractive, well-fitting, and functional suits. You don't need thirty. If you are a lady, bathing suit organization is slightly more complicated because you most likely want to feel confident and fashionable at the beach or pool, and that means options. Have a variety of colors and styles to match the clothing and accessories you bring with you. But if you have every color of the rainbow, it's time to put a halt to your bathing suit buying habit. Don't hold on to a bikini past a year that doesn't fit, hoping you'll fit into it again. If you lose that weight, reward yourself with a new suit! When organizing your suits, keep them arranged by style and then color in a drawer or basket in your **CLOSET**. If a suit is two pieces, keep them tied together so you never have to search for a top or bottom. If you like to hot-tub, as Mrs. O.C.D. does, it's helpful to have a dedicated "hot tub bikini" because the chemicals and hot water in the hot tub tend to fade and stretch your suit. You don't want to ruin that brand-new bathing suit or exit the tub with a saggy booty because your bottoms have stretched out.

O.C.D. APPROVED TECHNOLOGY

Don't let your beach bag or backpack end up soaked because you put a wet bathing suit in there. Get a bathing suit bag. They are waterproof and stylish—another excuse to bring fashion to the beach or pool!

BATHROOMS can become one of the most disorganized rooms in a house. If what used to be your tranquil spalike bathroom now makes you feel dirty even after a shower, first throw away all but the most recent **MAGAZINES**. Then remove all of the products from the vanity **SHELVES**, the sink, the **DRAWERS**, the **CABINETS**, and the cover of the toilet tank and place them in the bathtub or shower. Go through the pile and pick out the items you use on a daily basis. Once you have these items, designate a spot for them that is convenient for how you use them. I consider the top drawers in the vanity and **MEDICINE CABINET** the place for daily-use items only, and everywhere else for storage and weekly-use items. Now go back to the shower or tub and pull out the items you haven't used in over a year, excluding unexpired medications and first-aid items, and throw them out. You don't need to save that glittery coconut-scented lotion someone gave you that you never use. You never use it for a reason. It makes you smell like a bad vacation. The remaining bathroom items are things you use and want to keep, so find a home for them in the vanity, cabinet, or lower drawers. Organize them by category and have drawers or spots assigned for these specific categories so items are never tossed in together and always remain easy to find. Bulky items such as hair dryers, curling irons, and clippers can be kept in a basket under the sink. Always return items to their place! You should be able to open a drawer or cabinet and grab exactly what you are looking for in the dark. No items should sit on your sink top except soap and a toothbrush, but it's even better to put your toothbrush away. Do you really want something that goes in your mouth near the place where you wash your hands? You know what you just did with those hands.

Reorganize your bathroom once a year, or whenever you feel like your bathroom is becoming overwhelming and dysfunctional.

> ### O.C.D. EXTREME
>
> I keep a special towel in the drawer next to my sink that I use only for wiping down the faucet and counter after each use. You'll never find a spot on my vanity! Also, every time I shower, I wash down the shower. I bought a detachable showerhead specifically for this purpose and have made it part of my shower routine. I clean while I get clean!

BATTERIES are a requirement in every home. You never want to be in a situation where you don't have the right battery on hand, trying to calm a crying child because Tickle Me Elmo went to sleep and you can't wake him up. In my work, I find loose batteries all over the home, in random **DRAWERS** and **CLOSETS,** never knowing which are fresh and which are dead. This isn't even safe: batteries can leak harmful battery acid, especially if they are expired or damaged. Keep all your batteries in the same place and know what batteries you need to keep stocked for the devices you have. Only stock batteries that you can use. You don't need a hearing aid battery if you don't have a hearing aid. Organize your batteries by type, in labeled **BINS**, and keep them in your **UTILITY CLOSET, LAUNDRY ROOM, GARAGE,** or **OFFICE**. Wherever you keep them, make sure it doesn't get too hot so they don't deteriorate, and check the expiration dates. Whoever takes the last battery of a certain type, make sure that person is responsible for replacing them, or for telling someone responsible to replace them. Don't be the person who runs out of batteries and starts stealing them from other devices. You are just delaying the inevitable: go out and get some batteries!

BEDROOMS are a sacred place where you need to feel comfortable being vulnerable. This is where you recharge and reset for the outside world so you can be your best. Don't risk being a Mr. or Mrs. Cranky Pants by having a chaotic bedroom. Take off those pants and put on your happy suit by making the space relaxing, peaceful, and without distraction. There should be little to nothing on your **DRESSERS, NIGHTSTANDS**, or any other area, except picture frames, a plant or two, candles, lights, and a book or magazine you are actively reading. All those other **BOOKS** should be on a **BOOK-SHELF** in another room. Have a set place to charge your phone, especially if you are using your phone as an alarm clock. Resist the urge to use the space under your bed as storage, even though it's out of sight, because you'll still be aware of it and it will distract you. It's better to buy **FURNITURE** to use as a storage solution, like a bedside dresser instead of a nightstand, or an ottoman with storage at the foot of your bed, than to start using the space under your bed. They even make headboards that double as storage devices, so be smart and seek out these kinds of solutions for your bedroom. If your home or **APARTMENT** is small and you absolutely must use the space under the bed for storage, limit it to simple items like bed **LINENS** or guest towels so that you don't start to view your bed as a storage space you sleep on. If your home or apartment is that small, you may be using your bedroom as an **OFFICE** as well. If this is the case, make sure that area is separate and consider using a storage bench or ottoman to hide **OFFICE SUPPLIES**.

Every night before you turn in, give a quick glance to your bedroom and make sure it is reset for the next day. Take the time and have the discipline to put all of your **CLOTHES** away and return any item that is out of place to its home. You'll feel great waking up in the morning knowing that everything is in its right place instead of thinking your dresser exploded in the middle of the night.

B

■ ■ ■ ■
AN O.C.D. SUCCESS STORY

It takes a little bit of time for people to believe me when I tell them that clutter affects their quality of life. It's chaotic and distracting. I reorganized a bedroom with a client who was resistant to getting rid of some of the clutter in her space. She had photos, candles, books . . . all acceptable items for the area, but in too great a quantity. I told her to trust me and just try it out for a week. At the end of the week, she told me she was sleeping much better in her simplified bedroom and she decided to keep the excess items out permanently. Disorder creates a negative energy that follows you even into dreamland!

> **O.C.D. EXTREME**
>
> When I make my bed, I tuck in my sheets as tightly as possible and then use a lint roller to collect all the hair and dust that accumulates during the course of the night.

BELTS provide the valuable public service of keeping our pants up. They are easy to organize and maintain. As always, start by getting rid of belts you no longer wear, are too worn out, or don't fit. Don't be the person wearing a belt that is hanging on to your waist for dear life. Once you have your collection of belts, dedicate a space for your remaining belts in your **CLOSET** or **DRESSER**. If you have **DRAWER** space, you can roll your belts tightly and put them in the drawer in a single layer so it's easy to see what you have and grab it. You can also buy a basket and keep your belts rolled up in there if you don't have drawers. If drawer space isn't an option, and there isn't room for a basket, buy belt hangers and use different ones for your brown belts, your black belts, and your colored belts. Just make sure to put your favorites at the top because those are the ones you will want to grab most often.

> **O.C.D. EXTREME**
>
> Make your own belt hangers by twisting a wire hanger to form an s-hook. Cheap and easy!

BIKINIS (see BATHING SUITS)

BILLS should be as paperless as possible. The truth is, you really don't need to save very many bills. We all hate bills, yet we can't seem to let them go. (Admit it, most of us miss Bill Clinton!) You might be saying, "What if I need copies of my bills someday? What will I do?" Bills, like most statements, can be accessed online from the source. But how often do you really need to do this? Most companies now offer online statements and bill pay. Enroll in these programs and when bills pop up in your **E-MAIL IN-BOX**, pay them as soon as possible. Then file the e-mail payment confirmation in an **E-MAIL FOLDER** labeled "Paid Bills 2014." Obviously, you'll create a new folder every year. Create subfolders for each type of bill: phone, cable, gas, and so on. Resist the urge to enroll in auto-payment of your bills. You should always be aware of what you are paying and where your money is going. Service prices rise consistently, promotional periods end, or mistakes are made, and auto-payment can make you miss these increases and an opportunity to try to lower your bill. If you are unable to pay your bills online, keep paper bills on your **DESK** in a **BIN** specifically for unpaid bills until you are able to address them, which should be as soon as possible, but at least once a week. Keep supplies like **ENVELOPES** and stamps in a nearby area to make this process efficient. If you are constantly up on your bills, you won't ever miss a payment and get hit with late fees. Scan a copy of only the January, June, and December bills and save them in DOCUMENTS → LIVING → YOUR HOME ADDRESS to make sure your bills remain consistent throughout the year and in case you need to reference your account information. Shred the rest. Most credit card companies offer a year-end summary online to help you with your **TAXES**, so don't worry about saving every month's statement. With a little organization and some good judgment, you can break up with the Bills in your life and move on to Toms, Harrys, and even Michaels.

BINDERS should be used when you want to store information on a particular subject for easy access, like when you are a governor and want to **RESEARCH** female candidates for your cabinet. A more appropriate example would be a recipe binder with your favorite **RECIPES**, a **SHEET MUSIC** binder if you're a singer and have a lot of music, a school binder for a particular course, or a **TRAVEL** binder for places you may want to visit. Binders should never be used to store loose, random **PAPERS** or multiple subjects. They must always have a specific subject. Use clear sheet protectors to keep your information safe and neat, but visible. Make sure you have a table of contents at the front of your binder and update it as you make changes so you always know where to find things within the binder. Keep your binders on a **BOOKSHELF** and label the spines with a label maker. Nowadays, with small laptops and tablets, you may even want to scan the contents of your binders as PDFs and create digital binders viewable on your electronic device. If you do create digital binders, make sure you use scanning software with OCR (optical character recognition) so that your text is searchable and editable. Look for the option to scan with OCR and make sure it's checked. Save these digital binders in DOCUMENTS → SUBJECT → BINDER NAME along with any other related digital files on the topic.

O.C.D. APPROVED TECHNOLOGY

Brother makes a line of label makers called the P-touch. They are intuitive, easy enough for a child to use, and available at different price points depending on your needs. I like them because they feature a full QWERTY keyboard, which makes labeling fast and easy, and allow you to create labels in a variety of widths, sizes, and fonts for different applications.

BINS are the O.C.D. Experience's preferred method for easy storage. Bin there, done that! For long-term storage, use clear plastic bins, so you can always see the contents, that have lids that are airtight. Make sure each bin is labeled with its contents on the front of the bin. Create an **INVENTORY** list of everything in the bin so that you know everything that's in there. Print out this list and stick it on the bin, but you should also keep a digital copy. This makes finding items in storage much easier. Smaller bins can also be useful in the **BATHROOM, CLOSET,** and **OFFICE** to divide larger spaces and make it easier when you need multiple items for a task: you just grab the whole bin. For example, you can keep all your **HAIR ACCESSORIES** in a canvas bin under the sink. When you need to do your hair, you just pull out the whole bin, get styled, return everything to the bin, and put it back under the sink. Canvas bins are also useful in the closet for **SCARVES** and **BELTS,** as well as seasonal items like **SWEATERS.** Office items that aren't used often, such as a label maker, extra supplies like paper clips, pens, markers, and so on, can all be kept in one bin in a supply closet. It's better to use a bin to store like items than to keep an assortment of items all over a **SHELF.** Items in a bin are much easier to keep organized and maintained. When in doubt, bin it out.

BIRTHDAYS should be added to your **ADDRESS BOOK.** Forgetting a loved one's birthday is a stain on your relationship, and I hate stains, so stainguard by keeping organized. Don't rely on social media to remind you. People don't always add their birthdays to their **SOCIAL NETWORKING** profiles, and you may not check it on that day. Every time you meet someone new who is important enough or that you actually like, add their birthday into their individual contact along with their other information. If you don't see the field for birthday, click "other fields" and you should see it. Then enable "birthdays" on your **CALENDAR** and you'll always know when it's somebody's birthday who is important to you. At the beginning of every month, you can look through all the upcoming birthdays and plan to buy gifts or cards as necessary.

■ ■ ■ ■

AN O.C.D. SUCCESS STORY

Nothing makes people feel unimportant like having their birthdays forgotten. I worked with a client whose system for remembering birthdays was her brain and the random Facebook reminder. So basically, no system at all. She missed a lot of birthdays. You can't remember them all, and Facebook will only remind you of someone's birthday if they've put it in their profile, which not everyone does, and only if you check it at the right time. I showed my client how simple it was to add birthdays to her contacts and then calendars. Now she can act as thoughtful as she really wants to be.

BLU-RAY (see DVD COLLECTION)

BOATS are tight spaces that must be expertly organized and maintained. If the Skipper and Gilligan had been better prepared, despite their short tour, they'd never have been lost, although it was quality entertainment. Your boat has numerous supplies for safety. All of these items must be regularly checked for expiration and functionality. You do not want to be in a situation where you discover during an emergency that your life jacket has a hole or your fire extinguisher is broken. Before every outing, check all safety equipment and replace what is necessary. Keep a flashlight with some extra **BATTERIES**, some good rope and flares, a small tool kit for at-sea repairs, and a first-aid kit in a waterproof boat bag. You can even keep some extra gas on your boat for long trips. Keep all paper items like navigation charts, insurance information, and safety manuals in a small watertight bag. Most boats have very limited storage, so use that space wisely and label what should go in each area. Keep extra towels on the boat, as well as garbage bags and a gallon of potable water. Make a checklist of everything on your boat and keep a paper copy on the boat in a plastic sleeve, as well as a digital copy on your computer/smartphone. This list guarantees your peace of mind and will be invaluable in an emergency. If you have an organized boat, it will allow you to stay calm, cool, and collected in sticky situations. Safety first. Update your list when you add or remove items so you're constantly up-to-date. At the end of each trip, remove everything except the emergency supplies from the boat and rinse the boat down. This way, it'll be ready to go for the next outing, where you almost land that trophy marlin before it gets loose. You were so close!

BOLTS (see NAILS)

BOOKMARKS on your **COMPUTER** should always be added with a short and simple name. By default, bookmarks are given the name from the header of the Web page, which is usually too long and won't be fully displayed in your bookmarks menu, or ambiguously short. Is it at all useful to have bit.ly/gjlemu in your bookmarks? No, so rename it. Your browser will have a rename feature in your bookmarks manager. Pick a name that makes sense to you so you can find what you are looking for quickly. Also, use the sort-by-name option in your bookmarks so that instead of organizing your bookmarks by date or order of addition, they are in alphabetical order, which makes finding them much easier. No matter which Web browser you use, it is imperative to know where your bookmarks are being saved. Newer browsers allow you to put bookmarks in permanent tabs or at the top of your browser bar. But less is more on your browser window, so keep it simple and only add bookmarks to this area for sites you use often. For everything else, create folders or groups for your bookmarks based on category so you aren't scrolling through a huge list every time you want to visit a page. This also makes it easier to delete all the bookmarks for a completed project with a single click. You just delete the entire folder instead of having to do it one by one. Check your bookmarks menu regularly and delete any bookmarks for pages you no longer visit or that no longer exist. Create an account with your browser to take advantage of the **CLOUD** synchronization feature so your bookmarks will be available on any computer or device you sign in to. If you don't sync to the cloud, export your bookmarks regularly and include them on your computer backup so you never lose them. Remember, don't bookmark anything you wouldn't want someone to know you were looking at, even if it's on your personal computer. Not everyone will understand your fascination with unusual poodle grooming techniques.

BOOKS can be organized in various ways depending on the size of the collection. Everyone has their own specific way they like to display their books. As long as you aren't building Jenga-style book towers, book organization is open to some personal choice. My favorite method is to organize them by genre and then by size, but you can also do it by color, thickness, alphabetically by title or author, by person in your home, or even by what you've read and what you haven't. Your book collection is not just an opportunity to organize but also a chance to create a visually pleasing display and to showcase your knowledge and background on a particular subject or genre. Whatever method you choose, first pull all of your books off the **BOOK-SHELVES** and identify what you don't want to keep. Keep anything that was life changing or eye opening, like Mantak Chia and Douglas Abrams's *The Multi-Orgasmic Man*. This is a good time to clean off those dusty shelves. Donate, sell, or have a book-swapping party for the books you don't want. Keep a master list on your **COMPUTER** of all the books you keep and add or subtract from it every time you get a new book or give one away. There are even Web sites and **APPS** you can use that are dedicated to cataloging your home **LIBRARY** using the ISBN number of the book. Then put the rest of the books on your shelves according to your method and you have the start of a well-organized book collection. Always put oversized books on low shelves so they are easier to grab and so they don't pose a danger of falling on your head. Keep books you access often in easy-to-reach spots. If you need bookends, you can stack a few books horizontally against their vertical brethren and that'll do the trick. Always know how much space for books you have in your home or **OFFICE** and make sure that you don't exceed it. You never want piles of books taking over your space, even if you are a bibliophile.

■ ■ ■
AN O.C.D. SUCCESS STORY

One of my clients had way too many books and no more space to keep them. Together we got rid of some very impressive books that were difficult for her to part with. We also bought her a Nook and got rid of books that she was okay only having digitally. When she saw her new, beautifully inviting library, she quickly forgot her overstuffed collection and used the room more. She started actually reading the books in her collection instead of fearing the book towers might crush her in an earthquake.

◼ ◼ ◼ ◼

BOOKSHELVES are primarily for books or we'd just call them shelves, but they can also be used to feature personal effects like picture frames and tchotchkes. These items should only be there to enhance the bookshelf's appearance and not because they are being stored there or because you don't know where else they should go. As described in the **BOOKS** section, books can be organized in numerous ways, but the most important thing is that the books should complement the bookshelf, not crowd it or make it look stuffed. If you have a stuffed shelf, get another shelf if you have space, or it's time to get rid of some of your books. Label areas on your bookshelf according to how you organize your books. If you have numerous freestanding bookshelves, consider spreading them around your space instead of putting them all side by side to encourage creative flow. Always make sure your bookshelves are sturdy, secured, and accessible. You don't want your bookshelves toppling over on a visiting neighbor or on a child who thinks he is part monkey.

◼ ◼ ◼
O.C.D. EXTREME

Don't let the height of your bookshelves boss you around and dictate where you have to keep certain books. When I moved into my apartment, I demolished my built-in shelves and rebuilt them from scratch to fit the height of my specific books.

BOXES have a way of piling up: moving boxes, office boxes, product boxes . . . we live in a boxed world and need to think outside the box, literally. While it's good to keep some collapsed boxes or small assembled boxes on hand for transporting or donating items, don't save every box that makes its way into your home! Only keep product boxes for things that cost over two hundred dollars (excluding shoe boxes, ladies—get rid of them), and then only as long as the return period or as soon as you are confident you won't be returning the item. You can keep boxes for items you plan on selling later on, but break them down. Keep stronger, thicker boxes and recycle the thin or damaged ones. Store your boxes in a **UTILITY CLOSET** out of sight and away from things you access on a daily basis. Never store boxes in a damp or dirty place because they can lose their integrity, unless you wrap them in plastic. If you are someone who uses boxes regularly for shipping, perhaps for that online business, make sure to have a section of your **OFFICE** closet designated for shipping supplies. Most shipping companies provide branded boxes for this purpose free of charge. As for **MOVING** or office boxes, you only need a few for those special occasions. When it comes to preparing for a move, make sure you have an accurate count of how many boxes you will need by going through your belongings and deciding what you will be moving. Hundreds of dollars can and will be wasted on the over-purchasing of boxes. Save your money to decorate your new place and to buy or build systems that bring you one step closer to organizational nirvana.

BRAS support you, so support them with proper organization. Bras can be kept in one drawer in your **DRESSER** or **CLOSET**. If you have everyday bras and very special bras, you can create separate **DRAWERS** for them if you feel like you have enough bras to do so. A suggestion for bras and **UNDER-WEAR** is to go through them once a month and check the wear and tear. If there are holes or rips, if the material is thinning, or if they are just falling apart, it may be time to get rid of them or move them to the exercise drawer. Just like you don't want to see holes in your men's underwear, they don't want to see any in yours, ladies.

An active woman should have around eight bras, not including **LINGE-RIE**. There are many different types of bras for different **NEEDS** and outfits: convertible bras, demi bras, plunge bras, sports bras, and T-shirt bras. You know how you dress and live and what feels comfortable, so tailor your collection to your needs. In addition to colors, all ladies should have the basics: black, nude, and white.

Keep your bras laid out in a drawer with the more frequently worn bras in the front. If space is tight, wrap the straps into the cup, fold the bra in half, and stack your bras into each other. For those bras that you decide to keep, each month have a "bra garden." This is when you wash and then lay your bras out to dry on a towel since bras should not be dried in a dryer. Laying them out instead of hanging them will help preserve their shape and increase their longevity. This is also a good time to organize your bras so that when they are done drying, you can put them away without the extra work.

This can also be a great time to invite your boyfriend or partner to give you input on what he or she would most like to see you wear next!

BROCHURES are things you should look at once and throw away, unless they contain a **COUPON** you are sure you'll use by the end of the week. If you are sure, keep the brochure, but people hold on to way too much paper that shows up in the **MAIL**. While it can be fun to browse **CATALOGS** and brochures, this will only tempt you into buying something you don't really need, which is what gets us disorganized in the first place. Generally, if you need something, you'll actively seek it out. If you are really thinking about purchasing an item you saw in a brochure, find the item online and save it as a **BOOKMARK** or add it to your **SHOPPING LIST** to purchase. If it is an offer for a service and you are interested in booking the service, book it and add it as an **APPOINTMENT** in your **CALENDAR**. This will eliminate the extra paper and give you the time and opportunity to look back at the item and make a decision. You can finally pull the trigger on that tufted organizational storage bench you've been dying to purchase.

BROOM CLOSET (see UTILITY CLOSET)

BUDDY LISTS (stop using this '90s term and see **SOCIAL NETWORKING**)

BULBS (see LIGHTBULBS)

BULK ITEMS (see QUANTITY)

BULLETIN BOARDS tend to become a place where you stick anything and everything, which results in an ugly mess hanging on your wall. Smear a bunch of glue on the wall, grab your **GARBAGE** can, and hurl the contents at the wall to achieve the same effect. A bulletin board should only be used for reminders, monthly schedules, emergency phone numbers, and a few photos. It's not for **RECEIPTS** you haven't scanned or **BUSINESS CARDS** you haven't entered into your phone yet. Nothing on your board should ever be covered by anything else. If it is, you need a bigger board or you need to go through everything on the board and start fresh. You can use bulletin boards for other purposes, like **ASSIGNMENTS** or work projects, or to inspire creativity (see **VISION BOARDS**), but designate an entire bulletin board for that purpose. Don't combine your boards or you won't be able to quickly spot the information you are looking for. Multiple bulletin boards that are smaller in size are good because they will help you keep each board to its purpose, but don't go crazy. While cork flooring is soft, durable, and eco-friendly, you don't want an entire wall lined with cork in your home.

■ ■ ■ ■ ■

AN O.C.D. SUCCESS STORY

Years ago, the O.C.D. Experience partnered with an event planner to create O.C.D. Events. The woman I partnered with is a creative visionary, but she didn't have the best system for organizing her materials for each event. I got her in to the habit of using bulletin boards and dedicating a board for each event in her pipeline. She loves that she has a way to view all of her materials at once so she can always see the big picture of an event instead of just its parts. Now her level of organization matches her creativity.

BUNKER is going to save your behind come the zombie apocalypse. If you have the space and can afford to stock it, building a bunker or converting an existing space into a bunker, fallout shelter, or panic room will give you peace of mind and a safe place to go in the event of a catastrophic emergency. Once you go in, you may not be coming out for a while, so make sure you are organized and have everything you need. Your bunker is the one place where "what if"s are allowed. Depending on your space, decide the duration of time you'll be able to stock your bunker for. Then go out and buy everything you'd need for you and your family to survive that amount of time: food, toiletries, **MEDICINE**, clothing, entertainment, **BAT-TERIES**, and so on—your typical **EMERGENCY KIT** on steroids. Anything you buy should be nonperishable and be able to run on batteries, of which you should have plenty, unless you have a generator. Keep everything organized in categories on labeled **SHELVES**.

I've seen all different kinds of spaces transformed into bunkers, like a sauna stocked with a month's worth of water and protein bars, survival gear, weapons, gas masks, and even bulletproof vests. I even had the privilege of consulting with someone who built a complete underground shelter for eight people, stocked with a year's worth of water, food, cots, machine guns—you get the idea. Whatever you put in your bunker, make sure it's appropriate for your **NEEDS**. You need to feed, clean, clothe, and potentially defend. Think about your family and what you hope to gain from having the security of a bunker. Remember: only tell the people you want in your bunker about your bunker. Otherwise, the ill-prepared will be showing up on your bunkerstep when California becomes an island after the big one hits and anarchy strikes.

BUSINESS CARDS can be a very easy thing to keep organized. They can also wind up being little useless piles of paper clutter. How many of you have stacks of cards on your **DESK**, in your car, or on your **NIGHTSTAND**? Save yourself from paper cuts and bleeding, reduce your Band-Aid expenses, and enter the digital world where business cards can be exchanged and returned to the owner in no time.

"Nice to meet you. Here is my card. Look forward to talking with you soon." Now is your moment to shine! Take the business card, walk to a quiet corner in a room, and input it into your phone. If you aren't comfortable doing this yet, because you aren't fast enough on your phone, practice! Remember, input only the necessary information that you will need in your contact. Not many people use a fax machine these days, so skip the fax number and ask for it later if you really need it.

Now go back to your new contact and hand them their card back. If they ask you for yours, be one step ahead of them and tell them you have already sent them an e-mail with your contact information.

If you haven't mastered the two-minute business card dance, then get in the habit of making sure any business card that is given to you is transferred from paper to digital in less than seventy-two hours. This is enough time for you to transfer all the necessary information from the card to your **COMPUTER** or **SMARTPHONE**, where you will actually get to utilize the information.

Get rid of business card portfolios that encourage you to hold and save all those business cards you've collected. You don't need an extra folder in your life, especially one with an obsolete purpose. Information is only powerful when it is at your fingertips.

Send a follow-up e-mail to the person who gave you their card to start a dialogue and acknowledge that you have already put their card to use. If you have yet to make the jump to digital and like holding on to people's business cards, start doing things differently now! The longer you wait, the more behind you'll end up as technology advances. You don't want to be the only one seeing "unknown caller" on your holographic communications implant because you didn't take the time to input someone's business hypercard! Changing your ways will save you time in the end and certainly energy in the future.

■ ■ ■ ■
AN O.C.D. SUMMARY

Organize: Whether you keep the actual card or not, quickly digitize it. If you keep them, have a specific location to hold the business cards until you digitize them.

Create: Using your favorite scanning iPhone app or inputting it into your computer, create a digital filing system that is quick and easy to manage. I like using TurboScan and Google Contacts.

Discipline: Do not let a card sit around for more than seventy-two hours because the pile of cards will become overwhelming and you will be neglecting possible new business opportunities and contacts. Update information immediately upon receiving it.

BUSINESS RECEIPTS (see RECEIPTS)

C

CABINETS should have a specific purpose and must be maintained for that purpose. Just because *cabinet* contains the word *net* doesn't mean it should catch everything and anything. No matter what cabinet you are dealing with, whether it's in the **KITCHEN, BATHROOM, OFFICE,** or **LIVING ROOM,** each cabinet should be home to a specific group of items. For example, let's look at a kitchen cabinet: define it as a cabinet for **SPICES, CANNED GOODS,** and flavorings. You should never put glasses or **DISHES** in this cabinet. Get into the habit of making sure this cabinet is for those specific items only. If you have trouble staying organized, create labels to remind you where each item belongs. Then pay attention to those labels! When you take something out of the cabinet, put it back exactly where you found it. Every couple of months, you should do some simple maintenance to make sure everything in your cabinets is where it should be and not expired. Trust me, you do not want to know what a flour beetle is, and if you do, hopefully you'll find out on Wikipedia and not in your kitchen. Remember, the O.C.D. Experience is about organizing and creating the discipline to maintain that organization. Discipline yourself and you'll never have to think twice about where things go or where to find them.

AN O.C.D. SUCCESS STORY

I talk a lot about designating specific purposes for your spaces. But those designations should still be within the context of where that space is located! A client who just happened to be one of my best friends had indeed designated one of his kitchen cabinets for a specific purpose. But it had nothing to do with the kitchen! He kept unprocessed paper documents in his cabinet. Clearly in the wrong place, and hidden behind a door, he sometimes paid bills late. I convinced him to move his unprocessed documents to his desk to scan and process them quickly. As a result, he now pays his bills on time and can always find what he is looking for. Designate your spaces for specific purposes, but make sure they are relevant to the room they are in!

CABLES (see CORDS)

CALENDARS will help you organize and distribute your time and energy effectively, if used properly. If used improperly, you might find yourself at the wrong place at the wrong time, like spending an hour on the freeway to get to a business meeting and then discovering your meeting is scheduled for the following week. I use my calendar every day and make sure that I sync it with the people who are close to me and work with me. Keep your calendar organized in such a way that anyone could pick it up and get to every scheduled appointment without a problem. This means no shorthand. Put down all of the relevant information for every event, even if you think you'll remember it: event name, time, date, location, phone numbers, addresses, and any relevant notes. If your **ADDRESS BOOK** is always updated, there is no reason to duplicate that information in your calendar. Don't do double work. If you still handwrite your calendar and haven't joined the digital age, that's okay. But remember, the moment you lose your calendar, it's gone. No backups. Your life will suddenly tumble into dysfunction. Which kid goes where at what time? When is that root canal? Which days do you need to be "extra sensitive" in your relationship? Help! For a busy household, consider using a whiteboard for an easy-to-see-and-edit solution. Just make sure it's hung high enough so your kids don't erase it. When you add to it, make sure it is legible and use colored pens for different areas of your life. For example, use red for work, blue for personal, and green for health and exercise. Using different colors will make it easy to see how you balance your life and adjust your priorities. Most of us shortchange our personal time. If you are using a **COMPUTER** or phone to keep your calendar organized, it's much simpler and more powerful than a handwritten calendar. Aside from backup capability, these devices give you the option to make multiple calendars for personal and business use. You can sync your calendar among all devices, and even with other people, such as your spouse, children, or employees. Just make sure your default calendar is set as your own and not someone else's. You can choose your default calendar view as daily, weekly, or monthly, but I recommend keeping it on the daily view because your events are easier to see. Change the time frame as necessary when you want to see a bigger picture of your schedule. You can also take advantage of the invite attendee feature, which will allow you to send e-mails to people with event information that will then automatically update their calendar. Set alarms on your calendar to remind you of important meetings an hour or two before, or however long you need, so you have time to mentally prepare. If you are a busy, on-the-go person and have back-to-back **APPOINTMENTS,** make sure you leave yourself enough travel time so you aren't late. If you can, schedule your appointments so that you don't have to run all around town, unless you are trying to lose weight. Whatever calendar system you use, just make sure you update it regularly and with all relevant information, back it up, and synchronize it between your device and computer. Make sure you adjust all of your calendar preferences to accommodate your **NEEDS** and how you want your calendar to function for you. This will lead you to a functional and organized life.

AN O.C.D. SUCCESS STORY

My friend bought some concert tickets months in advance of the concert to surprise his wife. He kept the tickets in a drawer and of course, relying only on his brain, forgot about them. He remembered them only the afternoon of the concert. At the last minute, he had to call his wife, ruin the surprise, pull her out of a meeting, and have her rush home. They were late to the concert, and the thoughtfulness of his surprise was negated by his irresponsible methods of remembering events and appointments. I have since helped my friend move to a digital solution and actually get credit from his wife for being thoughtful, using the calendar on his smartphone to set appointments and reminders. He hasn't missed an event since.

CAMPING EQUIPMENT (see SPORTING GOODS)

CANNED GOODS take a long time to expire. Unfortunately, this means you often end up with what looks like a fallout **BUNKER**. It's important to organize your cans so you know what you have, can actually use them, and don't end up buying extra stock at the grocery store. Check your cans and then make a **GROCERY LIST**! Don't just head to the market and wing it. You'll wind up with stuff you don't need. All of your cans should be in one area, subdivided by type (soups, vegetables, broths, fillings, etc.) and then by product. If you have deep **CABINETS**, consider using tiered can racks to maximize space and efficiency. Depending on how many cans you stock, you can also use clear Uline bins for easy organization. Using **BINS** like these will allow you to know exactly how much of an item you can fit, so when you get low, the reorder process is simple: if the bin can fit ten cans and you have two left, you go to the store and buy eight! Once you have all of your canned goods in their proper place, make sure that the labels are facing out so you are never confused about what is in your cabinet or **FOOD PANTRY**. Put cans that expire soonest in the front so you use them first. Go through your cans once a year and dispose of anything expired. Expired cans that contain high-acid food, like tomatoes, can actually explode when you open them because of the buildup of hydrogen gas (H_2). Don't get a blast of spoiled diced tomatoes to the face. Donate any unexpired cans that you just won't use. If you won't be eating those lima beans, a canned food drive would be delighted to free up your space.

CAR (see AUTOMOBILE)

CARRY-ON BAG (see PACKING)

CASSETTE TAPES are never coming back into style, unlike the situation with vinyl **RECORDS**. You should not have any of these. If you do, convert them to a digital format or simply repurchase the album digitally if it's available. If you must have the original recording, there are many inexpensive USB devices that can be purchased to convert your cassettes into digital formats using your **COMPUTER**. Convert and file them with the rest of your **DIGITAL MUSIC**. The sooner you get those tapes converted, the better you'll feel knowing that all of the information will be preserved. You can graduate from making mix tapes for your crush, skip **CDs** entirely, and hand them a thumb drive with the greatest '50s love songs. Now that's romantic!

CATALOGS are just **BROCHURES**' fatter older brothers. A good rule of thumb for these types of materials is to browse and purge. Once you flip to that back cover, head for the **RECYCLING** bin. Everything in a catalog can be found on the Internet, so it's not necessary to keep any catalog after you have browsed through it, and never keep it for more than a week. If you are interested in keeping an eye on a particular item, go to the company's Web site, type in the model number or name of the item, and **BOOKMARK** it for later viewing. Never toss catalogs in with your **MAGAZINES,** or they will inevitably overstay their welcome in your home. Be a good neighbor: if you see catalogs sitting around in a common area **MAIL** space, recycle them. Just give your upstairs neighbor a chance to grab them first so you don't have to explain why you recycled his Victoria's Secret catalog.

CDs are on their way out as digital downloads take over, but many of us still have that large CD collection. See these CDs swiftly scrapped. Say that five times fast. CDs can be digitized with a single click using almost any music software and then backed up to the **CLOUD** or a **HARD DRIVE** and synced between your devices. You'll find yourself listening to a lot more music. Stick it, rip it, and ditch it: when you are done importing the CDs, put them back in their case, sell them, use them in an art project, or donate them to a local library or charity. You also don't need to digitize everything. As you go through your collection, consider that you'll probably never listen to that DJ Jimmy Jamz and the Freaky Bunch album again. So don't bother digitizing it. But before you begin this process, make sure to set the import options on your software to suit your organizational **NEEDS**. You can choose how your files are named, where they are stored, how they are tagged, and how are they organized. You may even have the option of what kind of music file to import them as—MP3, WAV (waveform **AUDIO FILE** format), M4—but the most common file to use is MP3. Create a master **MUSIC** folder prior to the large importing process so you'll know exactly where your music is kept. Once your collection is digitized, there really is no reason to hold on to the discs, but if you insist on keeping them, there are two ways to organize them. The simplest and most compact way is to toss the jewel case, unless it's signed, and keep your CDs alphabetized in a Case Logic CD notebook, which can hold from twenty-five to five hundred discs. This process is most effective when you've decided not to buy any more physical CDs, so the books don't have to be reorganized every time you add to the collection. Sliding everything over is time-consuming and tedious. If you want to display your CD collection for others to see, you should alphabetize the collection by artist for simple searching. Find **SHELVES** that go with the decor in your home or **OFFICE** or make shelves that are custom to your taste. For signed CDs, consider framing and displaying them on your wall. Always put CDs back where they go once you're done using them, or else your easy-to-find alphabetized system will quickly deteriorate and you won't be able to find the album you are looking for. Why settle for Tupac when you can have The Notorious B.I.G.? That's right, I said it . . .

AN O.C.D. SUMMARY

Organize: Pull out all of your CDs. Get rid of any you no longer listen to.

Create: Choose your storage method: as digital files, in a CD book, or on shelves. If you choose digital, keep everything in your music folder and ditch the discs and cases after import. If you choose to use the CD book or to display your collection on shelves, keep your collection alphabetized.

Discipline: Always put your CDs back in their proper place. If you digitize, make sure you are choosing a consistent format and saving in a consistent location.

CELL PHONE (see SMARTPHONE)

CHANGE is necessary to grow, but all pocket change will do is just weigh you down. Don't sort your pocket change by pennies, nickels, dimes, and quarters. Just put it in a jar at the end of each day as you empty out your pockets, **PURSE**, and **WALLET**. Make sure you don't use a jar that will be too heavy when it's full. You don't want a water jug full of change you can't move out of your house. You can pull out a handful of quarters every now and then to keep in your car for parking meters, but most parking meters are rapidly being updated to accept **CREDIT CARDS**. The moment the jar is full, take it to your closest coin-counting machine and enjoy what feels like free money! Also, a lot of the Coinstar machines at your local pharmacy will give you the option of a gift card in lieu of cash and take less of a fee. I recommend going this route and buying things you need from the pharmacy at this time, such as toothpaste, soap, vitamins, and detergent, because you will always need these items. Free money or free toiletries—what a great choice!

CHILDREN'S BEDROOMS are the place to teach your child early on how simple and rewarding organization can be. And to read them *Cloudy with a Chance of Meatballs* while pretending it's just for them. Kids grow up fast, so their rooms will require constant reorganization, but always make them a part of the process to empower them and teach them good discipline. Ask them their opinions. This will get them thinking about organization and you'll reap the benefits for years to come. Make it easy for them to maintain their room themselves. The most important things to think about when organizing a child's room is how you want them to use the room, height appropriateness, and room to grow.

If you have a separate **PLAYROOM**, then let the bedroom serve only as a place of work, learning, and rest. Keeping **TOYS** and **GAMES** in the playroom will eliminate distractions and make it easier for your child to work or sleep. If you must keep toys and games in the room, make sure they are sectioned off to one area. You don't want toys taking over the bedroom. Discipline your child to return the toys to their assigned place by the end of each day. It may seem harsh, but tell your child that whatever toy isn't worth respecting and putting away isn't worth keeping and will be thrown away.

All children should have an assigned space to do homework. This shouldn't be in the **KITCHEN** or **LIVING ROOM** where they will be distracted by the hustle and bustle of the family. If possible, it should be in their bedroom in a quiet area where they can focus. Encourage them to maintain their **DESK** like you would your own: have a **BIN** labeled **CHILDREN's SCHOOLWORK**, which will also help you keep track of their **ASSIGNMENTS**, and a few pens or pencils in a cup. Everything else should be in **DRAWERS** in assigned and labeled spaces. Keep to this simplicity or soon your child's desk won't be visible beneath the mess and you might lose a pet in the pile.

When it comes to buying **FURNITURE** for your child's room, think about storage. Does the piece have enough storage and is that space manageable? What will be kept in it? And is it big enough to continue being functional as your child grows?

Kids are short, so keep that in mind when you organize their space. Don't organize it for yourself; organize it for them. That means height appropriateness and accessibility, especially in the **CLOSET**. How can your children learn to maintain organization and discipline if they can't reach the closet rod? Hang hooks on the back of doors that are height appropriate for your child's bags and quick grabs.

Your child's room can contain age-appropriate **BOOKS**, comforting **STUFFED ANIMALS**, and some **ART** that accents your child's personality, but keep it contained and constantly reevaluate what is still appropriate for your growing child. A thirteen-year-old no longer needs a baby monitor in his or her room. Give the kid some space!

CHILD'S PLAYROOM is the place for your child to play and do creative projects, like exploring the artistic potential of dried macaroni. Make sure you keep the room organized for that purpose and use it as an opportunity to teach your child good organizational habits. As in the case of your **CHILDREN'S BEDROOMS**, everything should have a place that is labeled. Designate specific areas for **TOYS, GAMES** and puzzles, **BOOKS**, dress-up, and **ART SUPPLIES**. Encourage your children to maintain the discipline of returning things to their proper areas. The whole room should be gone through in anticipation of every gift-giving holiday and birthday. Go through this process with your children to figure out what they no longer play with. Instead of asking them if they want to keep something, offer them a choice between two items and only keep the one they pick. This will teach your children to have healthy attachments to their possessions and keep their playroom manageable. In an ideal world, this room should be shoe-free to keep it clean and sanitary. Your kids' faces will probably have a close relationship with the floor, so keep that dog-soiled shoe sole out of that space!

CHILDREN'S SCHOOLWORK will be coming home frequently and for many years. If you don't have a system for dealing with it, you'll be shocked by how quickly your home will turn into the Metropolitan Museum of Finger-Paintings. Don't indulge your parental instincts to keep everything they ever produce. Schoolwork should be viewed and discussed with your children as soon as it comes home. This will keep you aware of your children's **ASSIGNMENTS** and performance. Make a decision at that time if you want to hold on to that work. Trust your instincts on work that is unique or special to you or your children, or shows that a new milestone has been reached. Take a picture of the work with a scanning app on your phone. Create folders to store the schoolwork and download the pictures to DOCU-MENTS → CHILD's NAME → SCHOOLWORK → TITLE OF ASSIGNMENT → DATE. Then toss the paper unless you really think it's a masterpiece worth saving a hard copy of. Have a plastic **BIN** labeled "Schoolwork" for each child and keep the hard copies in there. Once that bin starts overflowing, it's time to go back through all the work and get rid of some of it. It will be easier to get rid of work that seemed precious in the moment when you see your children's collection of work as a whole. Maintain the discipline to do this whenever the bin gets full and *never* start storing work outside of the bin. Store the bin in an accessible but out-of-the-way place so you do not have bins taking over your home. As for displaying the work, feel free to hang up what you are most proud of. If you use your **REFRIGERATOR**, limit it to one item per child. Explain to your child that when a new piece of work goes up, the old one has to come down. In addition to not wallpapering over your refrigerator, this will make the displayed items much more meaningful to your child. A drawing of a chicken made from a hand tracing is just another in the flock when they are all over the fridge.

■ ■ ■ ■
AN O.C.D. SUCCESS STORY

A client of mine lived in an area affected by Hurricane Sandy. Her garage flooded and everything in cardboard boxes was ruined. Luckily, I worked with her before the storm and helped her reduce the amount of children's schoolwork she kept. We put the rest in plastic bins, which survived the storm unscathed. Those precious memories are safe and still ready to pass down when the time comes.

CHILDREN'S TOYS (see TOYS)

CHORES should be written in a place viewable by all people responsible for completing them. Everyone will know his or her **RESPONSIBILITIES**, and everyone will know who doesn't get dessert when a chore isn't completed. This can be a whiteboard or chalkboard, a notebook kept on the **KITCHEN** counter, or even a digital document kept up to date. You can even enter chores into your smartphone **CALENDAR** as **APPOINTMENTS**. Since a lot of children have smartphones these days, use it to help them stay on top of their chores. You can use **SMARTPHONE** privileges as an incentive to get them to do their chores. Giving your kid a phone might not seem like such a bad idea when it can get work done around the house! Divide your chores up among the household. If you have no children, make sure that the chores are split evenly and that everyone stays on top of their responsibilities. If you have trouble assessing how chores should be divided, then start by sitting down and discussing it. Everyone will have a preference of what chores they like to do, which will make staying up on them much easier. The rest can be distributed evenly. Make sure that no matter what is going on in your life, you complete your weekly chores on the days they need to be done. If someone is out of town, pick up the slack by doing chores for them. It all comes back around. Completing a chore well doesn't take a lot of brain-power, so you can multitask as long as it doesn't affect your performance, or use the time to think about work, friends, and evening plans. There is a satisfaction to completing chores, and it will greatly benefit your organized home life. Stay on top of your chores so they will never be on top of you.

■ ■ ■
O.C.D. EXTREME

Vacuum in straight lines to create a pleasing pattern on your rug or carpet. Nothing screams fresh and clean like parallel vacuum lines!

■ ■ ■
O.C.D. APPROVED TECHNOLOGY

Want to empower your children to get their chores done? Download the Goodie Goodie app. It lets you, the parent, create chores and re-wards that sync to your child's iDevice. Easy for you, fun for them. They earn points for chores they can then redeem for either rewards that you set or for gift cards to their favorite stores. It's a win-win!

CLASSROOM organization is all about facilitating learning and teaching discipline by good example. As a teacher, you must set an example for your kids in how you keep your own **DESK** and **DRAWERS**. Disorganization has a way of spreading, so don't be the one who starts the outbreak. Every two weeks, have a desk check and give out little rewards to students who have well-organized desks. If they aren't organized, explain to them how they could better organize their desks for the next check. As for classroom lay-out, don't just accept what the last teacher or school staff had previously set up. Organization is all about what works for you and your students! Orga-nize your classroom so it doesn't feel like one enormous space, but rather separate learning areas: a reading area, a computer area, a hands-on play area, a **BULLETIN BOARD** area for important information, and a secluded area for you and a student to have semiprivate face time. Also designate a space for filing important student information like signed forms, tests, and **ASSIGNMENTS**. Have a folder for each student so that when a parent asks a question, you can easily pull the file and back up your answers with the actual work. If you are comfortable in the digital world, scan all those **DOCUMENTS** and keep them on your **COMPUTER** under DOCUMENTS → STUDENTS → STUDENT NAME. You should also have general folders for each day of the week to put work for each day of class to be completed by students. This way, if you are out sick, a substitute can jump in and assign the appropriate class work to your students without getting off track. At the end of each week you should plan and organize for the upcoming week. I know some classrooms are tight, but all of these suggestions are possible in even small spaces if you organize it right. If you are providing some of your own materials, **BOOKS**, puzzles, or **GAMES** to the students, keep these items separate in plastic **BINS** so they don't get mixed in with school property and so you can easily take them with you at the end of the year. Encourage students to always return things to their places immediately after using them. You can even assign **RESPONSIBILITIES** at the beginning of the year to get your students to play a part in the organization of your class-room. The promise of a pizza party is always effective.

AN O.C.D. SUCCESS STORY

Part of my success as a professional organizer is because I don't orga-nize for myself, I organize for my clients based on their usage and habits. I started this practice before I ever realized I'd be doing it as a career. When I was twelve, I noticed that although my teacher orga-nized the office supplies in the classroom, she didn't do so in a way that was best for the students who actually used them. Frequently needed items were kept too high. Supplies that were used together often weren't actually kept near each other. So one day I brought my label maker from home, stayed inside during recess, and organized everything according to how the students were using them, with my teacher's permission, of course. The process of gathering supplies for projects became much easier and faster. Don't just organize without considering whom you are organizing for!

CLEANING SUPPLIES are the fuel in your cleaning engine, along with the gyro you ate for lunch. Your supplies can be kept in a few areas depending on your space. If you have a **UTILITY CLOSET**, that's ideal, but under the **KITCHEN** sink works too. Wherever you keep your supplies, put those that you use on a weekly basis in a cleaning tote in the front of your storage space. The tote makes it easy to grab all the supplies you need and carry them with you around the house and clean efficiently. Put less frequently used supplies, like adhesive remover, spot remover, or silver cleaner, in the back of your space so you never have to move them to grab your weekly supplies, or even better, in another **CABINET** altogether. If you find that you have cleaning supplies that you no longer use or that are expired, get rid of them. If you have multiple floors in your home, it's good to keep a basic set of cleaning supplies, and even a vacuum, on each floor. This will save you time in running around the house and make you more likely to impulse clean on a regular basis, like when you just can't stand that spot on your mirror. CAR-cleaning supplies should be kept in the **GARAGE**, separate from housecleaning supplies. Try to fit all car-cleaning supplies in the bucket you use to wash your car. If you really baby your car with an array of products, designate a small area in your garage on a **SHELF** or in a cabinet and keep them there, but away from any food items. No matter where you keep your cleaning supplies, get in the habit of cleaning on a weekly basis to keep your space feeling fresh. If you feel comfortable eating off your floor, not that you should, that's a sign you are doing a good job. Please don't eat off your floor.

■ ■ ■

O.C.D. EXTREME

Rinse off your cans and laundry detergent caps, shake down your brooms outside, and wipe down the shelves you keep your cleaning supplies on. Nothing inspires you to clean like clean cleaning supplies!

CLOSETS that are out of control can be a terrifying sight! Don't give your skeletons a place to hide. Your closets will be distracting and overwhelming, and they will lose their functionality. Selecting an outfit should be a simple task but becomes daunting when you have to toss things aside, dig through piles, and aggressively shove hanging items aside because your space is overstuffed.

Closets come in many shapes and sizes, so you have to design a system that works for your specific space. But in general, a healthy closet has **CLOTHES** separated by type and color, all on uniform **HANGERS**, with enough space to easily see and access every item in your closet. To get your closet explosion back to this state, employ the O.C.D. Way.

Take everything out of your closet and go through each garment, one at a time. Most closets are overrun with an excessive amount of clothing that is never worn. Ask yourself these questions: What haven't I worn in over a year? What will I never wear again? What can be donated? What can be tossed? Are any contents in my closet distracting me from picking out the best possible outfit? Do I have room in my closet for this particular item? If you find it hard to make decisions, grab a trusted friend for their honest opinion or call O.C.D. for an O.C.D. Team Member!

Now make four piles: items you wear, items to donate, items to consign, and items to trash. Immediately bag the donation items. As you do this, for tax purposes, create a list of everything you are donating. You can treat the consignment items the same way, but make sure the bags don't get mixed up. Continually take out the garbage as you work to create a more organized, spacious, and calm atmosphere and to visually see your progress.

Now that you have the pile of clothes you think you are going to keep, it's time to start putting them on your uniform hangers. But don't put them in the closet just yet! As you grab each item, ask yourself one more time if you'll really wear it, if it really fits, and if you feel good wearing it. If you are just holding on to it because you "might wear it again," get rid of it. This is also a great time to get anything dirty or dusty laundered. Also consider making additions to your closet system based on what you are keeping. Never design a closet system before you know what you need to put in there! I've worked with so many clients who hire someone to design a nice-looking closet system without considering what they actually own and where things will go. The end result is a flashy but costly and useless closet. So ask yourself: Are you missing **DRAWERS** for your **SOCKS** and **UNDERWEAR**? Are you missing an extra hanging **SHELF** for the pants, dresses, or suits you are keeping? Have you always wanted a place for your leather chaps? Remember: the purpose of this process is to make room for the new and create space and functionality in the most frequented storage area of your home.

At this point you should have all the clothes you are keeping on their hangers, ready to go into your empty closet. Ask yourself how you want your closet to function. This means asking yourself how *you* function. We tend to have a daily schedule of how we wear our clothing. Perhaps you exercise first thing in the morning, shower, dress for work, come home, and put something on to lounge in. So arrange your closet to facilitate this schedule by organizing what you use the most often to be the most accessible.

Create sections for each type of clothing and arrange the sections by the amount of fabric for that type of item. For example, start with a section for tank tops, followed by sleeveless tops by strap size, then move into **T-SHIRTS**, blouses, long-sleeve tops, then jackets, and finally suits. This way, your closet will feel like it builds and has consistent growth as opposed to looking random and chaotic. Fold and stack **SWEATERS** instead of hanging them because they tend to get hanger bulges on the shoulder. See **BELTS, HATS, JEWELRY, PURSES, SCARVES**, and **SHOES** for good solutions on these specific items. But shoe boxes have no place in your closet. They take up way too much space and prevent you from actually seeing the shoes you own. So liberate your shoes from their bulky prisons and toss the boxes! If you're worried that your shoes will get dirty, just dust them every few weeks. After all is said and done, if you still find yourself with a jam-packed closet, consider other storage solutions like buying an armoire or **DRESSER**, or using the space under the bed. Or consider stocking your closet with only the items appropriate for the current season and storing everything else in moisture-resistant, lightweight, pH-neutral white polypropylene boxes in another location. You can find these online and they are specially designed for storing high-end clothing.

Once you've got your beautifully functional and organized closet, stay disciplined. Items must be hung back up in their designated spaces as soon as they come off your body or come back from the cleaners. Never put that cheap wire hanger from the cleaners in your closet. Always put clothing back on your uniform hangers. You should go through your closet once a year, and every time you spend too much at the mall, and donate items that you no longer wear. It should be much easier this time around if you've maintained discipline in your closet the O.C.D. Way.

■ ■ ■

AN O.C.D. SUMMARY

Organize: Pull out all of your clothing and divide it into four piles: wear, donate, consign, and trash.

Create: Divide your clothing by type and designate areas of your closet and dresser for each type of clothing. Make any necessary additions to your closet.

Discipline: Return your clothing to its designated home soon after it comes off your body or out of the laundry machine. When you buy new clothes, take the opportunity to purge your closet of clothing you no longer wear.

■ ■ ■

O.C.D. APPROVED TECHNOLOGY

Your closet hangers should all be uniform. My favorite hangers are the Slimline velvet hangers. They are strong, save space, are affordable, and have a luxurious look and feel. There are many different brands and colors, so compare prices.

■ ■ ■

CLOTHES create your image and I fully believe that we should dress for success. Your outfit should reflect your personality, not reveal the fact that your closet is disorganized and you couldn't find clothes that matched. How you organize your clothes should be specific to how you put together an outfit. You can organize your clothes by color, by type of item, by occasion, by recent purchase, or even by how frequently you wear that particular piece of clothing. As for how you distribute your clothing among your spaces, anything that can hang and is prone to wrinkling should always go in a closet. Foldable items should go in the dresser. See **CLOSETS** and **DRESSER** for instructions on how to fill those spaces in an organized way. Sometimes clothing is sentimental but no longer worn, such as a wedding dress, uniform, or a concert **T-SHIRT**. Keep these items in a **CONTAINER**, but not in your closet. You only want things in your closet that you will be wearing, period!

Once a year, but also depending on how often you shop, go through all your clothing and purge what you no longer need or wear. Ask yourself these questions: What haven't I worn in over a year? What will I never wear again? What can be donated? What can be tossed? If you find it hard to make decisions, grab a trusted friend for his or her opinion. Now make four piles: items you wear, items to donate, items to consign, and items to trash. Immediately bag the donation items. As you do this, create a list of everything you are donating for tax purposes. You can treat the consignment items the same way, but make sure the bags don't get mixed up. Continually take out the garbage as you work to create a more organized, spacious, and calm atmosphere and to visually see your progress. You'll be amazed how many bags of clothing you get rid of—people may wonder what's in all those bags. Maintain this discipline to keep your clothing collection manageable and you'll always dress your best.

■ ■ ■

O.C.D. APPROVED TECHNOLOGY

Garde Robe is a service that allows you to send in your less frequently worn clothing. They'll care for your clothes and store them while you don't need them, which is especially useful for seasonal items. They'll also provide you with a virtual closet complete with images of your clothing. When you request an article of clothing, they'll quickly send it to you anytime and anyplace. It's like cloud storage for your clothing!

C

CLOUD storage is a great way to back up, access, transfer, and share your files from anywhere in the world or just your **LAUNDRY ROOM**. Just like your **HARD DRIVES, E-MAIL FOLDERS,** and **COMPUTER FILES**, it needs to be properly organized to be functional and promote efficiency. That's why you are using the cloud in the first place—for quick and easy access on the go. Free cloud space tends to be limited, so you want to carefully select what it is that you send to the cloud. Don't waste your cloud storage space on your **MUSIC**—there are a number of music-specific cloud services that are very effective, like Google Play or iTunes Match. **DIGITAL PICTURES** can go onto a photo-sharing site like Picasa, but make sure before you upload that everything is labeled and already in organized folders. Uploading your music and photos to these services can save your cloud storage for your important **DOCUMENTS**. Make sure you have a local backup, which means on a physical hard drive where you live or work, just in case the cloud is inaccessible for any reason. If you purchased a significant amount of cloud storage for your digital life, organization is still important. Only upload what you really need. Just like on your **COMPUTER**, you want to have a clear and simple file structure so you can find what you need quickly and easily. I consider bringing up the file search feature a personal failure.

iCloud, Apple's cloud service, works a little differently than simple online storage. If you have iCloud enabled on your devices, it automatically syncs photos, contacts, **APPS**, notes, **MUSIC, MOVIES**, documents, and more. This is useful for effortless syncing between Apple devices, but also dangerous. If you have one disorganized device, suddenly you have four. This syncing can also become a privacy issue because photos you take on one device end up on the cloud, then on your other devices, then on your living room TV while you are hosting a dinner party and have Apple TV's photo screen saver enabled. Lesson learned. So make sure to manage your iCloud settings and structure on iTunes or iCloud.com so you don't automate disorganization and embarrassment. Make sure you are creating a full local backup of your iDevice to your computer.

Cloud storage is still an evolving concept and will undoubtedly change and improve over time. Stay on top of advances so you can always use the cloud as efficiently as possible. Remember that cloud storage can quickly deteriorate into e-clutter. However you use the cloud, make sure it's secure. Change your **PASSWORD** regularly. If you don't use a cloud service that automatically backs up new and changed files on your computer, make sure you are manually maintaining it and updating it every time you change or create a file. And of course, go through it regularly and delete what you no longer need. Clouds are light and fluffy, not sloppy and overloaded. Make the people who picked the name "cloud" for digital storage think they did a good job!

CLUTCHES (see PURSES)

COASTERS should be on any surface on which you don't want water damage. According to Larry David, we must "respect the wood." Organizing your coasters is simple: have as many matching coasters as drinks you'd expect to have in that area at one time. Keep that number in a coaster holder, which most coaster sets come with, or nicely stacked. Store the excess coasters where you keep your place mats for parties and large gatherings. Wipe down your coasters every month.

O.C.D. EXTREME

I'm always looking for ways to add new functionality or significance to items. Repurpose old tiles as coasters by adding felt pads to the underside, or get creative and make your own coasters from old pictures matted on art board and sealed with tabletop epoxy.

COFFEE TABLES should be clear of all unnecessary items such as piles of **CATALOGS, MAGAZINES, BILLS,** multiple remotes, and that almost-empty bag of microwave popcorn with only the unpopped kernels remaining. You want to be able to use the surface without having to clear it off. A couple of current magazines are okay, but this isn't a doctor's office. Have a **COASTER** set available if your table is wood. A candle, decorative item, or coffee table book can make the space more cozy and inviting. You can keep a single remote on your coffee table, but if you have multiple **REMOTES**, you really need a better solution. The less cluttered your coffee table is, the more you and your guests will want to be around it. You'll actually be able to have coffee on your rustic wooden coffee table. Wipe down your coffee table anytime it becomes overused and dirty. The more you clean frequently used spaces, the longer they will last and the nicer they will be to use.

COLLECTIBLES should all be cataloged, just like **ANTIQUES**, especially if you have a collection like Steve Carell in *The 40-Year Old Virgin*. Take a picture of all of your valuable collectibles and save the photos to DOCUMENTS → COLLECTIBLES → NAME OF COLLECTIBLE with a file name that describes that item. Store the pictures and the document in this folder for quick reference. You can send this information to your home owner's insurance company and add collectibles to your policy if they are very valuable. Some people like to display their collectibles in one room, some like to display them throughout their entire home, and some like to keep them in storage. But no matter where you keep your collectibles, make sure that they are in a safe place, out of a child's reach, and well protected. Keeping any collection organized and in good condition is valuable to the integrity of the collection for the future. Most people collect things because they value them and want to pass them down to family in the future. If you do display them as a collection, make sure each piece has some room to shine instead of cramming everything into a display space. Consider showing off your favorite pieces, like your new-in-box Ultimate Warrior wrestling action figure or your original Midge Hadley pregnant Barbie, and storing the rest, wrapped as necessary, in airtight **BINS**.

COMIC BOOKS should be kept in the plastic sleeve they came in when purchased. Heroes need protection too. If the comic didn't come in a sleeve and is of significant value to you, buy plastic sleeves or invest in a hardcover case. Being a collector is all about keeping your collection in the best condition possible. Don't be a supervillain to your comic collection. Organize your comic books by publisher, character, series, and then issue number. You can either display them or, like any valuable paper **COLLECTIBLE**, keep them in airtight **CONTAINERS** or drawer boxes in a cool, dark, dry place and with a silica pack to control moisture. Software also exists that allows you to digitally catalog your collection.

COMPUTER organization is often overlooked because files and programs don't take up physical space. Neither does time, but you're still careful with how you fill it. (Or you should be. See **TIME MANAGEMENT**.) Your computer is a tool of productivity and needs to be kept organized to be as functional as possible. Computers often come bloated with unnecessary software that takes up hard-drive space and clutters your program list. When you get a new computer, the first thing you should do is go through the preinstalled programs and delete anything you won't use. You can do this anytime by going into the control panel on a PC and clicking "add or remove programs." This panel shows you how often you use a program and the last time you used it. On a Mac, you just drag and drop the program into the trash. If you aren't sure whether you'll use a program or not, leave it and three months later, do another delete pass of your programs.

Now explore the control panel and adjust the settings. Computers offer many options and you should choose the ones that work best for the way you use your system.

Once your computer looks and feels right to you, stay on top of your files. Just as with your real desktop, files shouldn't pile up on your screen. Keep your files in a smartly organized folder system. Once in a while, go through your folders and delete files you no longer need, like that kinky video you should never have made in the first place. Always make sure you have a data backup solution in place so you never suffer a catastrophic loss from theft or a hard-drive crash.

COMPUTER FILES can be tricky to keep organized because every program tends to have a different default location where it saves files. As a result, you've got random files everywhere. Herd your files back into their proper corrals so they don't wander off and eat the grass from the neighbor's ranch. The first step to organizing your files is to have a digital scavenger hunt. Go through all existing folders to find your pictures, documents, **MUSIC**, and video files. Once you find these files, delete anything you don't need and move the rest into their appropriate folders. Music files go in the music folder by artist and album, picture files go in the picture folder by location and event, video files go in the video/movies folder by location, event, and date, and documents go in . . . you guessed it, the **DOCUMENTS** folder. Create subfolders to help you further organize your files and make them easy to find. This is a simple concept, but most people tend to have hundreds of mixed-up files in a single general folder. *Never* create a folder labeled "miscellaneous" or "to-do." These will become digital graveyards.

Some programs will even do the organization work for you—for example, most music programs—so check to see if that option is available. But don't assume that because files look organized within a certain program, they are organized on your **COMPUTER**. This is especially true with **DIGITAL PICTURES**. A lot of clients think they have their pictures organized because they are nicely displayed in a photo program. When they transfer their pictures to a new computer, they discover that they're faced with ambiguous file names and no file structure when they just want to show off the photos from their Disney vacation.

How you name a file is also very important. You should adopt a consistent file-naming structure for every document you create. That way, they'll be easy to search for and find in a list. A good rule of thumb is to name files with the title or description of the document and the date of your last edit.

Now that your files are in the right places and with proper names, make sure that all of your programs start saving new and downloaded files to the desktop by default so that you're in control of where they are filed. Put them where they need to go promptly and don't leave them on your desktop. No items should live on your desktop other than your **HARD DRIVE** icon, shortcuts to your most visited folders, and files you are currently working on. Too many items on your desktop will be distracting.

If you keep to these practices, transferring files to a new computer will always be a breeze. If you do get a new computer, take this opportunity to go through your files again and delete what you don't need. Then take the old computer and donate it. Just make sure to swap out the hard drive so you don't get your identity stolen or end up going to see a movie you could have sworn you wrote.

AN O.C.D. SUMMARY

Organize: Locate all of your files and put them in one folder to be processed. Go through them one by one, deleting whatever you don't need.

Create: As you go through your files, create the relevant folders and subfolders to organize them effectively. Change your file names so that you can identify the file without having to open it.

Discipline: Whenever you add or create new files, make sure to save them to appropriate folders on your computer. Don't let them just sit on your desktop or in a downloads folder. Keep your files backed up!

CONTACTS (see ADDRESS BOOKS)

CONTAINERS can be used for anything from flour in your **KITCHEN** to loose **CHANGE** in your **OFFICE** to **SEX TOYS** under your bed. Like sex toys, when used properly, containers are a useful tool. If you determine that a container and lid is the best solution for a particular space and purpose, get one that is appropriate in size for that application. Define containers for a single purpose and keep them properly labeled. Some people overuse containers, sometimes for things that don't even need to be contained! The end result is a plastic jungle. So always ask yourself if there is a better storage solution. When containers fill up, empty them, and when containers are empty, fill them up.

The one room almost everyone uses containers is in the kitchen, to store both leftovers and raw ingredients. Containers can be labeled by using dry erase markers or even chalk. Look into these options because it makes keeping things organized easy and noting expiration dates simple. Keep them together with the lids in one clean area of your kitchen. This area can be a deep **DRAWER** with enough room, the back of a **CABINET**, or even a large pot that might only be used once a year for that family clambake. Assess what your **NEEDS** are by thinking about the last time you used all of the kitchen containers that you currently have. Was there ever a time where they were all being used? Can you discard some of the older containers that will not be used? Get rid of containers that are missing lids, that have stains, or that have just been worn from excessive use. Stack the rest by size, largest at the bottom, for easy storage and accessibility. Lids can be stacked vertically next to the containers or underneath their partners, or placed inside one of the larger containers. Try not to keep the lids in a separate location from the containers. They are a family and you don't want to be a home wrecker.

CORDS are wires of any kind used for electrical needs. There are a plethora of different kinds, which can get very confusing: phone chargers; USB cables for cameras, printers, and external **HARD DRIVES**; telephone cables; coaxial cables; HDMI/video and audio wires for TVs and TV peripherals; extension cords; power strips . . . YIKES. I run into cable rat's nests in nearly every home I organize.

Some cords are indeed worth keeping. They are expensive and extras do come in handy. Most new devices or services will provide you with a cable so you only need one extra cable of each type in case of a shortage or failure. You can also keep additional cables for your portable devices in your **LUGGAGE** so you are always ready for a trip. You don't need cables for any device you don't use or don't have. I know that many people simply don't know what certain cables are used for or if they still need them. So when it comes time to tackle your cable rat's nest, grab every electronic device you own. One by one, see if a particular cable fits in any of your devices. *If it doesn't fit, get rid of it!* You got rid of your original Nintendo from 1985, along with the Light Gun and Gyromite, so you don't need that power cord anymore.

Store the extra cables (one of each type) that do fit your devices in an out-of-the-way **DRAWER** or in a bag or **BIN** that can be kept in your **UTILITY CLOSET**. Make sure this bag is labeled and that each cable is tightly wound so they don't get tangled. Electrical cords for outdoor use and heavy-duty items should be kept in a **GARAGE** coiled and hung or in a bin, always ready for use. Alternatively, keep the cord with the equipment or **HOLIDAY DECORATIONS** it's used with. No need to separate that extension cord from that Christmas tree.

Go through your cables once a year and purge those that are obsolete or may have gone with a piece of equipment you no longer own. When you are done using a cable, make sure to wind it and store it. Stay disciplined and the rat's nest will stay away.

When running cords in your home, keep them as out of sight as possible. It will be a glorious day for me when all our devices are functionally cordless and wireless. Until the day we can all forget the word *cord*, find the most logical way to run cords. Measure the distance of your cord run BEFORE you buy the cord so you buy the most appropriate length. Use cable ties or black electrical tape to keep them taut and tangle-free. With a label maker, label each cord on each end so that replacing a cord will take seconds instead of hours of trial and error trying to find both ends of the same cord. Take that extra thirty seconds to really make sure the cord is run well. A well-run cord makes a difference in the long run. I've seen some pretty scary cord bundles and nothing ruins the energy of a productive space like the feeling of being in a scene from *The Matrix*.

■ ■ ■ ■

O.C.D. EXTREME

I hate seeing cords, so if I have carpet, I'll pull up the edge, run my cable underneath, and then hammer the carpet back down. Voilá, no electric snakes! I also make my own custom-length cables so I never have extra slack I have to coil up. Most types of cables can be cut and then a new end put on with some simple tools from the hardware store. This is a great way to get exactly the length you need!

COUNTER SPACE needs to be clear to be functional, just like a windshield, so make sure the things you keep out are necessary and frequently used. Don't cause an accident. Are you juicing daily? If not, get that juicer in a **CABINET** and take back that counter space from Jack LaLanne. If you notice you don't use some things often and have the space to store them away, do it. You don't have to keep them out just for the sake of keeping things out. There's nothing naked about a bare counter. **BATHROOM** counters should be limited to hand soap, disposable towels, a picture or creative touch, and perhaps a candle and some matches to hide your shame. **KITCHEN** counters should be a blank canvas for food preparation and plating. Try not to keep bottles of cooking oil or **SPICES** on display, but you can leave out a bowl of fruit and small appliances that are used weekly, depending on your space.

COUPONS are as easy to organize as "clip and put away." For years, I watched my grandma spend entire Sunday mornings clipping coupons. Neighbors' newspapers were known to go missing from time to time. The one thing she did that was different from most clients is she used them or purged them. Don't let your coupons pile up.

I've worked with clients who use a large **BINDER** with plastic inserts to store their categorized coupons. Some common categories include baby, baking, beverages, breakfast, condiments, dairy, meat, pasta, produce, and snacks. Clients take the binder with them every time they go shopping. If you want to schlep around a massive coupon binder, and aren't ashamed of it, then this is an acceptable way to organize your coupons. But for a more subtle method, keep all of your coupons in a coupon wallet or small accordion folder with alphabetical tabs. Every time you clip new coupons and add them to the wallet or folder, go through the coupons in there to remember what you have. Make sure expired coupons are discarded and that soon-to-expire coupons are put to use. You can even have a section for coupons expiring this week or high-value coupons you really want to use. But there is no point taking time to cut coupons if you just stick them in a big bag to get lost in time.

For the digital guru, download your coupons from online or take a picture of each coupon and create an album/folder on your phone titled "Coupons." Before visiting your favorite store, take a peek in your album of the coupons that you have stored for that vendor. This will allow you to consistently keep your coupons updated and remind you which products you should purchase. Visit the company's Web site for any downloadable coupons and include those in your album/folder.

Keep your coupon system simple and maintained, and treat your coupons as you would your money. You'll never have to hand over that extra 99 cents for a frozen package of Bagel Bites.

AN O.C.D. SUMMARY

Organize: Take all of the coupons you have and alphabetize them. Get rid of expired coupons if you so choose, but some stores will still honor an expired coupon. Decide what method of couponing you want to use: tangible or digital.

Create: Dedicate either a small accordion folder or wallet specific for couponing, or create a digital system on your phone.

Discipline: If coupons are disorganized, you won't be able to find them, and that means passing up the savings. Refresh your memory as to what coupons you have before each trip. And remember, the more coupons you have, the less likely you'll find the coupon you actually need. Discipline yourself to keep coupons only for places you actually shop.

CRAFT ROOMS are a bit of an organizational paradox: they're meant for creativity, but you need to store a ton of different supplies and no one is inspired to make something beautiful in a chaotic space. Paint a picture while standing in your garbage can. You can't! Therefore, you should really try to decide what it is you'll be crafting in your craft room and stock only the relevant supplies. It will also help your creativity to choose a space with abundant natural light.

When reorganizing your existing craft room, get rid of everything you don't use. It'll just make it harder to find the stuff you do use. Then, based on what it is you do and your available space, set up different stations for specific purposes, like painting or sewing. This will limit accidents and also relieve the monotony of working at a single space for long periods.

Once you have your stations, ask yourself how often you use each item at that station and make the most frequently used items the most accessible. When you sit down, the things you use the most should be right at your fingertips. You don't want to have to get up and down too much for things that you use regularly. Put that energy into creating.

To store all those bottles of glitter and packets of confetti, stencils, and googly eyes, I like to use small, labeled **CONTAINERS** or jars kept alphabetically on mounted **SHELVES**, ideally near their relevant stations. But a craft space is about creativity, so feel free to design your own inspiring but effective storage solutions, such as putting up pegboards for holding tools and accessories, mounting a rod and hanging spools of **RIBBON** with zip ties, or keeping fabric visible and organized in a wall-mounted wine rack. Use your wall space as much as possible, but always keep it organized and efficient.

Clean up after each project and make sure you leave your supplies the way you want to find them for next time. It would be a shame to walk into a craft room to wrap a gift for someone and not be able to find that special paper. Don't keep scraps unless you have plans to use them on a particular project immediately. Also, constantly be aware of the **QUANTITY** of your supplies so you don't reach for something and discover you ran out because you forgot to restock it. Break the habit of going to the store and buying craft supplies on a whim because they are on sale. Just because they are half price doesn't mean you need to buy thirty packs of neon green pipe cleaners. Have a purpose when buying your supplies and carry out your creative endeavor before buying more and more and more . . .

■ ■ ■ ■

AN O.C.D. SUCCESS STORY

My friend's mother hadn't crafted for years, yet she had a large collection of supplies. After I helped her streamline the overwhelming collection of supplies in her craft room, she picked her hobby back up. Sometimes the very act of organizing can reinvigorate a passion!

CREDIT CARD RECEIPTS (see RECEIPTS)

CREDIT CARDS should be ordered only as absolutely needed and not because a company is offering you zero interest for the first twelve months, a free airline ticket, or 10 percent off at the cash register, even though it would help you justify buying those amazing **SHOES**. If you are the kind of person who is bad with money and bills, think about having only one credit card, and never order a new card because one is maxed out. If you have a business, you can have two credit cards, one for business and one for personal. If you are good with your **FINANCES**, and like to use multiple credit cards with rewards like mileage or cash back, or keep a card stashed away for emergency situations, pay those **BILLS** immediately so you never lose track and end up paying interest. However many cards you have, monitor those **ACCOUNTS** regularly for suspicious charges and fraudulent activity. The more cards you have, the likelier it is this will happen at least once. Scan the front and back of each card you own and save it as a password-protected PDF. If it ever gets stolen, you'll have the emergency phone number and account number to cancel it quickly. You can also just open up the file if your wallet is in another room and you're doing some online shopping. Always keep your credit cards in the same place in your **WALLET**. That way, you'll always know where they are supposed to be. If any are missing, you'll know right away without having to search through your entire wallet or **PURSE**. You can then call the credit card company immediately to cancel, or call out your teenager who took it.

■ ■ ■
O.C.D. EXTREME

Why have one layer of security when you can have two? Instead of signing the backs of your credit cards, write "SEE ID." Merchants will have to check your license to make sure you are who you say you are, stopping wallet thieves dead in their tracks.

CUBICLES at your workplace are a true testament to who you are as a person. Show your colleagues, your bosses, and your Skype buddies that you are an organized and reliable employee. Your cubicle is already small enough; don't shrink your work space further by leaving unnecessary items out on your **DESK** or stuffed in your **DRAWERS**. If you already have a messy cubicle, start sorting! Pull everything out of drawers and file **CABINETS** and off your desk. Make a "keep" pile and a "junk" pile. If you even think you can get rid of it, do it! Don't save old pens, old **PAPERS**, loose paper clips, dirty rubber bands, or anything that should be sticky but isn't. Toss the **GARBAGE** and you'll be able to start organizing your cubicle. If you inherited the cubicle from someone else, make it yours quickly. Always claim your space so you can take power of that space. It is nearly impossible to do so with someone else's old baggage holding you back.

The best way to organize your cubicle is from a seated position, since that's where you'll be most of the time. Sit down in your chair and decide where the best place is for your phone, your **COMPUTER**, and any supplies you use often. Don't be afraid to ask the IT guy for longer **CORDS** to move your electronics. You need to be comfortable and your company should accommodate that. Don't be the person whose cubicle looks like an office supply store. Keep only what you need and use daily on your desk, and weekly, in your drawer. Leave everything else to the supply closet. Everything you need should be within arm's reach, unless you have unusually short arms. You shouldn't have to roll your chair for anything you use on a daily basis.

If you can file your papers digitally, you'll save even more space because you won't need a **FILING CABINET**. But if your **OFFICE** is behind the times, organize your filing cabinet and use it diligently so that there are only a few or no papers on your desk. This will also protect you and your privacy because you can lock your file cabinet. For active projects, you can use stackable, tiered trays on your desk, but don't start using them as a place for random papers. Label each tray for incoming work, outgoing work, and work in progress.

If you keep snacks at your cubicle, keep them in sealed **CONTAINERS**. Know that if you keep them on your desk, fellow employees will help themselves.

Print out a small list of commonly used extensions and numbers you may need throughout the day and display them in a prime location so they always catch your eye. Put up a few pictures and decorative items to make the cubicle your own. Before you know it, your cubicle will be the talk of the office, but more important, you'll work better if you make your cubicle a tiny but efficient and simple home away from home.

AN O.C.D. SUCCESS STORY

In a televised piece, I helped Miami news reporter Al Sunshine tackle his notoriously messy cubicle. He had twenty years' worth of reporting piled up! He was resistant at first, defending every item as historical and important. As soon as he starting seeing actual desk space, he changed his tune. Functionality trumps chaos any day!

D

DATA (see **COMPUTER FILES**)

DECEASED'S BELONGINGS can be a huge weight for a family and any loved one when a passing occurs. I remember when my grandmother passed how hard it was for my mom to look at her things. My grandma's stuff sat in her room in my parents' house, and the thought of walking into or near the room could make my mom cry. A little over a year later, I came home for **THANKSGIVING** and my grandmother was brought up. Good memories, bad, funny to a point where we were making fun of her, and all of the little things she did that made us all laugh. I seized the moment and took my mom into her room and started the process of going through her things.

It is very important to *take your time* with a loved one's belongings, if you need the time, and go through everything they left behind before purging and throwing anything away. It will be like peeling an onion for some. Some people let these items sit for a year while others wait even longer. It is important that you go through the natural grieving process before trying to organize these items, but make sure that time doesn't turn into three, even four years, because their belongings are something that you need to deal with in order to have peace with their passing.

Just like you would in your **CLOSET**, grab everything and organize it into groups: things you or a relative will keep, things that will be donated, things to be distributed according to a will, if there is one, and trash. Ask a friend or a relative to sit with you and go through the belongings, if that will make it easier. If it's fallen on your shoulders, by will or circumstance, to decide what to do with it all, consider asking relatives if they want some of the belongings before you throw away or donate the items. What may not be sentimental to you may be for others. But if they have trouble deciding, set a date for people to make decisions by and to come collect what is theirs, or the process could drag on for years.

We all have different ways of handling grieving. Keep a few of the belongings to remind you of your loved one, or discard everything that comes into your possession. Donate items that have no emotional connection to you and you know could benefit someone else.

Scan and document letters and special photos and **PAPERS** from your deceased relative. I know that I want my kids and their kids to see my grand-mother's photos and letters that I scanned with my mother that day. The process of scanning and documenting their belongings will also be a mourning process in itself. When done, the natural movement of feelings and emotions will have run their course.

The most important part of this process is that you deal with it. You accept the passing. You deal with the belongings. Deal with the responsibility passed down to you, and do it with grace and strength. Natural emoting will occur, and allowing your emotions to affect you during this process is healthy and valuable. When you are done going through these belongings, you'll come out of it with some memories, some new keepsakes, and less clutter in your life, mind, and spirit.

■ ■ ■
AN O.C.D. SUCCESS STORY

My friend lost his mother many years ago to cancer. For years, her belongings sat boxed up in a storage unit. I helped him go through the unit and understood the emotional significance. While almost every item in there was sentimental in one way or another, we worked to determine which items held extra significance. For him, it was cleansing to remember the story of those lesser items, but then to let go of them. The now manageable items of profound significance were able to come home with him and serve as a fond reminder of his mother instead of collecting dust in a storage unit. He was also able to share those items with his new fiancée, who had never met his mother but was now able to better see a picture of who she was. He let go of the extra expense of storing items that he no longer needed and was able to add emotional value to his life by bringing items into his home that were truly irreplaceable.

D

DECKS should be arranged so that **FURNITURE** is placed clear of walkways, doors, and **GRILLS**, and never too close to the edge. This will make people feel comfortable sitting and relaxing instead of leaning back and rolling off the deck. Your deck is no place for accidental somersaults. If you move furniture around, for whatever reason it may be, always make sure to move it back to its original place. A lot of clients bring music-playing solutions from inside their house out to the deck every time they entertain. It's best to have a permanent outdoor solution so that you don't have to waste time moving equipment or run the risk of something outside getting ruined. Design the best placement for speakers and **CORDS**. The device doesn't even have to be expensive, just effective (see below for some suggestions). Have some baskets or **BINS** for children's **TOYS** in set locations so your kids can learn the discipline of cleaning up after a day of playing outside. Having baskets will make it easy for them to just drop their toys in the baskets. Don't use glassware on your decks. It's much easier to pick up a plastic cup than pieces of broken glass, hoping that you got every last shard before someone steps on it in what tends to be a barefoot area. If you have the opportunity to build a deck from scratch, consider building in organizational components for storage and efficiency, such as a bench with a lifting lid, or buying furniture that doubles as seating and storage to house outdoor **TOOLS**, toys, paper products, grill accessories, and matches. But make sure that toys are kept separate from these items. If you keep any pool supplies on your deck, make sure you keep them secured and out of children's reach by housing them in a locked mini-shed or small **CABINET**. Don't be that person who lets your pool net lie out on your deck to get gross and mildewed. Keep it in a clip on the wall, just as you would your nicely wound hose. Your deck should be a place you yearn to escape to. The more organized and clean your deck is, the more you'll yearn for that fresh air, and the more satisfied you'll be when you get it. Stay disciplined and earn that yearn!

O.C.D. APPROVED TECHNOLOGY

If you don't have the cash to wire up a permanent outdoor sound system, consider buying a wireless Bluetooth speaker. Rather than trying to lug your home audio system in and out every time you have a BBQ, pick yourself up a portable Pill or Beatbox made by Beats by Dre. They have great sound and plays your smartphone's music playlist from up to thirty-three feet away.

O.C.D. EXTREME

If you have a raised deck, cut yourself a trapdoor set up on hinges, so you can crawl underneath your deck and clean. To keep those spaces between boards clear of debris, use the narrow attachment head that comes with your vacuum.

DEPOSITS will take little time at the bank if you arrive prepared. Endorse your checks before you walk out the door and write your account number and "for deposit only" on the back in case you lose the check between home and the bank. Endorsing your checks at home will also save you from experiencing the dreaded dead pen you always find at the bank, or worse, the pen that has miraculously escaped from its metal chain! If you make deposits at an ATM, this is especially useful because many ATMs don't have pens. To save even more time, you can have deposit slips at home, but make sure you have a designated space for them in your **OFFICE** or home. If your bank still requires a deposit slip, you won't have to make a stop at the slip kiosk and can breeze through the line. No matter how you make your deposit, resist the urge to deposit your checks in a single transaction. It may save time in the moment, but it will cost you time later on when you do your accounting, see one large deposit, and have to figure out where it came from. Depositing as individual transactions will make it much easier to look back on where your money came from. If you use the option of having your bank deposits e-mailed to you, instead of taking the waste-of-paper printouts (which you shouldn't), make sure that you set up a folder in your e-mail program for bank deposits. This will make tracking those deposits very simple if you ever need to find them later on. Show your bank how organized you are when they make a mistake on your account, unless, of course, you are playing Monopoly and It's in your favor, in which case, pass Go and collect two hundred dollars!

O.C.D. APPROVED TECHNOLOGY

Skip the bank entirely! Most major banks now offer smartphone applications that let you deposit checks just by taking a photograph of the front and back of your check! Use this amazing functionality to save time. Just remember to double-check the information on your check against what the app says and make any corrections to the amount, account number, or routing number. As soon as you get confirmation that the deposit was accepted, shred the check.

DESKS are specific to each person, so the best way to go about organizing your desk is to ask yourself what you need readily available at your fingertips. Of all the spaces I've seen that can turn into organizational nightmares, desks are at the top of the list. Sometimes, I don't even realize there is a desk underneath the piles. The irony is, this is your primary work space! This is where you need to be your most efficient, and therefore your most disciplined! Some people have the instinct to keep every possible office supply and tool at their desks. This will not make your work space more efficient, unless your job is to distribute **OFFICE SUPPLIES**; they will simply distract you from your work.

Take everything out of your desk **DRAWERS** and put it all in one pile. Get rid of the **GARBAGE**, then separate the pile by the things you use daily, the things you use weekly, and the things you didn't even know you had. Put the supplies you never use in the supply closet, donate them, or toss them. Then move on to the other supplies. It is not necessary to have more than three pens, three pencils, a stapler, a pair of scissors, a box of paper clips, and a notebook. There may be other supplies that are specific to your job, but only you know what they are, so use strict judgment when keeping a supply.

Post-it notes have *no place* in an organized life. They lose their stick, fall off, and get lost. Instead, keep a single notebook to jot down those quick reminders. Use two different color pens: one to write the list and one for crossing out. This makes it easier to see what you've completed. It's also satisfying to reach for your "cross-out" pen. I find that black and blue work best. Use a supply cup on your desk so you can keep your pens, pencils, and scissors readily available to you. As for your daily work, get a three-tier tray for your **OFFICE** and place it on your desk. The top tray is for people to drop things off during the week such as **MAIL** and incoming work. The middle tray is for work in progress and where you put your notebook at the end of each day. The bottom tray can be assigned to your most important project at that moment. Be specific and label what each tray is for so people don't put your work and mail on your desk. As long as you are disciplined about keeping your boxes organized, you will be more efficient. The goal is to keep your desk as clear as possible unless you are using it for work at that moment. File or scan **PAPERS** immediately so they never pile up. The cleaner your desk is, the easier it will be for you to find things and work more efficiently. Don't be a desk Houdini: never let your work space vanish before your eyes.

AN O.C.D. SUCCESS STORY

Back when I was an intern for a talent agency in New York, I realized people needed some help learning how to maintain their desks to function more effectively in their offices. Due to the nature of the business, everyone had piles of scripts everywhere. Post-its covered computer screens noting client availability. It was a mess! After I convinced the president of the company to try out my system, he was so impressed by his increased efficiency that he took it upon himself to go around the office ripping Post-it notes off of people's screens and throwing them out. As for the scripts, the names of projects were written on the spine so that they could be stored on bookshelves alphabetically and easily located. As technology advanced, we eventually set up a system to scan all incoming scripts into a digital database. The agency still uses these systems today, and agents actually have desk space.

DESK SPACE can be plentiful and can be minuscule. No matter how much space you may have on your desk, the less you keep on it, the better. Think of your desk as a good friend— would you pile junk on top of your buddies, weighing them down? Just because you have the space doesn't mean you have to use it all. Improve your friendship with your desk and keep it as clear as possible. Maximize your work flow by addressing the things on your desk before it's covered with **PAPERS**. If you are in an environment where you may not be in control of how much work is placed on your desk, designate space on your desk for incoming work, in-progress work, and outgoing work. You can also use tiered trays with a polite note to your coworkers to place items in the trays and not on your desk surface. Make sure completed work is taken off your desk, filed, or handed to the appropriate person who needs it. Your desk space is *your* space. As is true with a friend, if you treat it with respect, others will notice it and treat it with respect also.

AN O.C.D. SUCCESS STORY

Sometimes it's hard to get my clients to clear their desks because of their attachments to their possessions. In certain circumstances, and with permission, of course, I help them by starting backward. I follow the advice of rapper Akon and "smack that all on the floor." I literally brush all of their belongings off the desk and onto the floor. Once my clients see their clear and functional desk space, they know they have to have it. From the floor, we throw away trash and old office supplies, shred old paper, and deal with everything else appropriately. Sometimes, it's easier to organize when you are looking at a clear canvas instead of trying to imagine clarity beneath a chaotic mess. Start with functionality and go from there!

■ ■ ■ ■

DESKTOP ICONS should be few to none. I've worked on desktops with so many overlapping and scattered icons, I can't even find the recycle bin! Your desktop is the first sight you see on your **COMPUTER** and the gateway to your productivity, so it's the first place that needs to be organized. It's no place to create a pretty icon collage. Computers have file folders for a reason, so make use of them and create them when necessary. No items should be on your desktop other than your **HARD DRIVE** icon, shortcuts to your most visited folders, and files you are currently working on. Too many items on your desktop will be distracting and can make your computer load more slowly. Everything on your desktop should have a place, even if it hasn't found it yet. Go through your desktop and put files in the appropriate folders and subfolders. See **COMPUTER FILES** for tips on folder organization, because the desktop isn't the only place you have icons that need organizing! You will start to notice, if you have a very cluttered desktop, that there will be some items that you don't even need or remember. Delete these items and continue organizing your desktop until it is clear and functional. Any time you save or download a new file, put it where it needs to go promptly and don't leave it on your desktop. Once you are done, find a nice image to use as a background because you'll actually be able to see it. That picture of the Crab Nebula is totally awesome and inspiring!

■ ■ ■ ■

AN O.C.D. SUCCESS STORY

I have seen some crazy desktops. One client in particular had his entire screen covered with icons, some overlapping others. When I went through them, I noticed he had multiple copies of the same files. He told me he could never find them, so he just redownloaded them whenever he needed them. What a waste of time and memory! We cleared his desktop, moved everything into appropriate folders, and now he never has to download the same file twice.

DESKTOP WINDOWS on your **COMPUTER** can become chaotic if you do not have your own system for minimizing and maximizing. Finding the spreadsheet you are working on can be a guessing game if you have too many windows open, and it was due an hour ago! First, make sure you have a good pop-up blocker enabled so windows aren't infesting your desktop as you browse the Web. Once you have that controlled, ask yourself what you're focusing on and close or minimize every window that isn't serving that focus. Constantly be aware of your active and open windows and close those distracting you from being productive, especially if they have flashing banners advertising local singles in your area. Most operating systems include some kind of window organization option to see what windows are open and available. On the Mac, you can swipe three fingers up to see all open windows and three fingers down to get back to your active window. On a PC you can press the Windows and Tab buttons on the keyboard simultaneously to engage flip view, which will show a Rolodex-style view of your windows. Having too many windows open is a drain on your system and can slow performance.

DIAPER BAGS are for your baby's necessities, not for your stuff. That's why they don't call it a mommy bag or daddy bag. Your diaper bag should contain bottles, enough diapers for a day's outing, a small container with some baby wipes, a changing pad, a change of clothing for the baby, a **PLASTIC BAG** for dirty clothes, a burp cloth, baby food and baby utensils if necessary, a pacifier, hand sanitizer, mini sunblock, a few small **TOYS** and a book, and a twenty-dollar bill. Look for a bag that facilitates organization with divided sections so you can assign each section to a specific supply. Put your **BABY ACCESSORIES** back in their place in the bag as soon as you are done using them. You don't want to be searching for that pacifier when the baby is screaming in a restaurant. The bag should always be stocked and ready to go at a moment's notice. Restock it immediately after returning home from an outing and make sure you have all the necessary supplies and that they are clean. Get any half-eaten baby food out of there. The Gerber baby is cute, but not when you see him on a half-empty jar of moldy pureed peas. As you learn what your child truly needs, adjust the bag accordingly.

AN O.C.D. SUCCESS STORY

When I was working with Bryce Dallas Howard and Seth Gabel, I had my first encounter with a diaper bag. They had a fantastic assistant at the time, also experiencing the diaper bag for the first time, so we partnered up to figure out the best solution for her and Bryce and Seth's needs. What we discovered is that we'd come up with a solution that would work well for a while, but then we'd need to change it up as the baby grew and needs and preferences changed. There isn't always a right way to organize permanently, sometimes only a right way for right now. Organization requires flexibility. As needs change, or something isn't working for you anymore, so must organization change. Find a solution that works now, and be flexible and open to change when it is necessary.

DIARY (see JOURNAL)

DIGITAL MUSIC organization can be very rewarding once it is complete. You get to listen to music you didn't even know you had. You may not remember buying that Color Me Badd album, but now that you know you own it, get funky to it! The whole point of having music is to listen to it, and you won't do that if all your music files are jumbled up, misplaced, and mislabeled. Collect all of your music files and put them into your **MUSIC** folder so the **COMPUTER** knows where to look for your tunes. Keep this folder as the main hub for your music and make sure that every program that needs to access your music is pointed to this folder. It may be smart to keep this folder on an external **HARD DRIVE** so you free up space on your actual computer. Most programs have smart tags these days and can figure out titles of songs, albums, and artists. They'll even organize your music folder for you with artist and album subfolders if you check the box in preferences that says "keep my music files organized." The only trouble you may run into is if you copied a large amount of music from a friend who had a disorganized collection without ID3 tags. This is a good reason to buy your music legally—it will always have the correct information. But if you do have a mess of untagged files, download a program made for the purpose of correcting and adding information to song files rather than trying to listen to and tag all those files yourself. No one has the time for that. Once you get the music on your computer in good shape, you now just have to worry about the new music you are importing onto your computer. Once again, make sure you import to where your music files are now kept and organized.

An organized music collection will make it easier to create great playlists. Having playlists ready to go will allow you to play preselected music for specific occasions without having to DJ at your computer or device all night. This is especially useful when you are driving or hosting a party and don't want to be distracted by messing around with your computer or device. You can create playlists manually, by dragging each song into the list, or create "smart playlists," letting your program fill your song list based on music tags of your choice. **iTUNES** can even create a "genius playlist" for you based on your previous listening habits. Just make sure you give your playlists good names so that you remember what they actually are!

Nowadays, it's becoming less and less necessary to actually store large amounts of music on your computer. A lot of services allow you to upload your music to the **CLOUD** and sync and stream it to all of your devices. But this assumes you are always connected to the Internet, so it's still a good idea to keep all of your music on an external hard drive as well as uploading it to the cloud. Don't forget to back up your drive! Your music is a precious possession that serves as a history of your life. You can download it again, but that means you are paying for a song you already owned. Don't pay twice for your favorite make-out song!

O.C.D. APPROVED TECHNOLOGY

Get your personal collection of music on the cloud for free with Google Play. It will allow you to upload up to twenty thousand songs for free. Then you simply log on to your account from any device and listen to your music without the hassle of wires and without taking up any of your device memory!

DIGITAL PICTURES should be how you keep *all* of your pictures, unless you want to make a tangible **PHOTO ALBUM**. Loose photos are photos that get damaged, lost, or never looked at, so get them scanned! Like any other digital file, they need to be properly named and kept in a digital folder system that helps you organize and find your photos with ease. You'll never find the picture of you and that Elvis impersonator if it's in a folder with every other picture you've ever taken with the file name "DSC_01789." Prove the King is still alive and get organized. Whether you organize by date, event, city, category, or people's names, make sure you always stay uniform and consistent in your digital photo filing. For example, I organize my photos in folders in the following categories: Cards, Family, High School Memories, Justin Klosky, Los Angeles, Miami, New York—which are all cities I've lived in—Trips, Out of USA Trips, and Weddings. Take the time and create subfolders based on events for your pictures in your Pictures folder and continue to update these folders.

Download photos from your camera within a week of taking them. This will keep organizing your new photos manageable. It's overwhelming to try to do this with a month's, or even a year's, worth of photos on your camera. Your camera is not a **HARD DRIVE**. The longer you wait to transfer your pictures, the harder it will be to remember where you took them, when you took them, and why you took them. When you import new photos, take advantage of the "batch edit" feature in your photo viewing software. This will allow you to rename all the photos from a trip or event in a single click. Once downloaded and renamed, create a subfolder for those pictures in your Pictures folder in the appropriate category. Don't let your photo program decide where your pictures go! Show your software who's boss and direct it where you choose to store your photos. If you have control over the organization of your pictures, you will know where they are located. This will also help you when switching to a new **COMPUTER**. This information applies to your phone as well. Every two to four weeks, pull the pictures off your phone and name them by date range using batch edit. For example: "iPhone Snaps—July 2014." Remove those photos from your device so you can organize and properly label them on your computer. Then, if you want, you can add them back to your phone so you can view them on the go.

Back up your pictures! I've had to console clients who lost their entire photo library because it wasn't backed up and their hard drive crashed. Don't risk losing your precious memories! Back up to another hard drive or the **CLOUD**. You can use the same drive on which you keep your **DOCUMENTS** and **MUSIC**. In this digital age, you don't want to buy a drive less than one terabyte, so there is plenty of space to go around.

When it comes to synching photos between your devices, don't just sync everything. Your portable devices have limited space and a full sync is a quick way to fill it up. Create a folder specific for synching photos between devices and stick copies of photos in there that you know you want on your phone or tablet.

If you want to display your photos in your home, digital picture frames are a great solution. They'll maintain the folder organization you've already set up and give you powerful options for which photos to view and for how long. Keep a folder on your computer for copies of photos you want on your digital picture frame. But if you still like to keep actual printed photos in frames or albums, you can develop your photos through your favorite online service and even create photo books that are mailed to you. These books are very professional-looking and fairly inexpensive. This will also cut the cost of developing photos and buying many photo album books. You can remember which photos you've printed by using the star labeling function that most photo programs have available. That way, you'll never end up printing the same photo twice. You might look sexy in that shot, but one printout is enough.

■ ■ ■ ■
O.C.D. EXTREME

I have scanned literally every single photo in my family's possession. Using the facial recognition feature on my photo viewing software, I've tagged who is in every photo and made all photos searchable by person. Then I create digital albums of each person and give it to them as gifts!

DINING AREAS in your home are not just for daily eating but also for entertaining and offering the comfort of your own home to others. There's nothing comforting about dining next to a stack of **BILLS** ominously close to falling into your meat loaf, although eating them is one way to get rid of them. Don't let dining areas become multipurpose work spaces. It will prevent you from having a peaceful dinner experience. If your dining room has already reached this state, find an appropriate home for everything that doesn't serve the purpose of eating and entertaining. Less is more in this area. The more you have out on display, the more you'll have to move when it's time to eat, and the more you'll have to clean. If you have **FURNITURE** besides the table in this area, like a buffet, make sure that whatever is being stored is relevant to the dining area. Use this space to keep place mats, serve ware, fine china and silver, tablecloths, cloth napkins, and anything else you might use for entertaining in the dining area, but, as always, keep those items in specific and properly labeled places.

> ■ ■ ■
> ### AN O.C.D. SUCCESS STORY
>
> I had a client who would use his dining area as his desk. No matter how hard he would try to move from his dining room to his office, his work space always shifted back to his dining table. After some organizational therapy, we realized that it wasn't that he liked working at his dining room table but that his office wasn't a creative place for him and his desk was too cluttered to focus. We quickly cleared his desk, made room for the things that he truly needed, and added photos, awards, and vision boards for inspiration. Before he could get back in the dining room, he was streamlined, focused, and beginning to create in his office. Sometimes it isn't just the stuff that's the problem but the energy that comes along with the space you are providing for the stuff. Change your mind-set and your systems, and don't be afraid to rethink your spaces.

DIRTY LAUNDRY (see LAUNDRY)

DISHES should be washed, dried, and put away as soon as possible, and always by the end of each day. Start each day fresh with no dirty dishes lying around or sitting in the sink. To me, soaking is just procrastination. It may help get off some crusty or sticky foods, but we are all very capable of cleaning a pot with gloves, hot water, soap, and elbow grease right after the pot has been used. And I think food is easier to get off while it's still warm. Go through your dishes once a year and get rid of the chipped, old, or stained ones. Assess if it's time to purchase a new set. Having mixed and matched dishes while hosting can be embarrassing, so always make sure you have enough of a set to meet your entertaining needs. You won't have to play favorites and decide who gets the fine china and who gets the plate your kids decorated for you. If you have multiple sets, label where each specific set goes so whoever is putting them back continues to keep things organized.

AN O.C.D. SUCCESS STORY

My friends love to cook, yet they never made breakfast for themselves. It turns out that because they were leaving the mess in their kitchen overnight from cooking the night before, they never wanted to deal with it in the morning and skipped breakfast as a result. Breakfast is the most important meal of the day! I convinced them to deal with their dishes at the end of each night, no matter how tired. It was no surprise to find out that they were enjoying breakfast together much more frequently.

O.C.D. EXTREME

People love having me over as a dinner guest because I always do their dishes for them. I can't stand the possibility that they won't be cleaned until the following morning! Be a beloved dinner guest and help out with the dishes. If my host's dishware has patterns, I'll even line up the patterns once I put them back in the cabinet.

D

DISHWASHERS make cleaning your **DISHES** fast and easy. They do everything except return your dishes to their **SHELVES** Hopefully, they are working on that feature. If you have a dishwasher, there is no excuse for dishes to sit in the sink. Actually, there is NEVER an excuse for dishes to sit in the sink. Read the manual that came with your dishwasher. It will tell you the best way to load your dishwasher so that you can fit the most in there and it actually gets cleaned. This will stop you from having to do multiple loads and wasting water, energy, and your time. Organizing like items together when you load the dishwasher will make unloading a breeze. You'll be able to grab all of a similar item and bring it to its **KITCHEN** home in one trip. Make sure you unload the dishwasher as soon as the cycle is complete so that you always have a place to put your dirty dishes. You'll never have to look at dried, crusted scrambled eggs again.

AN O.C.D. SUCCESS STORY

Sometimes discipline can create ripple effects. One of my clients was frustrated that her husband would always leave dirty dishes in the sink. When I asked him why, he said that the dishes in the dishwasher were clean so he couldn't put them in there, and he didn't want to unload the entire dishwasher. I helped them make a deal: if she unloaded the dishwasher as soon as it was done, he would put the dirty dishes in the dishwasher instead of the sink. Her dishwasher discipline led to his sink discipline. Unload your dishwasher quickly so you always have a place to put that dirty dish.

■ ■ ■ ■

O.C.D. EXTREME

The dishwasher is a great place to sanitize things that aren't even used for food: sponges, jewelry, glassware, whatever! Just make sure it's in a secure spot so it can't fall down the drain.

■ ■ ■

DOCUMENTS on your **COMPUTER** should be organized similar to **DIGITAL MUSIC** and **DIGITAL PICTURES** and not like the file drawer you've crammed full of meaningless paper you thought you had to save. Create subfolders within your Documents folder to help you stay organized when filing and saving any document. I have folders labeled Business, Creative, Family, Insurance and Health, Living, Money and **TAXES**, Receipts, and Saved Voice Mails. Then I have folders within these folders to help me further organize my files. For example, in Money and Taxes I have a folder for each year, and, within that, a folder for donations, tax returns, tax documents, and stocks. However you choose to create folders, don't get so specific when creating subfolders that you end up with a single document in each folder. Also, make sure you are always saving your documents to the correct folder or dragging them over from the desktop. Resist the urge to print out documents. I know many people like the security of having an actual printed copy, but in this day and age of digital backups, it really isn't necessary. Even the IRS is going electronic!

For actual paper documents like bank and credit card statements, parking tickets and traffic violations, **RECEIPTS**, and payment confirmations, you should download and file the **BILL** from online (have it local—you never know when the Internet will be unavailable), or scan the paper copy, add it to your digital system, and shred the original. Scanning will also help you determine how important a document really is because you won't want to scan something that isn't necessary. Only a few documents should be kept in paper form: anything certified or notarized (which should be kept in a **SAFE** if you have one), receipts for major purchases until warranties expire, legal proceedings, government and personal documents like Social Security cards, birth certificates, death records, marriage certificates, passports, titles of ownership to your car or home, and wills. But scan these items as well and keep them in a password-protected flash drive in case of emergency. By taking the time to scan important documents, your **DESK SPACE** will remain clear, and you won't have to give up any real space to a bulky **FILING CABI-NET**. Stick a massage chair in that space instead as a reward for being so organized. That chair robot gives good shiatsu.

O.C.D. APPROVED TECHNOLOGY

Keep copies of your most important documents with you on a password-protected thumb drive or your phone. You never know when they'll come in handy, but you'll be glad to have them when you need them.

D

103

DORM ROOMS are every college kid's dream: their first place away from Mom and Dad. But for many, it might also be the first time they are thrust into the driver's seat of maintaining their own organization. For the freshman about to embark on this journey, or a parent of that freshman, my best suggestion is . . . take less with you! Only bring what you will absolutely need for school and enough of your sentimental items to make you feel at home while still allowing you room to grow. Call the school in advance to find out exactly what will be in the room. You may even be able to obtain a floor plan. This will help you plan what to bring.

College dorm rooms tend to be very small. In college, I could touch both of my walls at the same time. You'll quickly realize how important organization is in such a space. Use wall space and hang whatever you can. Use the **BOOKSHELF** provided for your **BOOKS**, **TOILETRY BAG** and **MAKEUP** tote, and sentimental photos. Try to buy items that serve multiple basic functions and don't bring anything with a highly specialized purpose. You don't need that panini grill. Mount a shelf or use stackable **SHELVES**. Take advantage of the space under the bed by using shallow **BINS**. If your bed sits directly on the floor, raise your bed up on blocks to claim that space. Use over-the-door hanging systems for your **SHOES** and towels. Use thin **HANG-ERS** to maximize **CLOSET** space. You can even add a second closet rod to double your space. Think vertically in every area because there won't be a lot of horizontal. Instead of a laundry basket, get a bag; bags take up less space and can better fit in any area. When they aren't in use, they take up minimal space. Though your room will probably just be a square, try to define spaces for food and eating, study, storage, relaxing, and entertaining. Sectioning the room will help you keep it organized. Keep snacks in **ZIP-LOCK BAGS** to prevent pests from sharing your tiny space with you.

Remember: you'll be home for **THANKSGIVING** before you know it, so you'll have an opportunity to fine-tune what it is you keep in your dorm room and what it is you leave at home. It helps to live in the space for a little while to know what you actually need. Also, Mom and Dad love to send packages your first year of school, so take advantage of that.

You will most likely be living with someone you have never met before. Reach out to that person and have a video chat before you head off to school. Together you can decide what major appliances and **ELECTRONICS** each person will contribute because you almost certainly won't have room for two of each. This will also save you both money. One of you brings the Xbox, and the other brings the PlayStation. When you both arrive, divide the space fairly so that you don't end up living in what feels like someone else's room. If you have a tough roommate, a simple way to divide the space is to measure. Inches are inches, no matter where they are. Create a list of **CHORES** you will each be responsible for. They don't need to be accomplished on the same day, but you need to hold each other accountable. Define purposes for shared spaces. This will help create boundaries and a better relationship with your roommate. College is about having fun and finding yourself, not wasting time looking for things in a disorganized room or fighting with your room-mate over whose turn it is to wipe the tomato soup off the sides of the micro-wave. The O.C.D. Way can help you find *your* way.

O.C.D. APPROVED TECHNOLOGY

Closet space is tight in any dorm room. Pick yourself up a Closet Doubler. It gives you two hanging bars instead of one. Double the closet, double the fun!

DOWNLOADS should be downloaded to your desktop and dealt with immediately. Keep your downloads on the down-low by getting them off your desktop and into the proper folder. If it's a program, install it and move the install file to the appropriate folder. I like to store all of my applications on an external **HARD DRIVE**, so if and when I need them again, I do not have to go through the process of redownloading them. If your downloads are **MUSIC**, video, **DIGITAL PICTURES**, or **DOCUMENTS**, file them in their appropriate folders. Like all **COMPUTER FILES**, you should deal with them immediately and not let them build up on your desktop. Don't use the default downloads folder or you'll inevitably let it become a place for miscellaneous file storage. Saving to the desktop will constantly remind you of which files need to be dealt with, while the downloads folder is out of sight, out of mind, and out of organization. Check your downloads folder monthly to deal with anything that might end up in there from a naughty program that doesn't know the downloads folder is a no-no.

DOWNSIZING is always a difficult process because it forces you to completely reevaluate the way you live and all of your belongings. Hopefully you are downsizing by choice. Perhaps the kids have moved out and you just don't need that much space anymore. If you are downsizing because times have been tough, try not to view it as a loss but rather as an opportunity to simplify.

Let's say you are moving from a 4,000-square-foot home to a 1,200-square-foot home. Your new space is just a bit over a quarter of your old space and will have less **CLOSET** and storage space. That means you should only bring about a quarter of your stuff. Sometimes organization is just simple math, so make your fifth-grade teacher happy and dust off those fractions and percentages.

It may be hard to think of letting go of your things. That is normal! Embrace the things that are the hardest and you will become stronger. Just because you've had something for years doesn't mean you need to keep it for years to come. You have to ask what is important to you. Now you have to ask what is *really* important to you. What can't you absolutely live without? These three questions will make downsizing easier. Do you really need that *National Geographic* collection?

To start the process, get in the right state of mind. Realize that we have built up a massive dependency on "stuff." We collect things to fill a void we may or may not know we have. But to reset your perspective, consider if your life would be so horrible if tomorrow you had to give away half of your things. Would you really suffer? Would your life stop after you gave up these belongings? *Of course not!* Once you believe this, you are then truly ready to downsize.

To start your downsize, create **BOXES** for all the things you use at least monthly. Pack these boxes in an organized manner with numbers on the outside of each box and a master list of contents corresponding to each numbered box. For more information on packing and moving, see **MOVING**. Once you have your boxes packed of the things you use monthly, start grabbing the things that have significant meaning to you and your family: heirlooms, **ANTIQUES**, **ART**, anything that has emotional value to you. Pack those items. But the hard truth is, you probably can't keep everything. If you are having trouble deciding whether to keep an item, pair it with another item and ask which you'd rather keep. This technique also works if you have children and need to pare down their belongings as well.

If you can measure your new space before moving in, it will help you decide what **FURNITURE** you should bring. Anything that won't fit or won't fit well, sell, donate, or give to family or friends. You can even include furniture along with the sale of your home. You might even want to consider selling all of your furniture and starting from scratch so you buy the furniture that really works best in your new space rather than trying to make your existing furniture work. Think about your new space and what you really need there. If you are moving from a five-bedroom home to a two-bedroom home, you won't need five TVs anymore! And honestly, did you ever really? Pack the one or two newest TVs and get rid of the others. Use this mentality with all of your other belongings.

Now you've packed your monthly items and **MEMORABILIA** and have a plan for your furniture. Usually, there will still be a lot left. You know what you will use yearly and you know what just sits around your home taking up space. Now is the time to be hard on yourself. You can't start fresh with an overwhelming amount of clutter. **STORAGE UNITS** are not an option for this process; they are a cop-out and will be a waste of money. Gift yourself the peace of a new beginning with only the things in your life that you value and are important. You know what those things are, so make the tough decisions and know that everything will be just fine. If that's hard for you to realize, throw on some Bob Marley and let him tell you that "every little thing gonna be all right."

■ ■ ■
AN O.C.D. SUCCESS STORY

I had a client who was hit hard by the recession and had to downsize. It was scary for his wife and him to be forced into that situation. They were afraid they wouldn't have all they needed in their new space. They hired me and I convinced them that with proper organization, everything would be okay. Though the process was difficult for them, they are happy and functional in their new home and would even say that life is simpler and sweeter.

DRAWERS in your home, BEDROOM, OFFICE, LIBRARY, or BATHROOM should always be assigned for a specific purpose. "Junk" is not specific. "Miscellaneous" is not specific, and also way too hard to spell. Make decisions on the best function for each drawer and don't put anything in there that doesn't serve that purpose. If you have a hard time figuring out how to allocate your drawer space, do this: go through all the drawers in your home, one room at a time, and take out all of the contents. Dump them on the floor in a pile. This works well because it actually forces you to deal with your belongings. Start to group similar items together until you have separate piles, throwing away trash as you go. You will start to see that many of your belongings have friends and serve similar functions. Some of those functions might not have anything to do with the room you are in, so relocate those items. These groups will define the contents of your drawers. It's up to you to figure out the best drawer location for the contents you have, but, in general, think about how often you use the items in that group and give the best drawer placement to things used the most frequently. This may be in the top drawer, with lesser-used items farther down the drawer totem pole. You may also choose to use drawer dividers or organizers if you have large drawers that are deep and wide, like those in a **DRESSER**. However you organize your drawers, make sure you do not get into the habit of throwing things into drawers they don't belong in. This is a guaranteed way to ruin organization, forcing you to start all over again. No one likes starting from the beginning after making progress. That's why I always hated Chutes and Ladders.

■ ■ ■

AN O.C.D. SUMMARY

Organize: Dump everything out of the drawer and onto the floor. Throw away trash. Sort like items together. Move things to better homes if you already have a space for them.

Create: Based on what you have left, designate the drawer for a specific purpose. Use drawer dividers to designate multiple spaces. Return appropriate items to the drawer.

Discipline: Return items to the drawer when you are done using them. Don't add anything that doesn't fit what you've designated the drawer for. When the drawer becomes unwieldy, repeat the entire process!

DRESSERS require a combination of organizational techniques. Earn your organizational black belt by using your mastery of **CLOTHES**, **CLOSETS**, and **DRAWERS** when it comes to your dresser. In general, the dresser should be for items that can't be hung, like undergarments, **BRAS** and **LINGERIE**, workout clothes, **SWEATERS**, **T-SHIRTS**, and shorts. Pull everything out of the drawers and assign the empty drawers of your dresser for specific types of clothing. Most frequently used items, like **SOCKS** and **UNDERWEAR**, go at the top. Label the inside of each drawer for the type of clothing that should be in it to help maintain organization for yourself and anyone else who might use these drawers. Consider using drawer dividers or organizers to create individual spaces within the drawers. You don't want socks disappearing beneath your underwear. Keep a fabric softener sheet in each drawer to keep your clothes smelling nice and fresh. And, of course, discipline yourself to put things back where they go. If you have **HOUSEKEEPERS** or others who help out in your home, make sure that you show them and teach them where everything gets put away. Organization is about communication. Don't end up with your spouse's underwear in your drawer. They won't fit and could be really uncomfortable.

■ ■ ■

O.C.D. EXTREME

I like everything to be visible in my dresser. Instead of stacking my shirts, I use the filing method, folding them and lining them up vertically. This way, I can see all my shirts, sort through them like files, and grab exactly what I want without making a mess.

DRY CLEANING produces a closet's most-wanted criminal: the paper-wrapped wire hanger. Always take your dry cleaning off this hanger, recycle it, and get your clothing on your uniform closet **HANGER**. After you drop off your dry cleaning, **RECEIPTS** should be kept on a **BULLETIN BOARD** or in a place where all members of the household can grab them. That way, anyone can pick up the dry cleaning when it's most convenient. If you know you will be the one picking up the dry cleaning, you can keep the receipts in your car so it is convenient for you to pick up the dry cleaning without forgetting the receipt in the house. Make sure you stay disciplined about picking up your dry cleaning so items aren't forgotten at the cleaner and you are dealing with your dirty **LAUNDRY** quickly and efficiently.

■ ■ ■

O.C.D. EXTREME

I set a reminder on my phone while still at the dry cleaners to pick up my dry cleaning on the day specified on the ticket. This keeps me aware of when my clothes are ready and prevents me from ever forgetting items at the cleaner.

DVD COLLECTIONS might end up being collections of shiny **COASTERS** once everything is available digitally, but until then, they can be organized in one of three simple ways. My preferred method, because I don't like to take up any unnecessary space, is to ditch the cases and put all of my media alphabetized into a Blu-ray/DVD binder. The easiest way to alphabetize a large collection, instead of trying to do it in the DVD case, is to lay all of them out on the floor with the spine facing up. Get them in the right order before you start putting them into the books. If the binder gets too unwieldy because you have a large collection, break the collection into multiple binders. You can divide by letters, or even make genre-specific binders. If you will be adding to your collection instead of purchasing movies digitally, leave space in between each letter so you can add movies later. Some people like to display their collection and view it as art. If you are one of these people, organize your DVDs and Blu-rays on **SHELVES** in alphabetical order. This is a functional and simple way, but not the most space efficient. The most advanced step is to digitize your entire movie collection to a large **HARD DRIVE** and use one of the many programs now available to stream your media through a home server and to your TV. For now, this is a luxury option and can be very expensive, but you'll feel like you are in a hotel. Just don't demand room service from your spouse unless you actually want to stay in a hotel.

■ ■ ■

O.C.D. APPROVED TECHNOLOGY

Want to get the hotel movie experience at home? Pick up a Kaleidescape system. It stores all of your discs and lets you choose your movies from the attractive on-screen interface. You can even stream to other televisions in your house that have Kaleidescape players.

DVRS are the best way to unchain us from having to be at the TV at a certain time, although I know some of you can't wait another second to see the newest episode of *The Amazing Race*. The more disciplined you are about keeping your DVR organized, the less time you'll waste in front of the TV. Make sure that your scheduled recordings are ones that you are still interested in watching or even still on the air. Before you set up your DVR to record every episode of a new series, record single episodes to see if you even want every episode. Adjust the settings to record only new episodes, otherwise you might find yourself with a DVR full of *M*A*S*H* reruns. Only set your DVR to record things you will watch because the more shows you record, the faster you'll fill up your DVR hard drive. A DVR only has a certain amount of space on it and when the space runs out, it will start to delete your recordings. Every now and then get rid of series recordings on the DVR that you will never watch again. Delete shows or movies you've watched right after viewing them unless you are saving them for a reason. Some DVRs give you the option of organizing your programs by folder. If it is available, use this feature because it's the best way to organize your recordings. Also, most DVRs have **APPS** for your phone that allow you to schedule recordings when you aren't home. Take advantage of this effective technology because sometimes you'll forget to record an important program before you get home and never know if Darla ended up getting a rose on *The Bachelor*. The more you maintain your DVR, the easier it will be to find the shows you want to watch and the more space you'll have to record them.

■ ■ ■ ■

O.C.D. APPROVED TECHNOLOGY

I still use TiVo even though most cable companies offer their own DVR boxes at a lower cost. The truth is, for reliability and ease of use, nothing comes close to TiVo's user interface. Grab yourself a box and sign up for service. You won't be sorry.

■ ■ ■ ■

O.C.D. EXTREME

Set boundaries with your significant other as to how long shows are allowed to remain on the DVR. This will come in handy if you are sick of scrolling through episodes of *Real Housewives* to get to the show you actually want to watch.

E

EBAY is a powerful tool for buying and selling goods. You'll find **ELEC-TRONICS, ANTIQUES, MEMORABILIA,** and even a grilled cheese with the visage of the Virgin Mary on eBay. As long as you use the service, you should keep your account maintained, in good standing, and up to date. Buying and selling your belongings will only take a few clicks. If you develop a good reputation in the eBay world by honestly representing products, paying and shipping quickly, and leaving feedback for buyers and sellers as soon as transactions are completed, you'll instill confidence in anyone you do business with.

Anytime you sign into eBay, there is a list of things to do to keep your account in good organized standing. First, make sure that you have an updated PayPal account linked to your eBay account because this is the fastest and most secure way to send and receive money. Keep all addresses and information current and validated. Consistently monitor your notifications because people might be sending you messages asking questions about your auctions. You don't want to keep people waiting on your listings; that will make them less likely to bid.

When posting an item for sale on eBay, make sure that you have an organized folder system on your **COMPUTER**. All items require pictures and a description, and you may have to relist an item several times before it sells, so it is a good idea to have folders for each item being sold that will contain your description and pictures of the item. Keep these folders organized by housing them in DOCUMENTS → EBAY → ITEM NAME. Once it sells, delete the folder or, if you have the space, archive it to your external **HARD DRIVE**.

If you run an eBay business and sell in high volume, make sure you have an organized system in your home to store merchandise and house shipping supplies. Categorize like items together and separate those that are currently being listed to help you remember your live auctions. By doing so, you can ship them quickly when the time comes. Set up a staging area where you can photograph your products. Also have a well-organized and clean shipping station. Be organized, maintain your listings, and keep an eye out for potato chips that resemble ex-presidents. You never know how much they'll sell for on eBay. Just keep your chips in an airtight **CONTAINER** so they don't get soggy: the crispness of your presidential potato chip can directly affect its value.

O.C.D. EXTREME

If you are really set on winning an auction, keep two bidding windows open on your browser. Use one to place a competitive bid, and have the other set and ready to go with a higher backup bid in case you get outbid at the last second. Sometimes you'll lose just because you don't have time to do anything besides hit enter before the auction ends.

ELECTRICAL CORDS (see CORDS)

ELECTRONIC ACCESSORIES for all devices should be kept together in one place. For example, keep all the lenses, batteries, cables, microphones, flashes, and **MEMORY CARDS** together for that fancy digital SLR camera you bought with more megapixels than you'll know what to do with. You will never get confused where something is because there is only *one* place it could be. Set that spot, label it, and continue to keep it organized. For accessories for smaller devices, like chargers, **HEADPHONES**, and earbuds, batteries, and transfer cables, keep these all in an electronic accessories drawer or **BIN** kept out of sight but accessible near your work space. Also, don't forget to put back any accessory you bring with you on a trip right when you get home. Every time you add a new device to your collection, take the opportunity to go through all of your accessories and make sure you still have and use the devices they correspond to. If you keep the charger from the Discman you got rid of, it's only going to confuse you in the future or short out another device when you try to plug it in.

■ ■ ■ ■

O.C.D. EXTREME

I keep a charger in every bag I use regularly, and even in places I visit frequently, like my parents' home in Florida: one less thing to worry about when packing.

ELECTRONICS are getting smaller and cheaper, which means they are easier to misplace, forget about, or accidentally swallow. You don't want to hear a ringtone coming from your belly, so your electronics should be organized in one place in your home or **OFFICE**. That way, you always know where to find them. Whether the electronics are cameras, camcorders, MP3 players, cell phones, or portable DVD players, make sure that you designate a **DRAWER** or space in a **CLOSET** for the devices, label them, and maintain the area. **ELECTRONIC ACCESSORIES** for the devices—such as chargers, power cords, or AV wires—should be kept nearby, or even in the same drawer with a divider or **BIN**. Make sure rechargeable batteries are fully charged before the necessary occasion so you never end up frustrated by a

E

113

dead device. Don't leave fully charged batteries sitting for long periods of time because this will drain battery life.

Every time you get a new device, go through the devices and accessories you have. Sell, donate, or give away any device you no longer use or that has been replaced by a new generation, unless you want to keep it as a backup device. Your nephew will love your old **iPHONE**. Just make sure you transfer and then wipe clean any media that might be on that device before you let it go. Wink wink.

E-MAIL FOLDERS, or in some programs "e-mail labels," should be set up to match your workflow and business **RESPONSIBILITIES**. Most people receive between 40 and 150 e-mails a day, many of them *not* about enlargement or weight loss. Sorting that many important e-mails can be overwhelming without an organizational system. Set up folders for anything you need to have quick access to, like projects you'll have to reference often. You want all the e-mails for a specific project in the same place so you can easily see its entire history and find the specific e-mail you need. For example, you might keep folders for Clients, Creative, Legal, Living, Money, **RECEIPTS**, Social Media, Vendors, and **WEB SITE**. You should also have a main folder labeled "* Saved E-mail—Year" for any e-mails that don't warrant a separate folder or aren't relevant to a specific project. The asterisk keeps that folder on top of the list, but make sure you put a space between the asterisk and the first word. File e-mails into these folders as soon as you've read and addressed them and they no longer require action on your end. You'll always be confident that you've taken care of your obligations and covered your ass. Chuck from Accounting won't be able to put the blame on you. If you still need to follow up on the e-mail, don't file it yet. But don't get in the habit of using a flag or a star to single out an e-mail, unless it is of the utmost importance. You'll overuse this function, it will lose all meaning, and all those flags and stars will just be distracting. Once your folders are created and you start to use them, go back after three months and see which folders are actually being used and which aren't. Archive the ones that aren't being used and then revise your system to make better use of the current folders and their contents.

Use your **E-MAIL IN-BOX** only for e-mails that you have yet to deal with and your e-mail folders for e-mails that you have read and dealt with. In a perfect world, your in-box should be nearly empty and never the storage area for all your e-mails. Some people think they can just save all their e-mails to a single folder and use the search function to find what they need. It never works out and you end up playing the "keyword" guessing game, costing you time and energy. You'd be surprised how many other e-mails contain the phrase you thought you were so clever to search for. Searching for "great organization" isn't going to find you that O.C.D. newsletter, even though it does indeed talk about great organization.

■■■■

AN O.C.D. SUCCESS STORY

It's amazing how many major companies don't have a policy for dealing with and organizing e-mail. When working on digital organization with clients, the first thing I like to tackle is the creation of an e-mail folder system that is unique and works for that company. When companies lack a good e-mail filing system, in-boxes are cluttered. As a result, order processing is much slower, client relationship management is less effective, and interoffice correspondence via e-mail is almost useless. Once I help companies implement a stronger folder and filing system, they run more efficiently and it becomes clear just how useful e-mail organization is to a business.

E

E-MAIL IN-BOX should be a place where your e-mails come in and leave as fast as possible. Think of your in-box as a NASCAR pit stop. Most of us check our e-mail every day and most of us have different ways of handling our e-mail correspondence. Sometimes we aren't ready, we're not in the mood, or we don't even have enough energy to reply to someone who has sent us an e-mail. Sometimes we have no choice because the e-mail is so pressing that our response is expected in a moment's notice.

Create separate e-mail addresses for different purposes, like personal and business. If you are using the same program for both on your **COMPUTER**, you will have the option to view these addresses as separate in-boxes. This will make separating your personal life from your work life much easier.

Set up **E-MAIL FOLDERS** for each in-box that will properly allow you to file completed e-mail correspondence. Do not get into the habit of creating folder after folder because this will only complicate your e-mail system and will overwhelm you. Less is more and being specific when filing is all about your own mind and process.

Don't feel rushed to answer personal e-mails instantly. We still have phones: if something is truly urgent, then your friend or family member will call you. But don't get into the habit of being the type of person who never answers their e-mails in a timely manner. It can be considered rude and lazy. If you are really busy, respond with a simple e-mail saying you got the message and will write back as soon as you can. Then write back as soon as you can.

If you have business e-mails in your in-box, stay on top of them. If you want to be respected as a businessperson and want people to treat you the same way back, then lead by example. Most people's businesses are their livelihood and letting an important e-mail sit because you just don't want to answer it is irresponsible. We all handle our workloads differently, so obviously what works for you is what matters most, but keep in mind that actions speak louder than words.

Deal with things promptly and make a disciplined habit of filing your e-mails from your in-box into designated folders. File anything and everything as long as those specific e-mails have been dealt with. Keep in-box contents to a minimum and make sure to be constantly creating new folders and using them as your business and personal life grows and changes. Opening an in-box that has very little e-mail in it is a rewarding and calming experience: Zen and the art of e-mail management.

O.C.D. APPROVED TECHNOLOGY

There is a plethora of e-mail clients out there. My personal favorite is Gmail for business or personal use. It's simple, easy to navigate, efficient, and customizable. You don't have to be a computer expert to use it. It effectively blocks spam, has powerful search features, and will keep you on time with its built-in calendar. It allows for multiple accounts and plug-ins, and constantly offers updates. It is also very simple to sync with your iPhone, iPad, or other smartphone quickly and easily.

EMERGENCY KITS should be kept in your home, **OFFICE**, and car in a large bag or **BACKPACK**. Obviously, different geographic areas are prone to different emergencies, so some custom tailoring is warranted, but a good emergency kit should keep you prepared for anything that may come for at least three days regardless of tornado, earthquake, or meteor strike.

First, make sure each kit has a list of emergency phone numbers and addresses in case members of your family are separated when the emergency occurs. Have this information on your phone as well. The kits kept in your home and office should be comprehensive and contain the following: at least a half-gallon of potable water per person per day; nonperishable canned food and dehydrated food items such as cereals, dried fruits, and nuts—avoid salty foods that make you thirsty and take into account any dietary restrictions for you or your family; a solar-powered radio; an LED flashlight with extra **BATTERIES**; a standard first-aid kit; a fire extinguisher; any prescription medications taken by you or your family; a pipe wrench for turning off gas and water valves; a waterproof bag containing at least a hundred dollars, paper copies of important **DOCUMENTS** like IDs, **CREDIT CARDS**, and insurance policies, a lighter, and matches, but remember, you don't want to use matches or candles until you are 100 percent positive there is no gas leak; a whistle; a set of clean clothes for each person; a good knife with at least a three-inch blade; and baby wipes. Keep your emergency kit in an easy-to-access place in your home, reachable in a moment's notice, but out of the way, and make sure everyone knows where it is.

The kit in your **AUTOMOBILE** can be less comprehensive to save space, but it should still contain a full change of clothes, including a pair of shoes, a twenty-dollar bill, a bottle of water, a flashlight, and a Swiss army knife.

Every few months, check your emergency kit and update it with fresher materials and based on any new needs you have. An outdated emergency kit isn't going to help you if you forgot to add the medication you now take to stop your brain from liquefying.

E

117

ENTERTAINMENT CENTERS are the landlords for our visual entertainment devices. Don't let them be slumlords. Since entertainment now comes from so many different devices, the entertainment center can become a chaotic place of precariously stacked equipment, cables, **REMOTES, MOVIES,** and **VIDEO GAMES**. As bad as it looks from the front, the back is usually an even scarier sight: a jumble of **CORDS,** cables, and wires, some that might not even have a device to go to. If you have a nightmare entertainment center with orphaned cables, sometimes unplugging everything, pulling it all out, cleaning everything, and starting from scratch is the best way to regain control.

Make sure that everything in your entertainment center screams functionality: if it doesn't provide or help provide your entertainment, get it out of there. Stack the largest components on the bottom and work your way up to the smallest device. Leave enough room for each component to breathe and not overheat; not doing so may damage your devices and poses a fire hazard. Keep equipment that functions together as close as possible, such as cable boxes and input switchers, or modems and routers. This will also aid in wire organization. Keep an eyeglass screwdriver nearby for doing hard resets on devices such as routers, modems, and streaming media players.

When you set up your entertainment center, think about the wiring behind the center. You want cables to have short, direct runs. Working your way from left to right, or right to left, plug in one cable at a time as neatly as possible. If you find yourself weaving through cables that are already plugged in, undo them and find a better way. Label both ends of your wires with a label maker. You do not want to be guessing which cables go to what if you ever need to replace a malfunctioning cable or add a new device. Use zip ties to pull up the slack, but make sure the bundle rests on the floor and not in midair, or else the weight will pull the cables out of the device. Plug in power cables last and always into a surge protector. To save energy when you are out of town, you can flip off the surge protector so your devices don't drain power. Energy vampires cost us money and a surge protector is their garlic. Make sure to use a separate surge protector for devices you want to continue to function while you are away, such as your **DVR,** Internet, and phone equipment. To provide yourself easy access for wiring and cleaning, put your entertainment center on Magic Sliders so you can easily move that heavy piece of furniture.

Remove components that are outdated or no longer being used, such as

VHS players. If you still have **VIDEO TAPES**, time to convert those to digital. For entertainment-related accessories, designate **DRAWERS** or **CABINETS** for specific items like remotes, video games, controllers, video game accessories, extra cords, or **ELECTRONICS**. Label those spaces and maintain the discipline of only putting items where they are supposed to go. Keep your **DVD COLLECTION** and other media separate from your entertainment center. The less chaos around your entertainment center, the more you can focus on the picture in front of you.

If you are buying a new entertainment center, know what components will be housed there. This is especially important if you are having something custom made. Measure each component and **RESEARCH** what kind of technology will be replacing your current technology in the upcoming years to make sure your unit will be future-proof. Those that bought or even custom built entertainment centers for square TVs right before flat screen TVs came out probably did some cursing. If you buy an entertainment center and know you will be **MOVING** a lot in the years to come, either for a **DORM ROOM** or a temporary **APARTMENT**, think about getting an inexpensive solution because repeatedly building, taking apart, and moving your entertainment center will eventually leave you with a wobbly piece of wood. Match your level of investment in your entertainment center to how long you plan on using it.

AN O.C.D. SUMMARY

Organize: Get everything out of your entertainment center that doesn't serve your entertainment needs. Convert any VHS tapes to digital. Get rid of components that are outdated or that you no longer use, as well as any orphaned cables that no longer serve a purpose. Group like items together, such as all of your video game equipment. Clean and dust everything.

Create: If you are buying a new entertainment center, measure your devices so you buy the right thing. Designate a space in your entertainment center for each type of device. Stack components with the largest on the bottom and smallest on top, leaving room for the components to vent so that they don't overheat. Plug in wires as neatly as possible, labeling each end of each wire. Plug everything into a surge protector and use cable ties to neatly pick up the slack.

Discipline: Make sure your components and entertainment center are cleaned every couple of weeks. Dust can damage your devices and creates a fire hazard. As you add new components and take out old components, remove wires and reorganize existing wires accordingly. Never get into the habit of using your entertainment center for random storage or to stick that DVD you are too lazy to put back in your DVD case or shelf.

■ ■ ■

O.C.D. APPROVED TECHNOLOGY

Placing Magic Sliders under your heavy furniture protects your floors and allows you to slide your heavy furniture around as if you are the Incredible Hulk. Give yourself the access to clean and organize even behind the heaviest bookshelf or entertainment center!

■ ■ ■

ENTRYWAYS are the first thing people see when they walk into your home or **OFFICE**, so make a good first impression. You want your home to be inviting, and a messy entryway is a quick way to rescind that invitation, so display proper organization and cleanliness.

The perfect entryway has a small area for **KEYS** and sunglasses, a shoe storage solution, and an umbrella stand. Everything else taken off or put on in the entryway should be going in your **ENTRYWAY CLOSET** or bedroom **CLOSET**. If you don't have an entryway closet, you can hang hooks for coats, **SCARVES**, **HATS**, and bags, but don't let the space become a giant closet. If you require that people remove their **SHOES** before entering your home, as I do, consider having a place to sit down to remove/put on shoes and accessories that has storage underneath. Use a mirror to make the space feel larger and for last checks before leaving the house. Flowers changed every few days are a nice added touch.

Make sure that anything taken off in your entryway, such as shoes, jackets, bags, or umbrellas, is put away immediately. You want the entryway as open and organized as possible for the next entrance. Think of it as a runway for airplanes: the moment the airplane lands, it taxis away, clearing the runway for the next plane to land and leaving nothing behind. Treat your entryway as your own personal runway that you want clear for any and all **GUESTS**.

O.C.D. EXTREME

An O.C.D. extreme household is a shoes-off household. Why would you want contaminants from the ground outside all over your clean floors and carpets? Take a cue from a centuries-old Asian tradition and provide your family and guests a place to remove and store their shoes at the front door. Request that they remove their shoes before entering. If you are having a party, put up a sign by the front door. This way, you won't have to repeat yourself over and over again, and if you see someone wearing shoes in your home, you can simply direct them to the sign.

ENTRYWAY CLOSETS are not just for *your* coats, bags, umbrellas, scarves, gloves, and **SHOES**, but also for your **GUESTS'**. Make sure you have room and extra **HANGERS** in your entryway closet to make your guests feel right at home. Don't insult your guests' garments: no one wants to shove his or her coat into a musty closet, so make sure your closet is kept clean and organized. It sets a good example to others and encourages them to respect your space, since you clearly do. Use **BINS** for gloves and **HATS**, hangers or wall hooks for **SCARVES**, **SHELVES** for **PURSES**, hooks for bags, and the floor for shoes. The entryway closet can also be a place to house a small toolbox for **TOOLS** for quick fix-its in the house. Go through your entryway closet and pull everything out once a year. Sometimes items will get left in there by guests, which should be returned or, if not claimed, sold on **eBAY**, or you'll find things that don't belong in the entryway closet at all and need to be relocated.

ENVELOPES of all shapes and sizes should be placed together in the **DRAWER**, **SHELF**, or **CLOSET** where you keep your **OFFICE SUPPLIES**. If you have the space, you can keep the envelopes in their boxes arranged by size. Stack the boxes, but cut open the front so you can grab what you need without have to shuffle boxes. If space is tight, toss the boxes and stack the envelopes with the larger, bulkier envelopes at the bottom and the smaller ones on top like a pyramid. You'll be able to tell what size envelopes are running low and need to be reordered. You will also be able to see what size envelopes you have to choose from and pick out the best size. Don't send a **GREETING CARD** in a manila envelope. It's a waste of good manila.

E

EXERCISE ROOMS in your home should be kept simple to encourage you to actually use them. I work with clients all the time that have gyms in their homes and nine times out of ten, they never use them while Bowflex laughs all the way to the bank. You only need a few machines, a set of free weights on a rack, a couple of **BINS** for storing your work-out accessories, a **SHELF** with clean towels and a bin for dirty **LAUNDRY**, a full-length mirror, and a mini-fridge for cold water and sports drinks. If you have a TV in your exercise room, make sure it's visible from all areas and that the wires have been well hidden. You need to be inspired and motivated, not looking at messy wires. Have powerful sayings on the walls or paint a wall a color that gives you energy. Having a plant or two in the space will keep it feeling fresh and improve air quality. Make sure the equipment you use is wiped down and clean and that you designate a small area for cleaning and maintenance supplies. Always discipline yourself to put all equipment and accessories back in their appropriate home when you are done using them. If you have a large space, designate areas for specific activities: weight training, stretching, yoga and Pilates, cardio, and admiring your hot body in the mirror.

Before you can discipline yourself to maintain your gym, you must have the discipline to actually use it. If you are going to have a gym in your home, or even a gym **MEMBERSHIP**, you need to figure out the purpose for it before you build it or buy it. Ask yourself why you intend to have the gym or membership and then set goals to achieve this intention. Hold yourself accountable to your intentions and work at them at least twice a week. You are not going to look great, lose weight, and feel your best without setting goals and achieving them. Set them and attack so you can finally fit into those skinny **JEANS** you saw at the mall.

■ ■ ■

O.C.D. APPROVED TECHNOLOGY

I love when companies build a better mousetrap, providing the same functionality as other products but in a smaller, more efficient package. Bowflex has done this with their SelectTech Adjustable Dumbbells. They take up the space of a single pair of dumbbells but allow you to select weight from 5 to 52.5 pounds. Get ripped without losing an entire wall to a complete dumbbell set!

F

FAMILY ROOM is for the family, so only keep items in there that serve the purpose of family bonding and entertainment. Find a better home for anything that doesn't fit this criterion. Don't let your family room become a general storage space. Everyone in the home should feel comfortable here. Keep this room calm and welcoming since it will be the area where most of your family interaction will take place. When you choose your **FURNITURE**, look for pieces that have built-in storage. Consider mounting **SHELVES** or adding a unit to add versatile space for your photos, books, media, and **GAMES**. Check out the game Quelf for a personal favorite of mine. Decide as a family if you will introduce a TV into this space. If you do, the room can also house your organized Blu-ray and **DVD COLLECTIONS**. **BOOKSHELVES** and **BOOKS** are a nice addition, but make sure the books are organized in a manner that makes you and your **GUESTS** feel inclined to grab them and explore. Have a few coffee table books on or near the **COFFEE TABLE** but not covering it in its entirety. It is important to keep surface space available so you and your guests have a place to put the things you are enjoying while using the room. And, of course, clean up these items when you are done. If your family room serves double duty, for example, as a **CHILD'S PLAY-ROOM**, break up the area to keep spaces defined. Make sure your children know that any **TOYS** that come out of their toy **BINS** go back in when they are done playing. However you choose to decorate is completely up to you, but don't overdecorate, because this will make the room less inviting and potentially feel like an Applebee's. As with all of your rooms, make sure that everything that goes in the family room has a designated space and that you always return things to their proper home after using them.

■ ■ ■ ■
AN O.C.D. SUMMARY

Organize: Before organizing your family room, take all of the items out and organize them into like groups. If a group of items doesn't serve a purpose for the room, find them a better home.

Create: Designate areas for each group of items in your family room. Label these areas if necessary to prevent future disorganization. Make sure the areas of your family room that you need for your family's well-being are accessible and comfortable.

Discipline: Place each item back in its correct space after you use it. Make sure you aren't placing items in areas where they don't belong. Don't let clutter from other areas in the home find its way into your organized family room.

■ ■ ■ ■

AN O.C.D. SUCCESS STORY

I worked with a client, a player in the NFL, who had a family of eight. Their house was so cluttered and disorganized that they had no place to all be together at the same time. How can you bond and be a tight-knit family if you can't even spend time together in the same room? After a comprehensive reorganization with the O.C.D. Experience, the entire family was able to enjoy one another's company in their newly functional family room.

■ ■ ■ ■

FAVORITES (see BOOKMARKS)

FILING CABINETS in the ideal O.C.D. world, where everyone has a scanner and paper is recycled back into trees, don't exist anymore, at least in a way that takes up physical space. I understand that people like to hold on to paper copies of certain documents, like **BILLS, RECEIPTS**, work, and statements to feel a sense of security. Certified documents are files that you cannot scan and shred, so keep them in a **SAFE** if you have one, or in a secure place in your files. Some people even like to use a safe-deposit box. Still, in the digital age, your physical filing system should be small and take up very little space because almost all of these items can be scanned. Really think about what you need to keep, since most institutions have electronic systems that go back many years in case of a dispute or problem.

If you do have a physical filing system, don't handwrite anything. It's hard enough for you to read your own chicken scratch, let alone someone else trying to find a file in your system. To keep things clear and legible, use a label maker to label folders and keep them alphabetized to prevent wasted time searching for things. Use hanging folders to create sections, and then manila folders for subcategories within that section. Keep all of the folders the same color with the same kind of tab. Put your documents all facing the same way. Consistency will keep your drawer manageable. Never overstuff your folders or let documents pile up higher than the folder label. I like having all the tabs lined up as opposed to staggered. Using staggered tabs doesn't really help you read labels any better and just makes your drawer look more chaotic.

If you ever have the option to receive electronic bills or statements, do it, because this will give you the flexibility to save these bills directly to your computer. If you have a physical filing system, only save the January, June, and December copy and shred the rest. Banking statements, investment portfolio paperwork, and credit card statements, if you are not getting them via e-mail or digitally, should be looked at and, once approved, shredded as well. **TAXES** should be kept for seven years and then can be shredded in a ritual where you curse the IRS. In a perfect world, with the way digital media and environments are taking over, it would be best to keep everything digital with a secure backup. Organize your digital **DOCUMENTS** on your **COMPUTER** just like you would your physical filing system, and don't forget to back up your files!

FINANCES are important to keep organized to help you understand where all your money went. If you have any money left after paying your expenses, you can decide where it can be spent and where it can be saved. You must have a system to organize your finances! Even if you have an accountant, it's helpful just for your own sanity and peace of mind.

Whether you handwrite it in a ledger, which of course I do not recommend, or use a powerful program like Quicken, which I do recommend, keep track of your spending. Quicken, or similar programs, will consolidate all of your **CREDIT CARDS**, bank **ACCOUNTS**, retirement funds, and trading portfolios into one place, allowing you to see where money is being spent and wasted. A lot of credit card companies will even export directly into Quicken, or have their own online labeling system, so you can track expenses and categorize them in preparation for paying your **TAXES**. Quicken, when properly set up, will even automatically pull your latest financial information from the Web and incorporate it into your report.

Using your program of choice, create a spreadsheet of all the expenses you have each month. A well-organized **DESK** is the perfect place to manage your **RECEIPTS**. Take a look at mandatory expenses, and then take a look at discretionary spending. Usually, the results are eye opening. Are you being wasteful? Do you need to adjust your lifestyle to reduce your mandatory spending? Do you need to downgrade your hamburger? Or, have you been living frugally when you don't really have to, and can afford that truffle burger? Now you can figure it out! This is also a good way to see all of your accounts in one place, such as bank accounts and department store credit cards. If you seem to have a large amount, maybe turn the cashier down the next time he or she offers you 10 percent off to sign up for a store credit card. The more consolidated your accounts, the easier it will be to keep your finances in check. You'll also receive a lot less paperwork, which will make organization less daunting. Less to start with means less to organize! Know your account numbers in case you ever need them in the strangest of situations. Have a master list of all of your accounts and numbers on your phone, but use a password-protected document.

Enroll in **ONLINE BANKING**, but don't set up recurring bill pay for anything that fluctuates from month to month. Money can be wasted, or mistakes or fraudulent activity missed, if you aren't staying on top of your **BILLS** and actively reading them. Your finances are one place where the mantra "out of sight, out of mind" is a dangerous philosophy. If you can, add in new expenses and purchases as soon as possible, but at least weekly. This is a good way to make sure receipts from purchases don't pile up or you forget what they were for. But you only really need to save cash receipts. Everything else has a digital record that can be imported into your financial planning program.

Remember, just because you have money doesn't mean you need to spend it. Be smart about how often you use your debit card. Try to discipline yourself on how much cash you take out of the ATM and limit yourself to a weekly allowance, which means you're only visiting the ATM once a week. For some discipline assistance, create a "discretionary spending" bank account and set up a recurring monthly deposit for your allowance. If you overdraft the account, ground yourself for the weekend and miss Arthur Gradstein's awesome Quelf party. Curb unnecessary expenses, which should now be easy to identify using your organized financial system. Control your finances so they don't control you.

AN O.C.D. SUCCESS STORY

I've seen stacks of financial documents that would shock and amaze, but nothing compares to the basement of a major Wall Street player whom I had as a client. In the basement of his country home, he had around thirty extra-wide, four-tiered filing cabinets filled to the brim with documents. That's 120 drawers. I went through every single one and shredded about 90 percent of the documents because they weren't necessary! Playing it safe, we ended up with six filing cabinets, leaving him and his family plenty of room to convert their basement into usable living space. To this day, I have not received a call saying they were missing anything important. Don't just save everything: really ask yourself what needs to be kept in paper form and what can be accessed online or just thrown out!

FIREPLACES can either be gas, wood, electric, or decorative. For working fireplaces, keep anything flammable away from the fireplace. This is no place to stack your **MAGAZINES** and newspapers unless you want to rebuild your home after the fire. At least you had that fireproof **SAFE** I told you to get, right? The only things that should be near a working fireplace are basic tools, supplies like starter blocks and matches, and **FIREWOOD**. Keep only a few logs nearby and the rest out of the house. If you have a wood-burning fire-place, clean it after each use. Make sure everything is cool, then scoop out the ashes and dispose of mostly burned logs. This will prevent campfire smells from permeating your home. Even though it produces no waste product, you still have to clean a gas fireplace to keep it safe and functional, although less frequently than a wood-burning fireplace. Make sure everything is cool and the gas is off, then vacuum out any dust or cobwebs and wipe down glass doors if you have them. Depending on the feel of your home, you may want to make the fireplace a cozy-up area and the central focus of the room. If you do, you can keep pillows and blankets out. Even if you don't make it a cozy-up area, it's nice to keep some blankets close by in a storage area or on the arm of your couch for that random snuggle. If you are going for a slick, modern feel, make sure the entire fireplace area is clean and bare. If your fireplace is decorative only, stock it with candles to create your own fire feature, or con-sider getting an artist from a local art school to come and paint a background

F

of a fireplace in your nook. They tend to work for food and/or alcohol, but just make sure you ask for ID first.

FIREWOOD should be kept outside, on your covered patio, or in your **GARAGE**. Stack it carefully in an area where you think your wood is safe from woodchucks, water, and thieves. Keep your firewood in a dry area so it's always ready to go for an impromptu s'more session. If you have to keep your firewood exposed, consider using a tarp underneath and covering your wood during the snowy winter months and rainy days. Keep only enough firewood inside the home near the fireplace for one evening's fire. No one needs a massive pile of firewood inside his or her home except for professional whittlers.

FOOD PANTRIES should be cleaned out and organized every six months or after every major trip to the grocery store or especially Costco or Sam's Club. I know you're exhausted from walking those mile-long aisles, but stick it out and get your **CANNED GOODS** in a row. Like a **REFRIGERATOR** and **FREEZER**, it is important to take *everything* out the first time you do a massive organization overhaul. You want to have complete knowledge of everything in your pantry so you don't overbuy, so you can keep things organized, and so you can actually find and eat what you have. Once everything is out, check the expiration dates. If anything is expired, toss it. If there are items in the pantry that aren't expired but you haven't used in over a year, donate them to your local school food drive or use them that week. If you find any cans that are bulging, rusting, or crawling, throw them away immediately because they may be hazardous to your health. Once you have the items that will be going back into your pantry, separate them into piles: beverages, paper goods, cereals, canned goods, baking items, snacks, and so on. Find an appropriate place in your pantry for these types of goods, label these areas, and stay disciplined next time you add to your pantry. Keep perishable items safe from bugs and moisture by using plastic **CONTAINERS** with sealable lids. Add **SHELVES** if you need more space. Stock the most frequently used items at eye level and less frequently used items higher up. If you keep appliances in your pantry due to a small **KITCHEN**, keep these heavier items down low so they are safe and save your spine. Consider using tiered can racks to maximize space and efficiency. Break down anything you buy in bulk, like paper towels, into individual items. Always keep labels facing out and stock items with those expiring soonest in the front. This will make searching for things much faster and help you use food before it goes bad, saving you money. This will also help you determine what you need at the grocery store because you will be able to tell which items are running low instead of having to roll the dice at the store and bring home that seventh can of cream of mushroom soup. Having an organized pantry will make shopping more fun and cooking less overwhelming.

FOYER (see ENTRYWAY)

FREEZERS should be cleaned once every two to three months and reorganized after every major trip to the grocery store. Get out your ice pick and goggles; take everything out of your freezer and put it in the **KITCHEN** sink. If your freezer is iced up, let it thaw out before you clean it, unless you actually enjoy ice picking. Grab a bunch of towels because a lot of ice turns into a lot of water. Using your favorite nontoxic cleaner, wipe down all surfaces and wash all ice trays. You can even dump your ice bin for fresh, clean ice. Now go through all of the food in your sink. Throw away anything with freezer burn or ice cream that's lost its texture. Now ask yourself if you really are going to eat what you have. Make a decision based on how long it's been in your freezer. If you can't remember when it was added, time to get rid of it. Whatever you decide to keep, just make sure you eat it or get rid of it the next time you clean out your freezer. If you have a large freezer, you have the luxury of saving more food or keeping chilled glasses. If your freezer is really big, like a stand-alone, consider using **BINS** to organize your food. If your freezer is small, such as in an **APARTMENT**, only keep what you regularly use and eat. Use the door for the most frequently used items. Stack boxes by size to make things easier to see and pull out. Make every effort not to waste food, but it's okay to throw things away that are no longer good or that you'll never eat. You don't need to keep that frozen Hawaiian pizza you never seem to bake. DiGiorno will get over it.

FRIDGE (see REFRIGERATOR)

FRONT HALL CLOSET (see ENTRYWAY CLOSET)

FURNITURE that is **ANTIQUE** or valuable should be documented and those records kept on file with your insurance company in case of an emergency or a thief who watches *Antiques Roadshow*. All other furniture in your home or **OFFICE** should be functional and useful. Certain furniture can be displayed as conversation pieces or art, but the point of furniture is to serve a functional purpose. Don't clutter a room because you are trying to use extra pieces of furniture from a previous address or that you inherited and don't know what to do with it. Every piece of furniture in your home should be there for a reason, so sell or donate what no longer fits or works. Never place furniture in front of a door or window. Place furniture thoughtfully so that you are not running an obstacle course to get to your bed, **DESK**, or couch. Always leave yourself enough clearance between furniture and walls, for instance, to get out of bed or scoot a chair back at the dining table. Furniture should be placed near other furniture that serves a similar purpose, for example, your dining table should be near your buffet. This seems like common sense, but I can't tell you how many times I organize homes with furniture serving like purposes placed far away or even in different rooms.

When buying new furniture, know exactly what space you are trying to fill and measure, measure, measure. Don't impulse buy anything and then hope to find a use for it. You won't. Also, measure your loading spaces! Just because it fits in your **APARTMENT** doesn't mean it fits in the elevator or stairway! When you look for new furniture, always consider pieces with built-in storage options. Furniture should enhance the functionality and decor of your home. Once it starts detracting, it's time to start subtracting.

If you have furniture in storage that is meaningful and you'd like to pass it down to children or other family members, make sure you are going to that storage facility twice a year to check on these pieces. **STORAGE UNITS** can be damaging to furniture if they are not climate controlled or if you haven't properly wrapped it.

O.C.D. EXTREME

In most cases, you can find a piece of furniture that fits almost perfectly in a space. But almost perfect is unacceptable when you are O. C.D. Extreme! If you really want something that fits perfectly, you need to have it made or do it yourself. I build my own desks to fit my work spaces and incorporate systems for cable hiding and management. Purchase the plans and follow the how-to videos for the O.C.D. Desk System on ocdexperience.com to build one for yourself!

G

GAMES are fun and entertaining, but only if you know where they are and can grab them easily. If you can't find Sorry!, you'll be the one who's sorry. Keep all games, puzzles, activities, and anything else used to liven up a party in the same area. This will put your choices right in front of you and your **GUESTS** so you can pick your entertainment quickly and without ruining the moment. I can tell you from experience, as I host game nights all the time, that being able to pull out that special game in seconds keeps the party rocking. You don't want to be searching for a game while your guests sit idly in another room. Find a **CLOSET** or space that is not frequently used so you aren't consuming space accessed on a daily basis. This is one of those times that buying furniture with storage provides a great opportunity to keep your games in social areas of the home, but out of sight and out of the way. Stack larger games on the bottom and work your way up to the smallest. If you have a large number of games and puzzles, organize them by type of game so you can find them quickly: board games, card games, erotic games, puzzles, strategy games, and so on. Make sure all the accessories are put back immediately when you are done playing so you aren't searching for that missing piece the next time you pull that game out. Keep **VIDEO GAMES** near your video game system. For children's games, designate a spot near your children's **TOYS** so your child will know where to find them without having to ask you. If they do ask, it will be easy to give your child an answer because the answer will always be the same. Teach your children the discipline of cleaning up their games after playing with them and putting them back where they go every time so it becomes a habit. As you teach your children, take this opportunity to take a dose of your own **MEDICINE** and remind yourself to maintain organizational discipline.

GARAGES, just like your dog, can be your best friend or bite you in the ass. I prefer it to be my best friend. Do you know what is in your garage? Can you access everything in your garage? How much time does it take you to find a single item in your garage? Most people use their garage as a large dumping ground with no thought of organization. Think of your garage as a home away from home. Like your home, you want to know where everything is and be able to make use of those things. When I was a kid, I was constantly organizing my parents' garage because they treated it like a **STORAGE UNIT**. As fast as I could organize it, they'd destroy it. To this day, I still fly home to Florida to help them go through their garage. We just recently pulled both cars in for the first time in years. My mom couldn't be happier! She even made me my favorite Rice Krispies Treats as a thank-you gift.

To tackle a disaster garage, lay a tarp down in a large area, such as your driveway or lawn. Pull everything out of your garage and put it on the tarp. Some trash should be immediately obvious. Get rid of it. If you have a lot of trash, consider renting a Dumpster. Separate all the contents of your garage into categories as you bring them out. This will be easier than rearranging everything once it's out because you'll have less working space. Just as when organizing your **CLOSET**, there will be items to donate, items to sell, items to keep, and items that have no business being in there in the first place. Find a better home for those items. Many people tend to stockpile projects in their garage: that chair you want to reupholster, those VHS tapes you want to digitize, or those pictures you need to scan. Deal with those projects now or set a date to complete the project. If it's not done by then, get rid of those items.

Now, for the things you are keeping, start grouping them with like items:

camping supplies, car cleaning, gardening, **HOLIDAY DECORATIONS**, sports equipment, tools, and so on. Take this opportunity to clean your garage well. Rent a pressure cleaner if you have to. It's not often that you have a completely empty garage, so take advantage of it. Now would be the time to have a **YARD SALE** if you are interested, but, whatever you don't sell, you must donate. If you were willing to sell it, you don't need it, and it shouldn't be taking up space in your garage, even if it represented your dreams of becoming a famous drummer.

Now create sections in your garage by asking yourself what you want the garage to be used for. If you like to build things and have a lot of **TOOLS**, then create a section of the garage as a work space designated for that. Find yourself the perfect tool chest that isn't too big or too small and organize your tools so that any guest could find a screwdriver or saw. If you are creating storage sections in your garage for bulk purchases, make sure that cleaning chemicals and food are not stored together. Food and chemicals do not mix! Also, keep your chemicals in a ventilated area. Make sure your garage is a safe environment by securing tools and any other dangerous equipment. Accidents happen! Even a loose bike can hurt someone. However you choose to define the space in your garage, now is the time to plan it out and add any organizational hardware and accessories such as **SHELVES**, clips, and pegboards for mounting tools, hooks for hanging bikes to utilize dead space, hanging baskets for children's **TOYS** and **SPORTING GOODS**, and lifts for storing seasonal items from the ceiling. If you have the budget, customize your garage by bringing in a third-party expert who will turn your garage into an organizational haven. There are companies these days that create custom work areas for your garage using weatherproof materials. If you find yourself in need of help, don't be shy—**RESEARCH** some of these companies to help you maximize your space. But remember: a garage should ultimately be used for storing your **AUTOMOBILES**. If you are planning on using the garage to house your automobiles, like most garages are built for, then make sure that your tools and designated areas are flush against the walls so you can park your cars inside without scraping the side of your car against a rake.

Use the walls of your garage for storage, since most wall space is dead space. You can hang anything from all-weather clothing, bikes, brooms, gardening equipment, ladders, strollers, tennis rackets, umbrellas, and vacuums. Go to your local hardware store and pick up a wall mount for

G

some of these supplies or research some DIY solutions to save you some money. Try to keep everything off the floor because it will become dirty.

Using **BINS** will make cleanup simple. They can house all types of equipment and gear and make things easy to find. Sealed bins should always be clear so you can see their contents without having to open them. When it comes to storage, we want X-ray vision. Always keep a bin designated for donation items. You'll use this regularly as you organize other areas of your home, and it will help you stay in the mind-set of donating items you no longer need that could be of use to someone else. Most charities will send a truck to pick up items for donation, saving you time and energy and giving you a valuable tax deduction. Just be sure to keep and create a master list of the items you're donating and attach it to your donation receipt for Uncle Sam.

Overall, make sure the things in your garage are items you actually use. If they're not being used, get rid of them! Whatever organizational choices you make, keep in mind that you want to be able to get to your belongings without having to go through an obstacle course. Your cars should be able to fit in your garage with ease and your children should be able to get to their toys and sports equipment without stress or risk of decapitation. Maintain your organization by returning things to their place and not allowing yourself to use your garage as a storage space.

AN O.C.D. SUMMARY

Organize: Take everything out of the garage like you are having a garage sale in your yard or driveway. In extreme cases, you might want to bring in a Dumpster. As you bring things out, dispose of the garbage and make a donation pile. Separate the remaining contents of your garage into similar items: sports equipment, seasonal items, tools, and so on.

Create: Create a floor plan for your garage as you would for your home. If necessary, add industrial shelving or a pegboard for tools. Designate sections for the items you will be keeping and prioritize accessibility based on frequency of use.

Discipline: Once the garage is clear and the floor plan is implemented, add to your garage only these things that fall into the areas you've created. If you remove something, make sure to put it back in its proper place. If you think of your garage as a functional place and not as a dumping ground, it will continue to stay a functional place.

■ ■ ■ ■

GARAGE SALE (see YARD SALE)

GARBAGE might seem like an odd thing to consider organizing, unless you are Oscar the Grouch, but even organizing your trash can benefit your life! For your day-to-day garbage, make sure you are sorting your recyclables from your true trash. Do this daily or weekly. Always follow local codes and dispose of paint and chemicals properly. If you are feeling philanthropic, put valuable items at the top of your trash or prominently displayed for your local neighborhood scavenger.

You should have a garbage can in your **KITCHEN, BATHROOM, OFFICE, GARAGE,** and **LAUNDRY ROOM**. Make sure the size of the can is appropriate for the space—you don't need a twenty-gallon can under your **DESK**. If you do, you need to overhaul your office supply use. Consider replacing the garbage can under your desk with a shredder. Empty your garbage cans when filled, but at least once a week.

During the organization of a major space like your garage, or when **MOVING**, you'll end up with much more garbage than you have space for in your weekly trash can. So get creative and use garbage to store garbage— fill boxes and bins you can't break down with other trash. Stack flat items. Not only will this reduce the volume of your garbage and the number of trips you'll have to make to the curb, but your garbageman will be grateful for your thoughtfulness.

■ ■ ■
O.C.D. EXTREME

I take my garbage out every day, even if it's not full. I'll do a lap around the house, emptying every can, spraying my Lysol, because I don't want anything stinking up my space while I'm sleeping. It's pleasing to start with an empty trash bag each morning. Also, I try to find trash cans that have lids for every room, even the tiny bathroom ones. Who wants to be staring at garbage?

GARDENS require a lot of care and maintenance to grow and look their best. Proper organization will help you become the envy of everyone on your block, or get that blue ribbon on your giant pumpkin. Just like everything done in the O.C.D. Way, first define your space. What will you grow? What will you need to make that grow? Make sure you have the proper systems installed and the best soil picked before filling the space. Choose a location near a spigot, and keep a hose on a hose winder for manual watering. Now you can start planting. Each time you add a plant, stick a sign next to it saying what it is and any important information like water and fertilizer requirements. Maintain your garden every so often by picking weeds, gathering debris, and checking the health of your plants. If you keep your gardening supplies and **TOOLS** well organized in your garage or outdoor shed, it will make maintenance of your garden fun and easy. Keep a water and fertilizer schedule for your plants and display it in this area. Mount your tools, gloves, and tool belt or apron together to keep them easily accessible. A pegboard is a great option. Always rinse your tools after each use to extend their usable life. Keep fertilizers together, arranged by nutrient ratio. Mulch, border stripping, pots, and any other less frequently used accessories should be kept on higher or lower **SHELVES**, lower if heavy or breakable. Any harsh chemicals, like those used for pest and weed control, should be kept in a well-ventilated area away from children and pets. Keep your garden organized and give your gardenias a chance.

O.C.D. EXTREME

Outline your tools on your pegboard with tape or paint so you, and anyone else, will know exactly where your tools go. Sometimes the simplest methods are the most foolproof.

GIFT WRAP supplies might take up a tiny corner in your **CLOSET**, or an entire station in your craft room if you have Martha Stewart aspirations. Either way, gift giving should make you feel good, and so should the process of wrapping that gift. It will be a joy if you have the proper tools and supplies readily available.

First, consolidate anything you use for gift wrapping: wrapping and tissue paper, scissors, tape, **RIBBON** and bows, bags, markers and pens, and cards. Make sure all of your paper is usable and undamaged, and that there is enough left to wrap something larger than a pack of gum. If there isn't, recycle it. You don't want to assume you have paper and then find yourself wrapping an expensive gift in newspaper at the last minute because you didn't have enough left on the roll.

Now pick a spot for your wrapping tools and supplies. Create a wrapping station if you have the space (see **CRAFT ROOM** for great ideas), or organize everything in a **BIN** you can pull out easily from a designated **DRAWER** or spot in a closet whenever you need to wrap a gift. If you do use a bin to store all of your supplies, separate and label them by keeping them in **ZIP-LOCK BAGS**. Anything that might be crushed easily can be kept in a hanging compartment bag on the side of the closet. If you keep many rolls of paper on hand, you can store them in an inexpensive plastic trash can. The upright storage makes paper selection easy: when you need to select your paper, pick and pull, and when you're done with the paper, roll and drop. You can also store your gift bags and tissue paper on the sides of the trash can. If you find yourself using a bin, a bag, and a trash can, make sure all of these items are kept together so your gift-wrapping supplies are always easy to grab. You'll be glad you are organized when you find out that today is your boss's **BIRTHDAY**.

■ ■ ■ ■
O.C.D. APPROVED TECHNOLOGY
If you take pride in giving beautifully wrapped gifts, consider buying a portable gift-wrap station. They store and organize all your gift-wrap essentials and can be hung in a closet or slid under a bed. I've even seen some with folding legs that double as tables. The Container Store offers a variety of options to suit your preferences.

GOLF BAG (see SPORTING GOODS)

GREETING CARDS bring joy, laughter, kind words, ten dollars from Grandma, and sympathy to or from friends and family. If you are the type of person who likes to keep the sentimental cards that people give you, I have two words for you: scan them. They won't take up any physical space, they'll be easier to file, and they'll be easier to share years down the line. You won't end up with that shoe box full of disorganized cards you'll never actually look through again. If you want to preserve the page structure of the card, perhaps for one with a risqué punch line, you can scan it as a multipage PDF. File your cards on your **COMPUTER** under DOCUMENTS → CARDS with a file name containing the name of the person who gave it to you, the event, and the year. For example, "Dave Matthews—My Birthday—2020." Then you can toss the original card after displaying it on your mantel for an appropriate amount of time.

It's also a good idea to keep a few unused cards and **ENVELOPES** on hand for that last-minute **BIRTHDAY** gift or holiday party. But you need to keep only one or two cards in your home for each major occasion. Don't worry about lesser holidays—sorry, Arbor Day. After every holiday, cards tend to go on sale, so this is a great time to snag some cards cheap to keep on hand. Keep your cards either with your **GIFT WRAP** supplies or **OFFICE SUPPLIES** in a small **CONTAINER**, accordion folder, or greeting card organizer. Once you give a card, replace the card. You'd be surprised how useful having a few cards on hand will be—and this is coming from a guy who doesn't keep much. You'll end up giving out more cards, and who doesn't like getting a card with a thoughtful message?

When you have a lot of cards to send out, for example, during the holidays, make sure you aren't leaving anyone off your holiday list. Keep a master list for your holiday card giving and cross-reference it with your **ADDRESS BOOK** for current addresses and phone numbers. This is the perfect time to kill two birds with one stone: making your holiday list and updating your contacts. Make your holiday list a few months in advance under the guise of updating your address book. People won't know the thoughtful reason behind why you are asking them for their information, keeping it a surprise. Make sure to get current e-mail addresses as well, because sending out e-cards is a great green alternative in a digital world. Send paper cards out two to three weeks before the actual holiday, because **MAIL** is more likely to find its way to the proper place if sent before the post office gets swamped. The sooner your cards get delivered, the longer they can sit on the recipient's mantel to remind them you care.

GRILLS don't require much, but what is required should be organized so you don't go to cook that beautifully marinated tri-tip and find you only have four charcoal briquettes left. You'll need a simple set of grill tools, a good stick lighter, a timer, a thermometer, a small fire extinguisher, a small spray bottle with water to control flare-ups, a serving tray, a flashlight or mountable grill light for night grilling, and charcoal or two tanks of propane in case one runs out mid-cook. If you are lucky enough to have a built-in grill station with storage, designate areas for your supplies and keep them labeled and maintained. If not, get a weatherproof **BIN** to keep all supplies. If your grill doesn't have fold-up wings, invest in a weatherproof table or cart to keep next to your grill. This will help in prep and service. Once you are done cooking, clean your hot grill while your meat rests, like a good grill master. Then grab that nicely stocked condiment bin from your **REFRIGERATOR** and enjoy! When you are done eating, clean all tools and return them to their homes.

G

139

O.C.D. APPROVED TECHNOLOGY

Don't end up with a half-cooked brisket! Leave nothing to chance and invest in a propane gauge so you know exactly how much is left in your tank. Running out mid-cook is a BBQ disaster! Also, pick yourself up an infrared thermometer so you can check the doneness of your meat without having to poke holes in it. Poking holes lets those precious juices run out and leaves you with a dry piece of meat.

GROCERIES will be brought home with you from the market into your organized home, so get a head start and organize your shopping cart while you shop. Take the extra moment to think about where a product is going in your cart instead of just tossing it in—this isn't *Supermarket Sweep*. While you are grabbing things, think about where they will be going once you get home and place them in your cart accordingly. The more organized your cart, the less time you will have to spend at home figuring out where things go. Always add frozen and refrigerated items last. Make sure when you check out that you place your items on the belt in the way you organized them in your cart. That way, the grocery clerk won't have any choice but to bag them that way. Don't let people rush you at the market. Stay calm, cool, and collected and take ownership of your organized cart. People are going to take notice.

When you get home and unpack your groceries, recycle your grocery bags (if you aren't using reusable bags). If you keep grocery bags for other uses in the home, fold them and store them in your designated location. Don't be the person who has three hundred plastic grocery bags under the sink. You'll never use that many bags before your next trip to the grocery store.

O.C.D. EXTREME

For smaller grocery shops, I like to use the self-checkout machines so I can control how things are bagged without feeling rushed. If the contents of my bags are organized, I can put them away quickly and efficiently when I get home.

GROCERY LISTS should be constantly updated as soon as you realize you need something. Otherwise you'll forget and come home from the market without your wife's whitening toothpaste. Nowadays, you can keep your list on your phone. There are great **APPS** designed for making a grocery list that allow you to share and update the list among members of your household, find and store **COUPONS**, and even scan bar codes. But a good old-fashioned magnetic pad on the side of your refrigerator works just as well, as long as you add to it immediately when you run out of something or plan a new menu. Be specific—include how much you need to buy and even brand preferences. If you keep an organized **FOOD PANTRY, REFRIGERATOR**, and **FREEZER**, it will be easy to tell what you need to buy more of. Double-check your list with these areas before leaving for the grocery store. Categorize your list by the type of product you are buying, such as beverages, dairy, fruit and vegetables, paper, and so on. This will make shopping much faster and you won't have to double back to aisles you've already visited. You may want to go as far as typing a grocery list template out on your computer with these categories labeled, stick it to your fridge, and write the grocery items under the specific category as you run out. If you are the type of person who does a small grocery shop daily for that night's meal, plan out what your **MEALS** will be at the beginning of the week or in the morning before you leave for work. You'll know exactly what you need to buy instead of deciding at the market. Discipline yourself into buying only what is on your list and just say no to that extra pint of vanilla Häagen-Dazs.

O.C.D. EXTREME

This tip requires intimate knowledge of your grocery store: organize your grocery list by aisle so you can plan your path through your market, working your way chronologically down your shopping list without having to jump around. You'll be so efficient, you'll think you're on an episode of *Supermarket Sweep*.

O.C.D. APPROVED TECHNOLOGY

The Grocery IQ app lets you create shopping lists quickly and easily. It lets you customize your categories, allows you to sync between devices, offers predictive input, and even lets you scan product bar codes to add them to your list. You can also add item details, like size or quantity. Grocery IQ will even provide you with coupons for your favorite brands.

G

GUESTS should always feel comfortable staying in your home. While a muffin basket is probably overkill, be a good host by making sure their room is clean and organized before they arrive. As much as your significant other wants to fill the guest room **CLOSET** with their overflow **WARDROBE**, just say no. Give your guests some empty **DRAWERS** and closet space with available **HANGERS**. Stock the **BATHROOM** with fresh towels, shampoo, conditioner, soap, a razor, toothpaste, mouthwash, a hair dryer, and a hairbrush. Provide some fresh flowers, a bathrobe, and an extra blanket and pillows. Give your guests a set of **KEYS** so you don't have to babysit them and so they can come and go as they please . . . unless they aren't trustworthy. Give them the tour of your home so they know where everything is.

You've been gracious toward your guests, so your guests should return the favor. If your guests will be with you for an extended period of time, give them specific instructions on how you like your house to be kept organized. If they're staying with you for only a day or two, just deal with it and let it go. You can reorganize soon enough. But in general, if you took the time to organize it, houseguests should respect it. Explain to them how to maintain order and organization in your home. Be specific about cleaning procedures and day-to-day upkeep so that your guests add to your home rather than make it more chaotic. Be honest about certain things that bother you or that you need done so there is no tension in your home. Little things like not leaving the toilet seat up, taking shoes off at the door, and putting things back in the appropriate place after they are used should be communicated before they become a problem. Your guests will appreciate this communication because no one ever wants there to be unspoken tension. If you have a home that has a lot of gadgetry, light switches, codes, or laser defense systems, create a house manual that your guests can refer to. Guests should always feel welcome (and safe from lasers) and you should always feel happy to have them back.

O.C.D. EXTREME

People love having me as a houseguest because I leave the room cleaner and more organized than I found it. If the room isn't orderly, I have to create order to be able to focus and sleep soundly. If there is stuff out on the bathroom counter, and it's my own private bathroom, I'll put it away and wipe down the counter so it's spotless. If you want to guarantee a repeat invite, go O.C.D. extreme (as long as your host is cool with it).

GYM (see **EXERCISE ROOM**)

GYM BAGS, more than any other bag except the **DIAPER BAG**, should be cleaned out after every gym visit. Those dirty, sweaty clothes and towels get very gross very quickly when kept in a zipped bag longer than they should. Your sweat isn't **WINE**. It doesn't develop in flavor with age. So get those clothes out, get them cleaned, and restock the bag so you are ready for the next workout. Your gym bag should house only the necessary items for your workout: a set of workout clothes or a change of clothes for after your workout, a lock, a towel, **HEADPHONES**, a hygiene bag, and a fresh snack and bottle of water. Keeping an extra pair of clean **UNDERWEAR** and **SOCKS** in your bag is always a good idea because you never know when you are going to need them. Your hygiene bag should include deodorant, a toothbrush, toothpaste, and any other products you need to feel like a clean and presentable human being. Put only what you will use and need in your bag and go through it after every workout to make sure everything is fresh and ready to use for next time.

AN O.C.D. SUCCESS STORY

My client had to go home after every workout because he didn't bring an organized and stocked gym bag with him to the gym. He had to run home to shower and change before moving forward with the rest of his day. What a waste of time! It also kept him from going to the gym as often because of the extra time it took. I convinced him to start keeping a gym bag ready to go with fresh clothing, toiletries, and supplies. Now he can stop at the gym on his way to work or whenever he feels like it.

H

HAIR ACCESSORIES like barrettes, clips, headbands, extensions, pins, rollers, and ties can be found in some scary states of disorganization: randomly tossed together, some wrapped in tangled strands of hair like a rubber band ball. Why would you want to reach into a chaotic **DRAWER** to grab anything that goes on your head? Give yourself peace of mind by feeling good about what literally goes on top of it.

Hair accessories should be organized by size and type. Smaller items should be kept in small plastic **CONTAINERS** or jars, separated by type. These jars should all be kept together on a **SHELF** or in a **BIN** or basket, depending on your space. Headbands can be kept in a clear, plastic travel bag.

For larger accessories such as hair dryers, curling irons, flat irons, and roller kits, use a basket that you can tuck away under your sink if you use those items daily, or otherwise keep them in your **LINEN CLOSET**. Never keep your hair dryer or curling iron out. Put it back every time you use it. The more things that are put away, the clearer and more functional you will be in your **BATHROOM**.

If you are a hair professional, consider buying an expandable train case. It offers portability and the ability to define compartments for different accessories.

For a creative and visual solution for your children's bathroom, hang a piece of **RIBBON** on the wall and clip their hair accessories on it. But do yourself a favor—pull the hair from the accessories after they come off your children and before the accessories go back on the ribbon. Your children's hair stops being cute once it leaves their head.

■ ■ ■

O.C.D. EXTREME

Have an outlet installed wherever you keep your electric hair accessories, even if it's under the sink. That way, you can always keep them plugged in. When you need them, you just grab them and hit the power button without having to fumble with power cords. With a bit of planning and the help of an electrician, you can create your own mini-salon.

HAIR PRODUCTS are sometimes a spur-of-the-moment purchase you never wind up using after that first trial despite the silken promises. Perhaps your stylist pressured you into buying some product. A suggestion for those impulse buys that have been sitting in your **BATHROOM** since their first and only use is . . . get rid of them. Give them to a friend or empty them out and recycle the bottles. If you're on the fence, put a sticker on the product with the date you last used it. When you check back, if it's been more than six months since you used it, toss it. For the products you use often, keep them in your **MEDICINE CABINET**, arranged by height, or under your sink. For the products that you use less frequently, keep them in a **BIN** or basket in your **LINEN CLOSET** on a **SHELF** with your larger **HAIR ACCESSORIES**, or under your sink but separate from your more frequently used products. Do your best not to clutter your bathroom with unnecessary supplies. Every so often, go through your products and do a healthy purge of everything you have stopped using or that is old and needs replacing. Give yourself the space to try some new and intoxicating head smells!

HALL CLOSETS are a storage luxury and, like this book, an exciting choose-your-own adventure. Depending on the location in your home and what it is you keep, they can have various purposes: **BROOM CLOSET, ENTRYWAY CLOSET, LINEN CLOSET**, suitcase storage, **GAMES** and recreation, and so on. But a hall closet should never be a multipurpose or miscellaneous closet. That just means it's a junk closet. Never throw something into a **CLOSET** just because it seems convenient at that moment. Define your hall closet for a specific purpose, then keep things neat and organized so they aren't busting out when you open the closet door. If you find yourself at the bottom of a hall closet avalanche, it's time to get everything out, sort through it, define your empty space, and find the right home for everything that used to be in there.

HALLOWEEN always seems to creep up quickly, so make sure that when it does you aren't haunted by it! Buy your candy well enough in advance from a warehouse store so you aren't stuck with the weird picked-over stuff. Take note of how many trick-or-treaters you had last year so you know how much candy to buy. Err on the side of too much or you might run out and end up with egg on your house. Those punks.

Get a jump on Halloween costumes. Two months away, lock in your family's costumes and go hunting early. Prices go up and selection goes down the closer you get to the holiday. As soon as October hits, pull those well-organized **HOLIDAY DECORATIONS** from your **CLOSET**, **GARAGE**, or **STORAGE UNIT**, and get them up to make the most use of them. But take them down within the week following Halloween, repack, and store them. If you spent a significant amount of money on costumes and can see yourself using them again another year, clean them, bag them so you don't lose any accessories, and put them in a labeled sealable **BIN** along with your decorations. Grab pumpkins about two weeks in advance and let them sit uncarved to start enjoying the Halloween spirit. You can even draw your design early, but don't carve until three or four days before the thirty-first or you'll end up with a saggy, brown jack-o'-lantern. To prolong the fun of the holiday, consider having a post-Halloween party to do a costume swap and eat any leftover candy you or your friends may have. Remember: the chaos of a last-minute Halloween is just short of a nightmare . . . on Elm Street.

■ ■ ■ ■

O.C.D. EXTREME

When it's time to carve pumpkins, instead of laying out newspapers, which are porous, have gaps between sections, and get ink on everyone's hands, roll out a plastic drop cloth. These are available anywhere painting supplies are sold. After the pumpkins are carved, you simply grab the corners of the drop cloth, fold it up, and put it in the trash. When carving, make sure everyone has their own tools and trash bucket so they aren't reaching or moving for things, spreading pumpkin guts everywhere. Halloween can be fun and clean.

HANDBAGS (see PURSES)

HANGERS become overwhelming and ugly when closets are filled with different colors, shapes, sizes, and girths. Make sure all of your hangers are uniform in size and color throughout every closet in your home. This will allow you to see the clothes you have to choose from rather than having your attention stolen by your hangers. Stay on top of those dry cleaner hangers and never let them make their way into your **CLOSET**. Dispose of them, or even better, give them back to your dry cleaner. Make sure that when you go to the store to buy your hangers, you buy some extra for the new clothes you will add to your closet. You always want at least five extra hangers in your closet at all times so you don't run out and feel tempted to double up two jackets on a hanger. Maintain a positive relationship with your closet and practice hanger monogamy.

HARD DRIVES are when you get stuck in L.A. traffic, but also the device where all your precious digital information is stored. They can be internal, which means inside your computer, or portable/external. For external hard drives, make sure they are properly labeled on the outside so you know what each drive is for. Just because you have a 500 GB (gigabyte) hard drive doesn't mean you should put anything and everything on it. The drive should be specific for a type of file. No drive is safe from crashing and failure, so always play it safe and keep everything backed up to another drive, off-site, or in the **CLOUD**.

Portable hard drives are getting smaller and smaller. Flash **MEMORY CARDS**, which are essentially tiny hard drives, and USB flash drives are easy to lose, so make sure you keep them in a designated space or with their device. These tend to be more for temporary uses like transferring information rather than for long-term storage, so use them for that purpose and then wipe them clean. I like to keep a small flash drive on my **KEY CHAIN** or in my **CAR** because you never know when you'll have to transfer a large file between computers and it really is the easiest way.

When replacing an internal hard drive during an upgrade, first transfer all relevant files off of your old drive. This is a good time to get rid of any digital files you don't need. You'll need an intermediate hard drive to accomplish this task. Ideally, this already exists as your backup hard drive, which should have a copy of every file on your **COMPUTER**. Both Apple and PC computers have file transfer wizards that are easy to follow and reliable. Once all of your files are on your intermediate hard drive, remove the old internal drive and replace it according to the manufacturer's instructions. Reinstall your system software and then import all of your files from your intermediate or backup drive. They'll still be nice and organized, assuming you kept your digital folders according to *Organize & Create Discipline* standards. If you choose to keep your old internal hard drives, which I recommend in the event of a hard drive crash, store the most recent drive in a secure, dry, airtight **CONTAINER** or fireproof **SAFE** so no damage is done to it. Label it with the computer it came from and the date of removal.

■ ■ ■

O.C.D. EXTREME

When it comes time to dispose of an old hard drive, you can electronically wipe your data by deleting everything or downloading a wipe program. But it's still possible for committed data thieves to access your data even after digital deletion! The most surefire way to make sure your data is secure is to physically destroy the drive. Cover your hard drive with a cloth or towel and hit it with a hammer until you hear the platter, the magnetic disc inside, shatter. If you shake the hard drive and hear rattling inside, you've done the trick.

■ ■ ■

O.C.D. APPROVED TECHNOLOGY

Solid-state drives (SSD) are becoming more popular. They have no moving parts, are faster when accessing stored data, and consume less laptop battery life. Currently, it's a luxury option because it costs more per gigabyte of storage, but if you want to keep your data on the Ferrari of hard drives, pick one up.

HATS are fun to organize, especially if you have a large hat collection you like to show off, in which case, hats off to you. There are numerous hat organization solutions available for purchase, such as hat racks, standing hat racks, and wall-mounted hat racks. A simple and cheap idea for your collection is to buy removable plastic wall hooks and use each one as a hat hanger on the wall of your closet or back of your closet door. This will use space in your closet that is normally not taken advantage of and is also a great way to be able to see your entire hat collection. It also makes putting your hats away quick and easy because all you have to do is drop them on a hook. If wall space isn't available, stack your hats by style and color and keep them in a **BIN** in your **CLOSET** or **ENTRYWAY CLOSET**. For the serious hat collector, keep your hats in stacked and labeled boxes to preserve their shape, and keep the boxes on the top shelf of your closet. If you don't want to label the box, label the shelf where the box goes and make sure you always keep the hat in that spot. Whether it's a beret, bowler, cowboy hat, derby, fedora, porkpie hat, or sombrero, an organized hat collection ensures you keep your head adorned with the best hat for the occasion.

HEADPHONES in this day and age are included with everything that is in any way audio related: **SMARTPHONES**, cell phones, MP3 players, home entertainment systems, and even that software that promises to teach you Portuguese in ten days. Keep all of your headphones in the same place you would keep your **ELECTRONIC ACCESSORIES** for your portable electronic devices. You don't need to keep every set of headphones that end up in your home or a set for every device you own. At most, just have one set of headphones for each specific purpose you'd use them for: exercise, which might be water-resistant headphones designed to stay on your head or in your ears during aggressive activity; media viewing, which might be larger, high-fidelity can-type headphones; and communication and portability, which might be your standard space-saving earbuds. You can keep an extra set of headphones in your **PURSE** or **BACKPACK** or the glove compartment of your car. Many headphones now include a built-in microphone to use with your phone. Keep a pair of these in your car at all times, but only put one earbud in while driving so you don't T-bone the ambulance you couldn't hear coming.

□ ■ ■
O.C.D. APPROVED TECHNOLOGY
One pair of great headphones is better than three lesser pairs. I like the Tour and Powerbeats headphones from Beats by Dre. They sound amazing enough for the most discerning audiophile, are designed to stay in your ears during exercise, and even have a built-in microphone and volume controls for use with your smartphone.

HEALTH RECORDS (see MEDICAL RECORDS)

HOLIDAY CARDS (see GREETING CARDS)

HOLIDAY DECORATIONS can be a struggle to find each year, but they won't be next year if you follow the O.C.D. Way. Don't ruin the holiday spirit with expletives because you can't find the blue and white string lights. Use an airtight **BIN** labeled for each holiday. If you have a lot of decorations for a specific holiday, you can have multiple bins, but challenge yourself to keep only what you truly need to achieve that holiday spirit. For delicate Christmas ornaments, wrap them in bubble wrap or keep them in an ornament organizer. This will save them from getting crushed. If you have room, store these bins in an out-of-the-way spot in your **GARAGE**, or on the top **SHELF** in a **CLOSET** or storage area. You will only be using these decorations once a year, so don't put them in a place that should be reserved for more frequently used items. After using your decorations, dispose of any that have been damaged, and then put the rest back nicely and ready to use for next time: replace any burned-out or broken bulbs, boil your candleholders and menorahs in hot water to get the wax off, nicely wind any string lights, and give everything a wipe down. If some of your decorations are used for specific parts of your home, like a certain length of string light, label it so that you don't have redesign your system again. Next year you'll enjoy the holidays without stress because you'll find all of your decorations with ease. Erect and adorn your Christmas tree in record time!

■ ■ ■
O.C.D. EXTREME

Nothing goes into a bin in my life without going on a master list of contents associated with that bin. Keep a digital list of everything you have in each holiday bin and keep that list on your computer. You'll never have to pull out multiple holiday bins again to find your Christmas stockings.

HOME LIBRARY (see LIBRARY)

HOME OFFICE is a great opportunity to set up your work space exactly how you want it without anyone else having a say. It's also a great opportunity to work in your **UNDERWEAR**, but please don't have Skype meetings while wearing your extra-casual Friday attire. Whatever your outfit, your home office should be a place that gives you peace of mind and promotes productivity and quality output. It should be inviting. Do everything you can to separate the feel of this room from the rest of your home. This room needs to function like any productive **OFFICE** you would work in outside the home. If the division between your living space and your home office is hazy, you'll be distracted by your home life and won't do your best work. Organizing your home office is all about you and your business. Set it up so that it functions for you and makes you want to wake up and work. Hang pictures in your office that are meaningful and calming to you. A plant or two never hurts to bring some life into the office. Have a few energy crystals, citrine in particular, if you believe in that sort of thing—I do.

Keep the tools and supplies you need to accomplish your work but without going overboard. You'll be surprised how long a box of paper clips and staples actually lasts in a home office, so have enough **OFFICE SUPPLIES** for at least one working month and a little extra in case you have someone working with you. Save time by ordering office supplies online to be delivered. Always have extra **BATTERIES** readily available for any office devices that need them, such as wireless mice and keyboards. The goal is to have what you need to function solely out of your home office without ever having to go to an outside facility, except to grab a burger from Five Guys.

Make sure you create organized systems for your **E-MAIL IN-BOX**, **MAIL, GARBAGE, BOOKS, DESK**, and **DOCUMENTS**, and maintain your files in your **FILING CABINET**, if you keep one. Keep only the necessary work on your desk that needs to be completed and deal with any new incoming mail and documents as soon as possible. Have a shredder close to your work area for shredding your scanned documents and the 99 percent of mail that ends up in a pile you don't need. A multifunction printer will do you justice for printing, copying, scanning, and faxing without taking up too much space. Keep it close to your work area so you aren't wasting time going back and forth to your printer. Mount some **BULLETIN BOARDS** for a visual way to track progress and help you stay organized, but don't let the bulletin boards become a catchall for things you don't know what to do with. If you want to have a hardwired Ethernet connection, make sure that when your cable provider comes to set up your cable and Internet, they know you will need a cable line in your office. Also, make sure that you have enough outlets in your home office for the equipment you use. If you're lacking, buy a top-of-the-line surge protector. As you run all of your equipment, try to hide the wires as much as possible. They are distracting! If you can, mount the surge protector on the underside of your desk along with some tubing to make **CORDS** and wires as neat as possible.

Try out different systems and configurations to find what helps you function at your optimal level. Sometimes it will take a few failed systems before you find the right one. Whatever system you end up using in your home office, don't buy too many organizational products: sometimes less is more and more will just distract you from the work you actually have to do, so enjoy organizational products responsibly and in moderation. Clean your office once a week and always stay disciplined in maintaining your organized systems. This will keep you focused and productive.

■ ■ ■

AN O.C.D. SUMMARY

Organize: Get everything out of your office and sort through it. Get rid of all trash. If something doesn't help you do your work, or doesn't belong in a home office at all, find a better home for it. Keep a month's worth of the supplies you need to do your work.

Create: Design organizational systems in your office to store your supplies and to deal with your workflow and incoming/outgoing materials. Remember, just because you try a system out doesn't mean it will work the first time. Continually revamp your system until it is effective for the way you work.

Discipline: Keep your desk clear by scanning and filing your documents. Go through mail daily. Clean your office on a regular basis. Order office supplies as necessary.

HOMEPAGES should be set to whatever you want to focus on when you open your browser. If your e-mail is the first thing you want to see, that should be your homepage. If excellent organization is the first thing you want to see, set your homepage to www.ocdexperience.com. Some people like to use personalized homepages that display various tools, apps, gadgets, and information. I think these can be useful, but only if your page and layout are thoughtful and concise. You don't need to see an unreliable five-day weather report, breaking **NEWS**, your **E-MAIL IN-BOX**, new DVD releases, a calculator, and a word of the day every time you load your homepage. It's distracting! Limit your information to a few important categories and place them according to what's most important. Homepages for the O.C.D. Experience are set simply to a Google search bar.

HOTEL ROOMS can quickly become a disaster if you treat them like there will be a **HOUSEKEEPER** picking up after you. Yes, I am quite aware that there probably *will* be a housekeeper picking up after you, but only once a day, and that shouldn't negate your desire to maintain order in your space. If you start throwing things around in your hotel room, it will define how you view your room for the trip: as a chaotic space instead of a luxurious getaway.

Save a couple of bucks by thinking ahead. Bring some of your favorite brands of water and snacks, or stop on the way to your hotel. This will give you more money to spend on spa treatments since hotels can charge up to six bucks for a bottle of water and your firstborn child for a bag of peanuts.

When you arrive at your hotel, unpack your **BAG**, unless you are staying less than two days. Take everything out, put foldable items in **DRAWERS**, hang up the **CLOTHES** that you don't want wrinkled, and even take the time to iron them or send them to be pressed if they need it. Put your **SHOES** in the **CLOSET** and your **TOILETRY BAG** in the bathroom. You can even unpack the items from your toiletry bag. Leaving a towel on the floor lets the cleaning staff know the towel is dirty, but that doesn't mean the towel has to be flopped out in the middle of your bathroom. The best place for dirty towels is under the sink.

O.C.D. EXTREME

When I stay at a hotel longer than three days, I let the housekeeping manager know some of my preferences. I ask them not to move my toiletries in the bathroom, even if that means not cleaning that specific area (which I do myself). I also ask them not to move anything on the desk or bedside tables. It bothers me when they reset the room after I have begun to stay in it because I've made it a space for me, not a clean slate for the next guest!

O.C.D. EXTREME

Don't trash your hotel room like a spoiled rock star or celebutante. If you maintain organization and cleanliness in your hotel room, not only will you enjoy your space more and find it more relaxing, but it will make packing up after your trip much easier. You won't have to search all over and under places to locate your things, and you can feel confident you left nothing behind.

Oh, and don't be the person who collects all of the shampoos and conditioners! Just grab a set to replace your current hair-washing favorites and leave the rest behind. You know who you are.

HOUSEHOLD CHORES (see CHORES)

HOUSEKEEPERS are there to assist you and help you maintain order and cleanliness. After your cousins come to visit, there's no one you're happier to see than Mildred and her rubber gloves. Housekeepers should bring calm into your life and help eliminate stress when it comes to your daily routines. If you have a housekeeper who does this, you are very fortunate and should make sure you treat him or her with respect and gratitude, especially when it comes to those holiday bonuses. If you aren't so lucky, it is time to give the housekeeper this book and help him or her learn some of the O.C.D. practices, or look for someone new.

Make sure you find your housekeeper from a reputable source or friend. The most important thing in your relationship with your housekeeper is trust. He or she will be in your home, sometimes alone, going through your things. *All* of your things. Discuss with your housekeeper how you want your things organized and how you'd like tasks completed and how often. Walk the housekeeper through each space and tell him or her what you expect to be done and if you have particular ways of doing things. To help your housekeeper speed through the learning curve, label your spaces. Having a cleaning manual or schedule can be very helpful because it leaves no room for confusion. This will make your housekeeper's job much simpler because he or she will always be clear on your expectations. Remember, housekeepers are professionals and probably have some great cleaning and organizing ideas of their own, so be willing to hear them out! They just might know how to save that sweater from last night's penne alla vodka.

Make sure your housekeeper has the supplies he or she likes and is familiar with, unless you have specific preferences, such as "green products." You should have a designated area for your **CLEANING SUPPLIES**, so make sure your housekeeper knows where that area is and how to maintain it. If you find yourself having to repeat things over and over and items still aren't in the right place, it's time to sit down with your housekeeper and explain that there is a disconnect in your communication. Show the housekeeper the space and tell him or her the issues you are having. Like any relationship, good communication is a must. Your housekeeper is probably not a psychic, although it's possible. If it happens again, steal a line from Donald Trump: "You're fired!"

AN O.C.D. SUCCESS STORY

I have worked with and trained many housekeepers to practice the O.C.D. Way. Any space that I organize must be maintained, and everyone who's a part of that maintenance must be trained. I've helped many housekeepers by teaching them how simple communication makes their jobs easier. Many housekeepers are intimidated by their employers, but when I empower the housekeepers to ask questions about process, organization, functionality, placement, and discipline, they end up excelling in their position and even having a better relationship with their boss. It is always nice to return to a client's home and receive a warm hug from the housekeeper!

HUSBANDS have an enormous responsibility to make sure their family is safe, supported, and loved. Help make this an easier task by giving him the backbone of an organized home and the occasional shoulder rub. In any marriage, your partner should be helpful on all levels. You should communicate and ask your husband his **NEEDS** when it comes to everything in a relationship, and that includes organization. Just because you have a certain way of doing something doesn't mean it's easy for your husband to mimic or follow your lead. Design a system that works for him as well. Be open to constructive criticism and trying new things to promote healthy organization and flow in your home that works for both of you. If there is something that you want organized or kept in a specific manner, just ask. If he has a problem maintaining a system, or vice versa, guide him or have him guide you through it. A common example in any home is a lack of organization when it comes to **LAUNDRY**. It is all about communication and discipline. Know the rules behind laundry, where it goes when it is dirty, where it shouldn't go, and when laundry gets done. All laundry should have a home and a logical place to go when not on your body. If you both stick to the rules you make together, clothing will never be lying around your home and insignificant arguments won't disrupt your relationship. If someone is slacking on any responsibility, don't be passive-aggressive. Just sit down and have a conversation that there has been a breakdown in something you are working on together and find the best solution to fix the problem together. Perhaps it's to set reminders in his entry "HUSBANDS" **CALENDAR** that read, "Remember to buy baby wipes." This will promote a healthy way of living as a couple and ensure that organization never breaks down between spouses.

AN O.C.D. SUCCESS STORY

Often there is a thin line between teaching organization and life coaching. Many times when I organize a home, I find that there is a tension between spouses—one tends to be more organized than the other. Organization, just like everything in a relationship, is about compromise and communication. As a couple, you need to design a system that works for both of you. I worked with a couple on the verge of divorce, but after we set up clear systems and processes in the house, life became easier and their relationship became less strained. I'm not saying that disorganization alone was leading them to divorce, but it was a major distraction from their being able to talk about what was really bothering them. They were too busy fighting about the stuff in their home instead of discussing and solving the real problems in their relationship. If you plan together and communicate effectively, organization will complement your relationship instead of creating discord.

I

iCLOUD (see CLOUD)

iCONS (see DESKTOP ICONS)

IN-BOX on your **DESK** should function just like your **E-MAIL IN-BOX**: anything that arrives in it should be looked at and dealt with as immediately as possible. You don't want to be the only one who didn't read the memo and doesn't know it's just a fire drill. Don't let work pile up in your in-box and don't let your in-box become a morgue for work you plan to get to. Never use it just to get rid of something sitting on your desk. It won't make it magically disappear. Go through your in-box frequently and make it a goal to see it empty at least once a week. It's a good feeling. At the end of your day, clear your desk off and place all unfinished work in your in-box. Make it a habit to address your in-box within the first hour of your next workday. An empty in-box gives you an opportunity to work on projects other than those in the piles that others have created for you, such as that idea that's going to revolutionize the company and get you stock options and a plaque.

■ ■ ■
AN O.C.D. SUCCESS STORY

The three-tiered tray that so many people have on their desks is shockingly misused. Some of my biggest success stories come simply from showing people how to properly use it to create a system that is effective for their workday. When I worked with clients at Pfizer Pharmaceuticals, I taught executive assistants how to simplify their workflow by using and labeling their bins. We dramatically improved flow and efficiency. And of course, desks were cleaner. When desks are cleaner across the whole office, the entire space feels calmer and leads to better energy.

INVENTORY organization is all about keeping track of what comes in and goes out of your business so that money is coming in and not going out of your business. If you don't have a professional inventory management system, you should keep a master inventory list that is organized alphabetically by product name for easy reference. Give every product a specific number that will correlate to the product name for easy processing. Once you have this master list, if you update it every time you add or sell inventory, you'll always know exactly what you have and what you have space for. Know your space so you know how much inventory you can store and don't overorder. In your inventory list, be precise on the quantity of the items you have in inventory, as well as how many of those items you have space for. For example, I have 289 cell phone cases, but space for 1,000. Assign a physical location in your store-room or warehouse for each item and label it. Heavy items should be on the bottom and light items on top. Always store your items in their assigned location so you don't end up with missing or lost inventory. Train your employees to follow these rules. Think about rewarding them with a pizza party. Maintain the inventory or assign someone that task, but someone must be accountable. Knowledge is power when it comes to inventory. You never want to run out of an item, so set alerts when inventory for a certain product reaches a certain level. A good rule of thumb is to reorder products when you hit 30 percent of available space. Your list can be kept as a spreadsheet or a document, or even in an inventory management software program. Whatever you use, record the product you are selling, its location in storage, the quantity you are selling, the quantity you have on hand, the price of the unit, the price you paid for the unit, the date sold, and any information you will need about your customers. You should also keep a master customer information document with all of your buyers' and suppliers' names, addresses, up-to-date e-mail addresses, and phone numbers. Cross-reference this list with your **ADDRESS BOOK**. Constantly keep these **LISTS** up to date and make sure you are always using this document when purchases are made.

These inventory organization methods also work in your home, even when you aren't selling anything. If you follow these methods for your home supplies, such as toilet paper rolls and laundry detergent, you'll always know what you have and what you need, and you never have to miss the added freshness of a dryer sheet because you will never run out.

Digital inventory, for example, the ad space you have to sell on your **WEB SITE**, should also have an organizational system. Just because it doesn't take up physical space doesn't mean it's not an asset. Ad space is generally sold in blocks of time, so make sure that on your master document you record this information. You should also keep a **CALENDAR** for easy reference to see when time is sold and when it's available. You may also be selling a product that has an unlimited supply, such as a software download. Inventory management will help you keep track of your sales and what products are performing the best. You'll know that your Dancing Sheep app isn't getting the response you'd hoped, but your Pigeon Simulator is totally taking off. Strategize and make changes accordingly.

Remember: knowing the **QUANTITY** that comes in with your order and the space you have for that item will always aid you in keeping a flawlessly organized inventory system.

■ ■ ■

AN O.C.D. SUCCESS STORY

When I worked with a major manufacturing company, I discovered that money was being wasted because there was so much overordering going on. Because there was no set place for inventory to be stored and no one knew where anything was kept, employees often ordered more inventory when they didn't have to or found that they were out of stock and unable to make a sale. Oftentimes, old inventory would be found later on and was outdated and thus wasted. The Japanese call this wastefulness *muda*. After empowering the staffer in charge of reordering and inventory quantity, I worked with them to reorganize the inventory and taught them when new inventory should be ordered. With a set place for everything, known to all employees, and a person accountable for maintaining the system, that company is now saving money and processing orders much more efficiently.

INVITATIONS are the precursor to any wedding, bar or bat mitzvah, birthday bash, holiday party, harvest jamboree, banquet, soiree, crawfish boil, gala, box social, karaoke slam, shindig, and disco blowout. These days, invitations can be physical or digital. If you are the one sending out the invitations, you'll first need a list of invitees with up-to-date information: home addresses for physical invites and e-mail addresses for digital invites. Keeping your **ADDRESS BOOK** current and accurate will make this process much easier. Alphabetize your list on a spreadsheet and include an RSVP column to mark off people who will or won't attend. This way, you will not only know numbers but also who has yet to respond. If you are giving your **GUESTS** food options, have a column for their preference as well. Basically, whatever information you are requesting from your guests, make sure you have a column for it.

If you send out digital invites, many services keep RSVP information and e-mail you updates as people respond. I still think it's a good idea to keep your own spreadsheet because these services are somewhat limited in the information they keep.

If you are sending out invitations with multiple parts, like people do for weddings, bar and bat mitzvahs, and other large events, make sure you order 10 percent extra of each element needed to cover your invite list. Now grab some friends and make an assembly line, with each person responsible for an element so no one receives an invite with a missing piece. How will you know if they want beef or fish if you didn't include a response card! Another option is to break the list down into letter ranges (A-E, F-K, L-P, Q-U, V-Z) and give each person a section of invites to be responsible for. Make a checklist next to each invitee's name and mark off each element as you put it in the envelope. It may seem tedious, but in the end it's better to have complete invitations rather than worrying about missing pieces.

It's much simpler to organize the invites you receive. As soon as you get one in your **MAIL** or e-mail, check your calendar and see if you are available and then decide if you even want to go. If attending the event requires **TRAVEL** and lodging, look into it to see if you can afford it. If the answer is yes to all of the above, add the event to your calendar immediately, no matter how far in the future it is. If someone will be joining you as your guest, send him or her a calendar invite so they have the information as well. If there is an RSVP card, fill it out and get it in the mail. Your host will love you for it. Now scan the invite, create a folder for the event in PICTURES → SPECIAL EVENTS, and shred the paper. After you attend, you'll stick any photos you took at the event in this folder as well. Book your flights and hotels after you RSVP if prices are good. Otherwise, set a reminder in your **CALENDAR** for two months before the event to look again and book. Don't get yourself in the position of debating flaking on an RSVP because last-minute flight prices are now exorbitant. Your soon-to-be-married college friend needs you to be an usher, so get the trip booked and brush up on your ushering!

O.C.D. EXTREME

Be sure to RSVP to the event and book your travel the moment you receive the invite. Often, I'll book my flight and lodging before even the bride and groom! That leaves me free to look forward to the event rather than worrying about the logistics at the last minute. It also saves me money because prices tend to go up the closer you get to your travel date.

iPHONE/iPAD/iPOD organization is all about maintaining your **APPS, ADDRESS BOOKS, CALENDARS, PICTURES,** and **DIGITAL MUSIC** without dropping your expensive device and cracking the screen. Nowadays, people tend to own multiple devices in addition to their **SMARTPHONE**. A good way to maintain organization across devices is to designate each device for a specific purpose. For example, your iPhone is for business and your iPad is for entertainment. That way, you can keep only the relevant apps and files on that device. However you designate the device, use folders to organize your apps into categories. You don't want them all over your device in no particular order. **iTUNES** is a useful tool for quickly rearranging your apps. The first thing you should do when you get a new device is to set up your preferences. Make sure your devices are backing up regularly, by plugging them into your **COMPUTER** or having updates sent to iCloud. Have on your devices only what you need—you don't need to max out their **HARD DRIVE** space with every picture you've ever taken. Know where each device sends your files when syncing with other devices and your computer. Keep your iOS software up to date. Set a **PASSWORD** to access your device and lock your phone. Our iDevices carry a lot of personal information that we wouldn't want strangers looking at. The choice of **UNDERWEAR** on my **SHOPPING LIST** is *my* business, and mine alone!

■ ■ ■
O.C.D. EXTREME

As soon as a company sets a release date for a new version of a product you own, and you want to upgrade, grab the original box and put your device for sale on eBay right away. You'll get the most money for it to apply to the new version. If it's a phone, and you are keeping O.C.D. Extreme, you should have a backup phone to use until the new phone is released. For other devices, just go without your device for a few weeks/months.

iTUNES can be a very complicated program with a lot of bells and whistles you never need to ring or blow. If you are truly interested in learning all the ins and outs of iTunes, visit Apple's Web site, www.apple.com/itunes. iTunes can automatically organize your **APPS, AUDIOBOOKS** and **AUDIO FILES, CDs, DIGITAL MUSIC,** and **MOVIES** for you. Where you need to focus your organizational attention is in the settings. iTunes has many settings that determine how things are organized and where they are kept. It even lets you choose what information is displayed and how files are sorted. You only want to display the most relevant information for each track. Unless you are a DJ, you don't need to know the beats per minute of your songs. iTunes is also the organizational portal for all of your iDevices. This is where you organize and choose what data makes its way among your **COMPUTER** and your **iPHONE**, **iPAD**, and **iPOD**. Make sure you explore all the settings in iTunes and make them work for you and your devices. You can be much more than a "default settings" user if you so choose.

O.C.D. APPROVED TECHNOLOGY

This is more of an unapproved technology. Don't always download an update just because it's available. Sometimes it's better to keep your existing version and wait for a second update to be released. This goes for iTunes, and technology in general. Let everyone else download the first update and discover flaws and bugs while you keep your smooth functionality. Sometimes when it comes to technology, early adopters are really just beta testers.

J

JEANS can take up a lot of space in a **CLOSET** if you hang each pair individually, so if you have a love affair with denim and want to save some space in your closet, fold your jeans and stack them on top of each other. Put your least frequently worn pairs at the bottom of the stack and your most frequently worn pairs at the top. Keep the pile organized by placing the jeans back on the stack after each use. If you are a jean connoisseur and have a type of jean for every imaginable booty shape and comfort level, stack your jeans by style and color. If you must hang your jeans, consider hanging them full length with hanger clips so you don't crease them or wear that area thin. As with any **CLOTHES**, once you have cycled through your newly organized jean pile, consider donating jeans you never wear to charity or giving them to a friend. Don't wash your jeans each time you wear them unless they are filthy. You probably didn't wear them for that mud-wrestling match, so extend their life by only washing them when necessary. Turn them inside out, wash them on cold with a gentle detergent, and hang dry.

O.C.D. APPROVED TECHNOLOGY

If your favorite and most beloved pair of jeans finally bites the dust due to a rip, not all hope is lost. Look up a denim repair shop in your area or send your jeans to the Denim Doctors in Los Angeles. I've seen them perform some impossible pant miracles.

JEWELRY is a precious possession, often handed down, collected on trips, given as gifts, or featured on hip-hop album covers. Do yourself the favor of organizing and cataloging your valuable and sentimental collection. You'll find yourself accessorizing better and getting to wear more and different jewelry. Start by gathering every piece of jewelry you own, no matter the value. Make two piles: jewelry you wear or want to wear, and jewelry you don't wear. Whatever you are willing to get rid of, do it. Take the jewelry you don't wear but want to keep because of its value or meaning and keep it in a **SAFE** or safe-deposit box. Make sure that you and a trusted loved one have the combination to the safe just in case something ever happens. Now separate the rest into real jewelry and costume jewelry, and then by type: earrings, bracelets, necklaces, **WATCHES**, rings, broaches, and pendants. Now assess the jewelry you have and determine the appropriate amount of organizing space you'll need. There are a variety of jewelry organizers on the market, from boxes to hanging systems, so knowing what you have will help you choose the best system. Whatever you choose, organize your jewelry by type and keep the pieces you wear most frequently at the top. Make sure you leave yourself enough space to add to your collection. Stay disciplined and return jewelry to its designated section after wearing it. Every so often, get your jewelry cleaned and checked so it sparkles just like the day it caught your eye and never loses a stone.

In the same way you would catalog your **ANTIQUES**, you should have a catalog with pictures, invoices, and insurance information for each specific piece of valuable jewelry in a safe place and backed up in case of a fire or emergency. Send this information to your home owner's insurance company. If the jewelry is over their coverage, think about getting a separate policy for specific pieces of jewelry, like those diamond-encrusted grills. You hear me, Lil Jon?

J

163

Purchase a closable mesh or plastic basket to use to clean your own jewelry in your dishwasher. Jeweler in the Dishwasher makes a good one. Only do this if you have your stone settings checked and secured regularly.

JOB SEARCHES come at an already stressful time. Perhaps you have a family to support. Maybe you are underemployed or unhappily employed. Maybe you're just sick of eating off the 99 cent menu. Something has to change. Reduce your anxiety and increase your chances for success by having a strong system in place to manage your submissions and responses. Ninety percent of job submissions and correspondence happens online and through e-mail, so make sure you are ready for this process. Get your résumé up to date and organized and keep it in DOCUMENTS → RESUMES. Search online for résumé templates, but keep it simple and easy to read. Consider contacting a recruiter to help you in your job search and ask him or her what your résumé should look like. If different recruiters have different preferences, or if you are seeking multiple positions, create multiple résumés, but make sure to label them clearly, for example, "Justin Klosky—Personal Assistant—2014," so you don't send the wrong résumé to the wrong person, Keep an editable version of each résumé, as well as a PDF version for sending out. Whenever you update the résumé, save over the old PDF version so it's always up-to-date.

Create a folder or label in your e-mail program called "Job Search." Within this folder, create "Job Search Sent" and "Job Search Received" and then, within those, specific companies and jobs you are interested in once a correspondence has been initiated. Make sure anytime you send or receive an e-mail about your job search, it is filed in the appropriate folder. This type of organization is called go-to organization. Putting things in the first place your mind goes to will help you find and access it much faster later on. Respond within twenty-four hours to any e-mail received because there may be many other people vying for the same job. Don't get passed over because you overslept after watching that *Breaking Bad* marathon all night.

You'll likely be using one or more of the many job search Web sites online. Make sure you have your username and **PASSWORD** for each site recorded in your **ACCOUNTS** document and that you set your preferences on the site to send you e-mail updates regarding your submissions. Once you are placed in a position, make sure you disable these notifications so you aren't bombarded and distracted at your new job. Also, update any profiles that contain your employment information.

Once you reach the point where you are setting interviews, set them as **APPOINTMENTS** in your **CALENDAR** immediately. Prepare by doing as much **RESEARCH** about the company as possible. Don't ask questions about salary until you get an offer or the interviewer brings it up. This is the fastest way to botch an interview: the last thing a potential employer wants to hear is you asking how much they will be paying you. Always follow up an interview with a thank-you e-mail. If you suspect your potential employer is old-fashioned, send a handwritten thank-you note instead. If you aren't sure, just ask what your interviewer's preferred method of communication is. Even if you don't get the job, maintaining good **RELATIONSHIPS** in your business life can lead to opportunities down the road. With any luck, you'll be working soon and looking forward to the weekend.

■ ■ ■
AN O.C.D. SUCCESS STORY

In addition to organization, the O.C.D. Experience has staffed and trained employees for other companies. Using the above methods, we've placed many employees in great positions with great companies. Reaching out to a staffing specialist is a great way to broaden your search and, most of the time, costs you nothing. Companies cover the bill.

JOURNALS are very personal and are meant to record your thoughts and states of mind at a given place and time, like how embarrassed you were when your roommate caught you bawling while watching *Beaches* (Hillary truly was the wind beneath her wings). Journals can be structured in many ways depending on your writing habits and style. The simplest way to structure a journal is to record the date and time you are writing before each entry. You want to be able to look back and remember when you were writing, so it's helpful to give yourself a bit more information. If you are the type of person who writes in their journal in the morning and then in the evening before you go to sleep, find ways to make the titles more creative than just saying "morning" or "evening." Note how the moment looked, how you felt, or where you were, and work this into the title. This will help transport you back to the moment when you revisit your journal. Once you complete a journal, use a label maker or write the date range on the side of your journal. File the journals in a secure place, such as a locked trunk, or stack them on your **BOOKSHELF** if you keep no secrets or you trust your company not to snoop.

Electronic journaling is becoming more popular as electronics have grown more portable. I am a fan of electronic journaling because its space saving, searchable, and secure. A **PASSWORD** is much harder to crack than that joke of a heart-shaped lock on your Strawberry Shortcake diary. If you use your **COMPUTER** to journal, be certain that your journal is constantly being backed up. There is no worse feeling than turning on your computer one day and finding that years' worth of entries have vanished due to a crash and you have no backup.

O.C.D. EXTREME

Scan your journals and save them as a PDF with the date range in the title. It takes a while, but it's worth it to have your journals saved digitally and to be able to keyword search through them. I convinced a client who used journals as part of his business to scan his completed journals. He went from having drawers filled with journals to having a digital system with a lot more free space in his office. It was also much easier for him to look back on specific projects by searching rather than thumbing through dozens of black books.

JUDAICA (Oy! See **RELIGIOUS ITEMS**.)

JUNK DRAWERS are found in practically everyone's home or **OFFICE**. Although I loathe the word *miscellaneous*, I do understand that sometimes little odds and ends need a home and just don't make sense anywhere else. So you can have one junk drawer. *One.* O-N-E. *The* best way to eliminate the junk and consolidate it to one drawer is to:

Dump your **DRAWERS** onto the floor in a place where you have some space to work. Sort through the pile and throw out the true junk. Some common junk drawer tenants are pens, Post-it notes, screwdrivers, **RECEIPTS**, napkins, menus, **KEYS**, **BATTERIES**, tape, screws, pet tags, and so on. Most of these items belong in designated spaces elsewhere in your home. Screws, screwdrivers, and other **TOOLS** (except an all-in-one screwdriver) can be put in your tool chest. Pet tags should be on your pet or thrown away if they are expired or out of date. You don't want a good Samaritan returning your Shih Tzu to the stranger living at your old **APARTMENT**. Batteries should be with your **OFFICE SUPPLIES** or **ELECTRONIC ACCESSORIES**. Most receipts can be scanned or thrown away. What you have left should now fit in a single drawer.

Just because it's called a junk drawer doesn't mean it can be messy and disorganized. Menus should be neatly organized in a folder but should really just be found online. Use a divider for accessories within your junk drawer to create some sort of organization. When things get out of hand, dump and purge, and if you can think of a better place for items in your junk drawer, that's where they should be. This does not include putting them in another junk drawer! Try to break the habit of randomly throwing stuff you don't want to deal with in a junk drawer. The goal is to properly deal with everything in front of you so you never even have a junk drawer.

AN O.C.D. SUCCESS STORY

I grew up with a bunch of junk drawers in my home until the day my parents went on vacation. I decided to give them a welcome-home present: I organized everything to the point that there were no more junk drawers. To this day, they've managed to keep only a single junk drawer. If they can do it, so can the 85 percent of you I know have multiple drawers filled with random stuff!

K

KARAOKE MUSIC offers you the chance to feel like Bon Jovi for three minutes. I bet Jon Bon doesn't waste time looking for his tracks, nor should you. Karaoke music should be organized like your **DIGITAL MUSIC**. Upload all of your karaoke tracks onto your **COMPUTER** and make sure to tag the tracks with the proper information from the CD because most often these won't turn up on auto-tagging databases. Isolate these files in a separate folder in MUSIC → KARAOKE MUSIC so that they neither get mixed in with your normal **MUSIC** nor get synced to your devices.

Certain karaoke machines require physical **CDs** to function and display lyric information. Make a CD book just as you'd see in a karaoke club: organize the book by artist, song title, genre, or even name of the CD. If your machine stores the actual discs, make sure you assign a disc number to each CD and keep your master list accurate and up to date. Otherwise, use your first instinct to set up your categories and start filing your CDs in your book. Keep a master list in the front so that when you open your book, you know exactly what you have and where it is. This will help you and your **GUESTS** find songs, even when filled up with liquid courage. Return each disc to its proper place in the book after use by labeling the slot and disc. Your guests will be able to help you maintain this intuitive system. Update your master list whenever you buy new karaoke music. You can save it as a PDF and send it to your **SMARTPHONE** or tablet to look especially cool at your own karaoke party. Maybe it will help people forget about how your voice cracked on the high note of "All by Myself."

KEY CHAINS should not be used as an opportunity to display every cute charm and gadget that's ever tickled your fancy. Stop being so ticklish and get your key chains under control. Key chains should hold a specific group of **KEYS**. You should have one key chain for your everyday keys, a key chain for a spare set of keys for your home and car, and a key chain for keys you use once a month to once a year, like those for a weekend home, parents' house, or **STORAGE UNIT**. Separate key chains can be used for work and home keys if the amount of keys you have is excessive. Better to break them up than lug around a janitor ring that barely fits in your pocket or **PURSE**. **FILING CABINET** keys and keys for special locks can be kept on one key chain also. You can buy key chains that have a section to write on with a plastic cover so you can label what those keys are for. Whatever key chain you use, make sure that all of your keys are kept in one area of your home so you always know where to find them. This can be in a lockbox, a **SAFE**, or even a secure **DRAWER** that has been neatly organized. You can keep a personalized accessory or thumb drive on your key chain, but don't go overboard. One is enough to make it your own. Drugstores and supermarkets are eager to get their member mini-cards onto your key chain. Scan these instead and keep the bar code as a picture on your phone. It works just as well and saves you space. The moment you no longer need a key, take it off your key chain and dispose of it or give it back to your ex. It always surprises me when people carry around a key they haven't used in years for a house they don't even live at anymore just because they didn't take the time to remove it. Unless you are planning to rob the tenant who moved into your old place, which is not O.C.D. approved, get rid of that key!

AN O.C.D. SUCCESS STORY

A client I worked with used to carry around a massive key chain with every key he might ever need. It took him forever to find the key he actually needed because he had so many to sift through. I broke his single massive key chain down into different context-based key rings for him. Now he doesn't have twenty keys bulging in his pocket and poking his leg everywhere he goes. He just grabs the set of keys he actually needs.

KEYS that are orphaned get no sympathy from me. They must correspond to a lock or go into a trash can. This includes keys from the past or that are not used anymore. If you have a bunch of keys but don't know what they unlock, take the time to go through every lock in your life and test every key. Once you find a match, label it with a number that corresponds to the key's use on a master list or color code the keys using rubber sleeves. Throw away any keys that you can't match up to a lock. Keep a master set of every key in your life. You'll never use any of these keys, but rather use them to make copies if you ever need them. This way, you'll never end up without a key that you need. Also, you should never carry keys with you that you don't use at least once a month. You'll carry way too many and walk around jingling like Santa's sleigh. By using the methods above you should never have trouble knowing which key is for what or find yourself unable to open a lock.

O.C.D. APPROVED TECHNOLOGY

My new favorite solution to ridding yourself of another key is the KEVO lock and app from Kwikset. Keep your phone in your pocket or purse. You can use the app, which will open your lock with Bluetooth technology or a key fob. There is even a feature where you can share your lock with friends or family to make accessibility simple on both ends. No more fumbling for your keys . . . just touch the lock to open for the ultimate in convenience.

■ ■ ■

O.C.D. EXTREME

Arrange the keys on your key chain in the order you use them during the day or for a specific process. I keep my daily keys in this order: car, building front door, mail key, front door bottom lock, front door top lock. I always know that the next door I have to open is the next key on the ring. I don't even have to look. I also have a set of keys for guests kept the same way. It's easy to tell guests how to get into my place. I just tell them what key to start with.

KIDS' BEDROOMS (see CHILDREN'S BEDROOM)

KIDS' PLAYROOM (see CHILD'S PLAYROOM)

KIDS' SCHOOL PAPERS/WORK (see CHILDREN'S SCHOOLWORK)

KITCHENS should inspire you to cook and eat, not run and hide. They need to be clean, warm, and inviting. No one wants to eat or prepare food in a dirty kitchen with cluttered **COUNTER SPACE**, open a **REFRIGERATOR** that smells, or reach to grab a fork, knife, and spoon and find that they aren't clean or organized. All **CABINETS** and **DRAWERS**, or sections in divided drawers, should have specific purposes and be maintained for that purpose. The kitchen cabinet you decide to put your **SPICES** and flavorings in should never have glasses or **DISHES** in it. Discipline yourself to make sure that whatever space you pick for specific items stays that way by returning things to their proper home after each use. Never put anything in the kitchen that isn't related to preparing, cooking, serving, or eating food or cleaning up afterward.

Every kitchen is different, but the best way to organize your space is to think of your kitchen in terms of stations: cleaning and washing, preparing, cooking, baking, serving, and storing. Then you can organize accordingly, using common sense. For example, keep pots, pans, and a utensil holder with your most frequently used cooking utensils near the stove. Dishes and glasses should be near the sink or **DISHWASHER** so you don't have to go very far when unloading. Cutting boards, knives, graters, and slicers should be near your prep space. Create a system like this and you'll never again have to run kitchen relay races to get what you need. You can flow easily through the entire process of making and serving a **MEAL**.

Everything in your kitchen, from silverware to cereal bowls, should be a complete set. This isn't a frat house—mismatched glasses, plates, and spoons have no place in an O.C.D. kitchen. Donate incomplete sets and buy a new set. Don't keep old sets as backup. You can have two sets of silverware and dishware: formal and everyday. If your formal set of silverware is real silver, make sure to polish it before using it. Designate a drawer for your silverware and organize it by type of utensil. Designate cabinets for your dishes and glasses and organize them by type as well. Keep sets together and label where they should go. The more formal and less frequently used sets should be kept higher up since you'll be reaching for your everyday set more often. Knives should be taken out of the bulky knife block and organized in a drawer or on the wall with a magnetic holder out of the reach of children. Throw that knife block away or use it as **FIREWOOD**. It takes up way too much space on your kitchen counter and encourages you to have more knives than you need. A note on knives: you really don't need knives of every shape and size. Save your money. A good small paring knife and a chef's knife will accomplish pretty much any kitchen task. If someone else cooks with you at the same time, have two chef's knives. Also keep a nice set of steak knives—they'll never go unnoticed.

If you keep cookbooks in your kitchen, designate a set amount of space for the ones you use most frequently. The rest should be on your **BOOK-SHELVES**. Even better, keep **RECIPES** on your **iPAD** or digital device and put it on a tablet stand or kitchen mount while you cook.

Lids for **POTS AND PANS** can be tricky—to keep them with their parent or not? That is the question. The pot/lid combination is much harder to store efficiently, so this is the one time I condone breaking up the set. Keep the lids together in a designated drawer or cabinet with lid dividers and stack the pots and pans.

Oversized items like cookie sheets, broiling pans, and giant pots don't always have an obvious home. If you are lucky, you have a narrow, vertical divided storage cabinet, a drawer under your oven, or extra space in your pantry for these items. If you aren't so lucky, you'll have to get creative. Store pans in the oven, but remember to remove them before you preheat and only do this if absolutely necessary because whatever you put in you'll have to take out every time you cook. Those oversized pots that just don't fit anywhere in your kitchen might have to be stored in the **GARAGE** or other storage space. To keep them as sanitary as possible, keep them in a garbage bag.

If you lack drawer or cabinet space, consider hanging things such as dish towels, aprons, potholders, even pots and pans or anything else you use on a consistent basis that needs a home. Try to hang these items near their appropriate station. Hanging items will also encourage you to keep them clean since they will be on display.

As with any room in your home or **OFFICE**, know your space! Don't buy that bulk aluminum foil from the warehouse store if it can't fit in the drawer you've designated for your foils, wraps, and resealable bags. Shove it in all you want, it's not going to fit and you'll have to practice making foil swans for your leftovers to get rid of it all. Maintain your kitchen every six months by going through everything and only keeping pots, pans, and equipment you use regularly. Replace **CONTAINERS** and Tupperware that are old, damaged, or missing lids. Constantly check food and **CANNED GOODS** for expiration dates. Keep your refrigerator, **FREEZER**, and **FOOD PANTRY** cleaned and maintained. Clean your kitchen meticulously once a week and wipe down the surfaces such as the stove top, top of fridge, kitchen counters, and sink after each use. Keep counter space clear and ready to prepare the next meal.

If you have the luxury of designing and building your own kitchen, make sure you really think about how it is you cook and how your family uses the space. Based on what you own, design smart storage solutions to make working in your kitchen a breeze. Think through where outlets will be, how they'll be hidden, and where you can store bulkier items. Make sure you measure your equipment before you hire a designer to create something for you. You don't want to spend all that money on a new kitchen only to discover your mixer doesn't fit under your cabinet!

Remember: the O.C.D. Experience is about organizing and creating the discipline behind maintaining it. Discipline yourself to maintain a clean and inviting kitchen and it will be a wonderful place for you and your family to gather and enjoy each other's company and meat loaf.

■ ■ ■
AN O.C.D. SUMMARY

Organize: Pull everything out of your kitchen: empty every drawer, cabinet, and shelf. Trash and replace any incomplete sets, anything that is broken, or anything that has missing parts. Take the opportunity to clean all cabinets and storage spaces.

Create: Divide your kitchen into stations: cleaning and washing, preparing, cooking, baking, serving, and storing. Designate and label your storage spaces based on their proximity to your stations. Organize your belongings into their new homes.

Discipline: Always return everything to its proper place. Keep your kitchen clean and don't let items that don't belong find their way into your storage spaces. Make sure everyone who uses the kitchen knows where everything goes. Go through your kitchen twice a year and get rid of anything you aren't using.

L

173

L

LAUNDRY, although responsible for 87 percent of unsolved missing sock cases, is easy to organize. It's as simple as having three separate and properly labeled baskets or bags in every bedroom closet or discrete location for colors, whites, and **DRY CLEANING**. If space is tight, you can have a single basket or bag, but make sure to separate your **CLOTHES** before doing the wash. I really recommend multiple baskets because sorting through a pile of dirty clothes is exactly that: dirty. Ideally, you should have baskets for lights, darks, and, if you have space, delicates. Once you get your laundry into the **LAUNDRY ROOM**, separate your delicates (if you haven't already) so you don't ruin them in a normal wash. If you have to travel to do your laundry, either down the hall in an apartment building or to a Laundromat, think light: buy small bottles of detergent. Take only the dryer sheets you'll need.

Consider buying a laundry backpack to free up your hands. Stop your laundry from piling up by setting a date for yourself to do your laundry. Just like any **CHORE**, whatever is happening in your life, do your laundry on this day. If you have a lot of clothes that require dry cleaning, perhaps because of your profession or taste, take them in the same day you do your laundry every week. If you only need dry cleaning once in a while, take it in when the bag gets filled or when you're en route to another errand, like a trip to the grocery store. Whatever your dry-cleaning needs, always take your dry cleaning off the cheap wire hangers and hang your dry cleaning back up immediately on your uniform **HANGERS** after picking it up. Tackling your dirty laundry will not only keep you feeling clean but will allow you to wear that shirt again that always gets you phone numbers.

LAUNDRY ROOMS need to be one of the cleanest places in the home since their main purpose is for getting things clean. Nothing deflates your sense of laundry accomplishment like realizing you've folded your clean white shirts on a dirty, dusty surface. Stay inflated by making sure the laundry room is only for doing laundry, ironing, and storing **CLEANING SUPPLIES** and a small set of **TOOLS** if you have the space. Don't use it as a general storage space. Get everything out that doesn't belong there. Designate a space for detergent, dryer sheets, fabric softener, bleach, stain remover, and any other laundry accessories, organized in the order you use it and ideally above the appropriate machine. If you don't have one already, consider installing a hanging dry line or rack. If you can, keep an ironing board in a **CLOSET** or on the back of the door. The iron should be emptied of water after each use and kept in a designated space in the **CABINET** with the cord wrapped around it. Keep a gallon of distilled water in your laundry room to fill your iron with.

This will prevent your iron from getting clogged up from the sediment in tap water. If you have enough space, keep an area clear for folding. Otherwise, fold your **CLOTHES** on a clean bed.

Make sure you are prepared by having your **LAUNDRY** sorted prior to doing your wash. The more prepared you are at your laundry machine, the less clothing you will ruin and the less time it will take you to complete the laundry process. Clean your machines every so often by taking a cloth dampened in hot water and wiping down the inside and outside of the machine. You'd be surprised how much detergent can clump in certain areas of the washer or how much dust accumulates on the top of a stacking unit. Your dryer's lint bin should be emptied out after every use as well. Make sure that your laundry area never has clothes piled on or around the machines. Get it folded and back into your closets and **DRESSERS**. Check between or behind your machines for those lost **SOCKS** so you don't have to downgrade its partner to a dust rag.

■ ■ ■
O.C.D. EXTREME
Once a year, I unscrew and remove the entire lint bin housing from the dryer and vacuum it thoroughly. Not all of the lint comes out of the dryer when you pull out the lint screen!

LEGAL DOCUMENTS (see DOCUMENTS)

LEGOS are one of the most painful things in the world to step on. Don't teach your child words they shouldn't know yet. Remember, "everything is awesome" in Lego world! Keep everything awesome by organizing Legos in a plastic **BIN** with a locking top. Label the bin "Legos" so no other **CHIL-DREN'S TOYS** are mixed in. Make sure the bin is large enough for the amount of Legos you have. Certain Lego sets have particular pieces that are unique for that set. If you buy these special sets, make sure to designate a labeled bin just for that set so no pieces are lost or confused. Keep the instructions that came with the set in the bin. Just make sure to explain to your child that the sets are different and need to be maintained as such. Teach them to respect their toys by making cleanup part of playtime. If your child is too young to understand, discipline yourself to only give your child one set at a time, make sure that the pieces don't get mixed up, and put away the Legos after each use. Start looking into graduate architectural programs for your structural genius of a toddler.

■■■■
O.C.D. EXTREME

As a child, I organized my Legos by shape, size, and color so I could quickly find the piece I needed to complete my masterpiece.

LESSON PLANS are important, especially if a teacher is going to be absent. While we all loved walking into our **CLASSROOM** as children to see a substitute teacher holding a movie, the point of school is to learn, and a lesson plan will ensure the learning continues. Think about the big picture for the entire year, what knowledge you hope to impart to your students, and any requirements that your principal, dean, or district has. Then break it down into weeks. Find time in there for fun days, games, and surprises: your students will appreciate it and it will recharge their minds to be able to absorb more information. Plans can be written on **COMPUTER** or in a lesson plan book. Organize each day according to time and subject. Begin each lesson with a focus skill—declare what specific skill it is you'll be teaching. The rest of the lesson should back this up. Next, note the chapter, lesson, and page numbers of the materials you'll be using for that lesson. Plans should include any follow-up work or review plans, which may be in the form of homework, guided reading, or independent work. Your weekly plan should be written so that anyone can read and understand it. You may get sick or have an emergency and you want a substitute to be able to continue teaching according to your lesson plan, not trying to decipher the hieroglyphics of your bad handwriting or shorthand.

■■■■
O.C.D. APPROVED TECHNOLOGY

Embrace the digital world and get your lesson plan online! You can include PDFs or links to all supplemental materials for each lesson. Use the cloud to create directories for all of the materials you need for each lesson. You can even accept homework digitally! Less paper is always better. Programs like Evernote, Dropbox, and Google Docs will help you accomplish this task, and instead of taking the time to answer hundreds of questions about your curriculum, you can simply direct curious parents and peers to your online lesson plan.

■ ■ ■ ■

LIBRARY is all about the **BOOKS** and **BOOKSHELVES**, but the room should be inviting and comfortable and should encourage you to pick up a book and journey into the world of Middle Earth. Have a couple of comfortable chairs, a side table or **COFFEE TABLE** for a drink and the book you are reading, a music player if you like to listen to **MUSIC** while you read, and, most important, good lighting. You don't want to strain your eyes reading that trashy romance novel. Eyestrain is not sexy. If you have tall shelves, keep a small step stool so you can reach those high-up books. Don't let books pile up—get them back on the shelf so they don't take over your library. If it's a separate room, consider making your home library an Internet-free zone. You can still read downloaded books on your tablet, but you won't be distracted by the Internet.

LIGHTBULBS represent a brilliant idea, but they are a dangerous combination for organization; they're bulky, they're fragile, they come in a plethora of shapes, sizes, and wattages, and they need to be replaced often. How many times have you had a bulb go out and discovered you have every kind of bulb except the one you need? Or you mix and match bulbs of different shapes or wattages in a single fixture? Eyesore! Get a handle on your lightbulbs.

The easiest way to do this is to do an **INVENTORY** of each light fixture in your life. This includes the interior of your home, exterior of your home, **GARDEN, GARAGE**, and even your **AUTOMOBILE**. Walk around with your **SMARTPHONE** and jot down the name of the light fixture and the number of bulbs, the wattage, style, and base type of the bulb. For example:

Front Entry Chandelier
    5 bulbs
    40-watt Frosted Candelabra Base

Back Hallway Sconce
  2 bulbs
  60-watt Clear Medium Base

You can find this information on the lightbulb itself. If it isn't on the bulb, or has burned off, take the bulb with you to the hardware store so you can match it or ask for help. Once you have all of the information, create a master list that you can store, or even laminate, in the area where you keep your lightbulbs. This is a good opportunity to see if you can switch bulbs in a certain fixture to match another fixture and buy fewer types of lightbulbs.

As for how many bulbs you keep, this really depends on your space. Chances are you won't have enough space to keep a replacement bulb for every bulb in your house. Try to have at least two bulbs of every type you use in your home. Replace a bulb as soon as it's burned out, and then replace the replacement bulb as soon as you can. As for bulb storage, you can take the bulbs out of their bulky packaging and keep them in a clear shoe **BIN** labeled by type. If the bulb is too big, keep it in the original packaging. Wherever you store your bulbs, keep them all together, organized and labeled by type. You'll never find yourself in the dark, wondering what you just stubbed your pinky toe on.

■ ■ ■

O.C.D. APPROVED TECHNOLOGY

Lightbulb technology is evolving. You can now buy eco-and-electric-bill-friendly LED lightbulbs for almost all fixture types. They are more expensive than traditional bulbs, but they last much, much longer and consume much less energy. Some, like the Philips Hue, even let you change the color of the bulb wirelessly! The lighting company RAB also makes a variety of sleek, intelligent LED fixtures. Let there be light!

LINEN CLOSETS are the first stop to having crisp, clean, comfortable beds and fresh towels in your home. If you keep an organized linen closet, you'll always be able to provide these luxuries for yourself, your family, and your **GUESTS**. Give your loved ones the simple joy of climbing into fresh bedding instead of wondering if Goldilocks has been sleeping in their bed.

Empty out your linen closet. Find a better home for anything that doesn't belong on a bed or in a **BATHROOM**. If you have the space, you can keep hygiene products, large hair care accessories, toilet paper and paper towels, an iron, a vacuum, and inflatable mattress in your linen closet, but only if you don't have a better place elsewhere. Now create two piles: relatively new items in one pile and older linens in another pile. Donate anything that isn't a complete set or that has holes or stains.

You should have two complete sets of sheets for each bed in your home. If you have children, you can have three sets for their beds because accidents happen. Have enough matching towels and hand towels for each bathroom. Keep two towels in addition to however many you need in the actual bathroom. Have enough beach towels for each person in your home, plus up to four extra, depending on how many guests you tend to host and how much space you have. Never use your bath towels at the beach. Keep two extra pillows and one extra comforter—preferably in a space-saving vacuum-sealed bag on the top shelf in your linen closet—for guests and for your inflatable mattress.

After you've purchased the complete sets of **LINENS** that you need, get rid of the old ones. This is also a good time to consider starting completely fresh with brand-new linens for every room and bathroom. Designate **SHELVES** for the linens for each room, bathroom, and function. Label these spaces so there is no confusion among family members or your **HOUSE-KEEPER**, if you have one. If you don't have the space, stack all your linens but keep those for certain rooms together in the stack, with smaller sets on top. Another option is to keep extra guest linens in your guest room. Don't overstuff everything into your linen closet. Extra wiggle room is the key to maintaining an organized linen closet because otherwise, anytime you pull something out, everything else comes out with it. This is not a place you want a five-for-one deal.

Every spring, or whenever you notice that your linen closet is looking disheveled, refold and reorganize everything. Fold, organize, repeat!

■ ■ ■

O.C.D. EXTREME

Keep a fabric softener sheet between your linen sets and a scented candle of your choice in your linen closet. My sheets and towels always smell fresh with a hint of berry! Just make sure you don't light the candle in your closet, unless you want to start fresh with a whole new set of linens, and potentially repair any fire damage to your home.

LINENS should always be clean and fresh so that you always feel clean and fresh. Who wants to dry off with a musty towel after a nice hot shower? If you raised your hand, please lower it. Sheets should be changed and washed at least once a week and after any particularly messy romantic night. Towels should be washed at least once a week or anytime you feel they are getting dirty or smelly. Keeping to this cleaning schedule will encourage you to rotate your linens with your extra sets, prolonging their life and providing a nice change of style.

When folding extra sets of sheets, keep sets together. Don't split sets among shelves. If you have the space, fold each item in a set and place them next to each other on the shelf so you can grab an individual item without disrupting the rest. If you don't have the space, stack the items in a set from largest to smallest: duvet, flat sheet, fitted sheet, and then pillowcases. Fold towels to fit the depth of your shelves and so they don't hang off the edge.

When your sheets and towels get old, replace them with something new! Resist the urge to keep old sets around as an extra extra set. Yes, I know it's tough to part with your Transformers twin set from college, but it's time. That's how you end up with an overstuffed **LINEN CLOSET**. Instead of throwing away old towels, consider cutting them up and using them as *shmatas* for household cleaning or car cleaning. When buying new towels, don't buy every possible size of a set—you really only need your bath towel, a smaller size to use as a hand towel, and a washcloth. Spare yourself the decision of whether you should dry your face with a 16" by 30" towel or 11" by 18" towel. They'll both get the job done.

LINGERIE should make an impression, not just when you wear that frilly little getup, but also in the way you organize it. Like any other **CLOTHES**, go through your collection and get rid of anything that you no longer wear; that is damaged, stretched, or worn out; or that was from a previous relationship. There's nothing worse than wearing an outfit that reminds you of how badly an ex treated you. Once you've sorted your collection, designate a space for your lingerie. If you have the room, keep it separate from your everyday **BRAS** and **UNDERWEAR**. Instead of keeping tops with tops and bottoms with bottoms, keep matching sets together. When you go to pick out your lingerie, it's much nicer to see it displayed like you would at Victoria's Secret instead of sifting through a jumbled pile. Organize it by style and color, and, most important, find occasions to wear it and mix it up! If it's organized and looks great in a **DRAWER**, you'll equate that with it looking sexy on your body and get inspired to wear it. Everybody wins!

LINKS (see BOOKMARKS)

LISTS, lists, lists . . . They can be a meaningless organizational disaster or an efficient way to optimize your time, energy, and **RESPONSIBILITIES**. If you have to make a list of all your lists, your lists probably belong to the former category. If you are the kind of person who uses a list to complete tasks and maintain an organized lifestyle, make sure that your list is simple, easy to maintain, and specific. Create separate lists for different areas of your life instead of one giant miscellaneous list. For example, keep a list labeled "Home Life," a list labeled "Work Life," and a list for anything you can get done or purchase online labeled "Online To-Do" or "Purchases."

I strongly suggest keeping your lists digitally on your phone. They will be able to sync to your **COMPUTER** and you won't have to carry around paper and pens. Digital lists are also easier to edit. There are many great **APPS** for list making that allow you to check off completed tasks, archive your lists, set alarms, and even let you create geo-reminders for items on your list that notify you when you are in that location. Review your list daily so you always know what's on it. Complete the most important tasks first. As soon as a task is complete, mark it as complete, which will archive it.

If you keep your lists on paper, which is really only okay when they remain at your **DESK**, the most effective way to create and maintain them is in a notebook. I can't stress how ineffective it is to write lists and reminders on **ENVELOPES, MAGAZINES**, scrap paper, or, worse, Post-its, all over your home. Keep it in your notebook and WACO: Write, Assess, Cross Off! Don't be a wacko, trust in WACO. Make sure that your notebook isn't massive so you can bring it with you if you need to **TRAVEL** for work. Have two separate pens: a color of your choice for writing down tasks and a red one for crossing out completed tasks as soon as they are done. Keep the colors consistent because consistency allows you to function more efficiently. For each new week, write the date and then your tasks below the new date. If you have uncompleted tasks from the previous week, move all of the uncompleted tasks to the new list. But I simply cannot recommend carrying around a notebook or paper and pen when you are out and about. Start utilizing

L

technology so you aren't sifting through your **PURSE** in the middle of a supermarket to jot down a task you just remembered. And men, where are you even going to keep your notepad? You'll have to sag your pants!

Stay on top of your list and complete your tasks. Watching your list get smaller and smaller is always a satisfying experience, so savor the moment when you get to cross something off.

■ ■ ■

AN O.C.D. SUCCESS STORY

It amazes me how many people in this digital age keep their lists spread all over their home or office on scraps of paper, napkins, envelopes, whatever! One of my old bosses used to do this. How on earth is this effective? I never judge, but it's my job to point out the truth of ineffectiveness. Is it better to run around your home searching for a list you kept on that old envelope that may have mistakenly been thrown away, or to keep the list with you at all times organized and synchronized on your phone? It might take some time to break the habit of randomly jotting down your list items on scrap, but taking the extra time to create a new positive habit will save you hours later on. I helped my boss use his smartphone for lists and he stopped misplacing them and always had them with him when he needed to reference them or add to the list.

LIVING ROOM, not to be confused with **FAMILY ROOM** if you have both, often becomes that extra room that sure looks nice but no one actually goes in. Most of us don't have the square footage in our homes to have a just-for-looks room, but we end up with one anyway because the living room is generally an undefined space in the context of the rest of the house. It's just another seating area, of which you already have plenty, and less comfortable and interactive than your family room, which features a television. Reclaim your living room by giving it a purpose. It can be where you and your **GUESTS** retire after a dinner party, a game room, a reading room, a room to play instruments, or even just an excuse to sit around a **FIREPLACE**. If you define the room and organize it as such, you'll actually wind up using it on occasion. Keep your living room actually lived in by making it a warm, inviting, and defined space.

AN O.C.D. SUCCESS STORY

Many clients I work with have large homes with both a TV-centric family room and a living room. One client's living room, although clean and nicely set up, was more like a museum than a functional space, even though the client frequently hosted parties. By simply reorganizing some furniture to create more of a social space, and storing board games nearby, the living room was redefined and became a comfortable and inviting space. Many of her parties now end with drinks, games, and good conversation in her living room.

LOCKERS, like a clown car, are small spaces that need to hold a lot. Lockers are an organizational challenge and the perfect space to implement the O.C.D. mantra of "Less is more." Say it with me: "Less is more." Lockers need to be a place for quick and easy access. The more organized and less cluttered your locker, the faster you can access your things and move on to your next task. Get creative: hang hooks, buy shelving systems to divide the space and then designate those spaces, purchase small magnetic **BINS** for accessories, or stick a mirror on the door for quick touch-ups. There is an entire industry devoted to locker organization products, but whatever you buy, make sure it's increasing your efficiency and not a novelty just taking up valuable space.

School lockers are usually small and have very little space for unnecessary things. To maximize the functionality of your school locker or your child's school locker, make sure you prioritize what's most important: books and schoolwork, not personal expression. Although there is room for this, it shouldn't be at the expense of school necessities. Organize the books and **BINDERS** upright in your locker in the order you have to grab them for class. Keep them that way. Think about the best times to visit your locker based on where your classes are. Visit your locker as much as possible to minimize the number of books and binders you have to keep in your **BACKPACK**. If you have a locker that isn't in a spot convenient for your class schedule, ask whoever is in charge of assigning lockers if they can switch it for you or find someone who may want to switch with you for the same reason.

It is not necessary to come and go from school every day with every one of your books. Keep in your locker the books you won't be using at the end of each school day for homework or study. This will make your backpack lighter and your vertebrae happier!

Gym lockers are most often just day lockers where you bring your own lock. These lockers should house anything you'll need during and after your gym time, but they should be locked securely because you never know who'll come around while you're rocking out on the elliptical. You need to focus while you exercise, and it will be impossible to do so if you are worried about who could be going through your belongings. If you have a permanently assigned gym locker, have the necessities you need in your locker at all times, which will make for a lighter **GYM BAG**. There is no sense carrying things back and forth between the gym and your home, except what needs to be cleaned. If you have a permanent locker, don't leave dirty gym clothes sitting in there because it will smell up your locker, contaminating your clean clothes. Always keep a clean change of clothes in your locker.

If you have lockers at your place of work, keep a bag with some cash for an emergency or the vending machine and a change of clothes, especially if you have to wear a uniform, but make sure you have a lock on it and don't mention your hidden cash.

Whatever locker you use, try not to keep precious valuables in it. Your locker is not Fort Knox, so keep valuables on your person. Keep your locker organized and clean. Wipe it down and clean it out when it starts to get dirty. Keep your locker combinations in your password-protected **ACCOUNTS** file on your phone so you never find yourself locked out with your homework on the wrong side of the door. Always replace the lock or reset the combination if you can so you are the only one who knows the combination.

■ ■ ■
AN O.C.D. SUMMARY

Organize: Pull everything out of your locker. Get rid of any trash, and sell or take home any books and binders from classes you've already completed. If you are starting with a new locker, assess what you have in terms of books and binders so you'll know what sort of system you'll need to buy or set up.

Create: Purchase the appropriate locker accessories that will best help you organize and maximize your small space. Designate shelves and baskets for specific purposes and organize your locker based on your daily schedule.

> **Discipline:** Always return things to their designated space. Only take what you need from your locker between each visit or for that night's homework. Keep your locker clean. Personal elements add a nice touch to make your locker feel like your own, but don't add them at the expense of functional space. Locker chandeliers are cool but wildly inefficient when it comes to space.

■ ■ ■ ■

LUGGAGE should generally be stored in an infrequently used room or **CLOSET**, or in a finished **BASEMENT**, and never carried emotionally. Store smaller luggage within larger pieces to save space, like a set of Russian nesting dolls. If you **TRAVEL** often, have one piece of luggage in an easy-to-access area of your home so you can grab it more quickly. A small duffel bag or carry-on bag in a coat closet or storage closet will do the trick. Make sure that your luggage is emptied out after each use so you are never searching for any of your belongings. Consider keeping a phone charger in your carry-on bag so you never leave home without it. You can even keep a separate travel **TOILETRY BAG** in your luggage so you don't have to think about packing your toothbrush, toothpaste, floss, deodorant, hairbrush, travel shampoo and conditioner, soap, razor, nail clippers, cotton swabs, and any other necessities when traveling. This will also expedite your **PACKING** process. Like most possessions, there comes a time when you need to replace your luggage. When you buy new pieces, look for luggage that is lightweight and easy to travel with and has organizational compartments. Before you purchase it, lift it up and wheel it around the store a few times while imagining that you just landed in Tahiti. Is it comfortable? Is it too early for a mai tai? As soon as you buy something new, get rid of your old luggage.

L

185

■ ■ ■ ■
O.C.D. APPROVED TECHNOLOGY
I love the bags made by High Sierra. They offer great organizational compartments and ways to divide the main section of your luggage. They are attractive, affordable, lightweight, and durable, with TSA-approved overhead, expandable, and rolling options.

M

MAGAZINE ARTICLES (see ARTICLES)

MAGAZINE SUBSCRIPTIONS can get out of hand if you aren't careful about how many you subscribe to. Just say no to that student selling door-to-door: this is an O.C.D. house and they'll have to find someone else to help them earn that top prize. If you are the type of person who loves to read **MAGAZINES** and has a large collection, or especially if you own a business with magazines in your waiting room, make a list of all the magazines you subscribe to. Create a document titled "Magazine Subscriptions" and keep it in DOCUMENTS → MEMBERSHIPS or FINANCIAL, whichever makes more sense for you. This list should include date range of subscription, cost of subscription, **MEMBERSHIP** number, and the customer service number for the magazine in case you move or want to cancel. Do this for both physical and digital magazines. Most companies send out renewal notices as early as four months into a subscription, which confuses some readers and encourages them to send more money when money isn't due. Don't let the magazines tell you when to pay! This list will help you control and maintain your subscriptions and also help you decide if you really need all those magazines coming into your mailbox and life. Update the list as necessary and take control of your periodicals, period. Or even better, exclamation point!

MAGAZINES should be read and tossed, or kept only until the new issue arrives. That's your cue to toss the old one out. It's not necessary to keep piles of magazines like you run a dentist's office . . . unless you actually run a dentist's office, in which case, I'm due for a cleaning. Otherwise, if you want to display some magazines for guests or casual reading, keep them in frequented areas of your home and only offer two or three of the latest issues of your choice. If you like to read on the toilet, you can have a couple of magazines in there as well, but make sure they don't sit there too long because anything near the toilet is, well, near the toilet. Moisture will also ripple the magazines over time and make the pages stick. Gross. If you collect a particular magazine for a very special reason, like *National Geographic*, keep them with the rest of your **BOOKS** in your home **LIBRARY** organized by publication date. If collecting magazines is required as **RESEARCH** for your business, like fashion, art, or exotic tattoo magazines, keep them in magazine bins organized by month. Replace them each year as the new magazines come out. If you subscribe to digital magazines on your e-device, create a folder or use Newsstand on the **iPHONE** so that all of your magazines are together.

MAIL should be checked and opened every day. Don't be rude to your mail: it traveled a long way to get to you, so the least you can do is open it. On the way from the mailbox to your home, you should be pulling out junk mail that should go right into the **RECYCLING**. If you want to stop seeing junk mail or care about the environment, consider contacting these junk distributers and having your address removed from their lists. Address the rest of your mail as soon as you can. Designate a space where you always deal with your mail, like your **DESK**, and sort it into **BILLS**, **BROCHURES** and **CATALOGS**, checks, correspondence, cards and **INVITATIONS**, **COUPONS**, **MAGAZINES**, packages, statements, and **RECEIPTS**. Depending on what it is, deal with the mail appropriately: scan, respond, shred, read, pay, file, or deliver to the intended recipient, but don't just let it sit. We all know how to deal with our mail; it just feels overwhelming sometimes. Stop allowing your mail to overwhelm you. Mail for children can be placed in their room or left in a central area of the home. Having individual mailboxes within a home can be a fun way to designate responsibility and ensure no mail is ever lost. If you go this route, make sure the mailboxes are in a central area and don't take up too much space. No matter what system you use for reliable mail sorting, deal with it, toss it, or shred it if it's at all sensitive, but never let it pile up.

For outgoing mail, designate an area in your home near the front door or on your desk for people to drop their outgoing mail. Whenever someone leaves the house, get in the habit of taking out the mail. Make sure you keep a ready supply of stamps and **ENVELOPES** so you never find yourself needing to mail something without the proper supplies. If you generate a lot of outgoing mail, consider getting a postage meter and having envelopes preprinted with your return address or a stamp. If you use shipping services for your outgoing mail, keep your account numbers in your **ACCOUNTS** document for easy reference. Arrange for a pickup at your home or **OFFICE** to save time. If you find yourself writing a lot of checks and mailing them to pay bills, stop wasting your time and money on stamps and envelopes and start paying your bills online. In general, do everything you can online and through e-mail. Outgoing mail is becoming less and less necessary, so let's send it out with dignity by at least keeping it organized.

MAKEUP helps you look and feel your best. You should be able to find that exact lipstick you want without settling for a second choice and ending up with the *sad* kind of pouty lips. Tomorrow, the moment you wake up, before you put on your makeup, don't just say a little prayer. Instead, take out all of your makeup and accessories. Now divide it by type: lipstick, eyeliners, blush, foundations . . . you know what we're talking about. While you are sorting, get rid of anything cracked, old, dry, or that you've outgrown. Now pull out the makeup and accessories that you are going to use daily and can't live without. Purchase or designate a portable makeup case or bag to be used for your daily makeup. Keep it accessible in your **BATHROOM**. This makes getting ready in a hurry less stressful and getting ready on the go very simple because you can just grab the bag without thinking. Keep it simple and only include the things you need to look presentable in a moment's notice: powder, mascara, lip gloss, eye shadow, eyeliner, blush, brushes, and anything else that is part of your daily beauty routine. Always return your daily makeup to this container. If you bring it out with you, make sure you return it to its home when you get back.

As for all that other makeup, keep an amount within reason, organized by type, in a middle **DRAWER** or **BIN** under the sink. This is your special-occasion makeup or backup makeup. By separating your makeup into these two categories, getting ready in the morning will be faster, and getting ready for the weekend or parties will be more exciting. You'll be able to find the things you want and put them away more easily, and you'll get a boost each time you get to reach for your special-occasion makeup. Time to bust out the Really Red lipstick!

Every month, clean the containers or drawers that house your makeup because they tend to get filthy. Maintain the discipline to never let your makeup collection spread across the entire bathroom again. You and your bathroom can finally make up over your makeup.

■ ■ ■

AN O.C.D. SUCCESS STORY

Having too much makeup can actually mean having less. One of my clients, who lives her life in the spotlight, regularly bought or was given makeup she never used. Her makeup collection grew so large, it was overwhelming and she actually used very little of it. When you have that much makeup, you can't possibly test it all or remember that perfect color! We sorted through her collection, gave away a ton of unused makeup, and she still has quite the impressive collection. Now, unencumbered by an overwhelming amount of options, she actually gets to wear her products and change up her look—a necessity when you are constantly scrutinized for your appearance.

MARIJUANA organization is becoming necessary as more states legalize medicinal marijuana. To be clear, the O.C.D. Experience condones the possession and organization of only medicinal marijuana, unless you are in a state that has legalized recreational use, in which case, enjoy responsibly. Dispensaries sell an impressive variety of marijuana, marijuana edibles, drinks, tinctures, and pills to alleviate whatever it is that ails you. That's between you and your doctor. Keep your purchases organized so you can always grab the medicine you need, especially when you are already medicated. Marijuana in plant form tends to fall between two categories: indica, which has more body and relaxation effects, and sativa, which is more cognitive, uplifting, and energetic. A lot of strains are hybrids that have different balances of these attributes. Keep your medicine organized according to this scale, with pure indicas on one side and pure sativas on the other. Keep your medicine in sealed containers, preferably glass, in a discreet, lockable, cool, dry place to help it last longer. If you have children, use childproof containers. Use dry erase labels on the containers to write down the date of purchase, strain name, type of strain, and notes on effects. Any accessories you need, such as pipes, papers, grinders, or vaporizers, should be kept in the same place or nearby.

Every couple of months, clean any glass accessories in the **DISHWASHER** to keep them clear and tasting fresh. Dispose of any marijuana that is old and crunchy. If you purchase edibles, purchase them only when you need them instead of storing them in your **REFRIGERATOR**; this way, no one might mistakenly eat them, especially your kids. When you go to a new dispensary, don't forget to bring your original certificate; otherwise, they will not admit you. Always keep a copy of your doctor's recommendation in your car with your insurance just in case you are pulled over on your way back from a dispensary.

O.C.D. APPROVED TECHNOLOGY

If you frequently use medicinal marijuana, consider purchasing a vaporizer, especially if your voice or lungs are important to your career or hobby. A vaporizer will provide a healthier way to ingest your medicine that will be less irritating to your lungs, throat, and vocal cords. Vapor is safer, more pure, less damaging, and less painful to inhale than smoke. When you burn the entire plant, in addition to inhaling the active ingredient, you end up inhaling irritants you don't need. When you vaporize, only the THC and other cannabinoids make their way from the plant into your lungs. For a well-designed and compact solution, check out the G-Pen vaporizer from Grenco Science.

MEALS tend to be a dull or even unappetizing experience if you don't plan ahead and get what you need. Dinnertime is not the time to play Iron Chef with that can of mushrooms, pack of hot dogs, and asparagus you just happen to have in your **KITCHEN**. Plan your meals for the week in advance. Organize your meals at the beginning of your week by setting a menu, making a **GROCERY LIST**, and shopping for your **GROCERIES**. If you are following any specific **RECIPES**, make sure you get everything you need and scale it up or down depending on how many you'll be feeding. Plan which nights you want to order in or go out to eat. If you like to save money, cooking at home is your best option. It also makes it much easier to stay healthy. When you cook at home and plan your meals, you can control calorie count, portion size, and nutrient intake. If you are the type of person who works from home, don't forget to schedule your own lunch break in your **CALENDAR** to keep yourself fed and functioning at your best. Have a full set of plastic **CONTAINERS** in your home so that if you like to prepare meals ahead of time or make enough for leftovers, you can fill them and label your meals for the week. You can designate an area in your **REFRIGERATOR** just for set meals for the week. This will make eating as easy as opening the fridge and grabbing whatever you're in the mood for, which probably isn't mushroom asparagus hot dog casserole.

■ ■ ■

O.C.D. EXTREME

Set up a family calendar that syncs to everyone's device. Add your family meals to it so everyone knows what time you are eating. You can even include the night's menu!

MEDIA LIBRARY is your entire digital collection of **MOVIES**, your digitized DVD **COLLECTION**, and CDs, videos, **PICTURES**, and **MUSIC**. This is where you'll find all your entertainment and precious memories, from *The Shaw-shank Redemption* to the pictures from your bar or bat mitzvah. Mazel tov! Create a folder for each type of media file: movies, music, pictures, and so on. Often, these folders already exist by default on your **COMPUTER**, so use them. Now find every media file on your computer and move it into the proper folder. Further organize each folder by creating subfolders, for example, MOVIES → COMEDIES. Whatever titles you choose, keep them clear and consistent.

A person's media library can take up a lot of hard-drive space, so it's best to keep it on a dedicated external **HARD DRIVE** and backed up on another drive. If your library is extremely large, you can even have multiple labeled drives for each type of media you have, such as a photo drive, a movie drive, and a music drive. You can also consider buying a family hard drive that is shared or networked; everyone in your home can upload his or her media to the family hard drive. That way, everyone can enjoy and stream everyone else's media. Just make sure everyone knows the rules of proper organization when importing, naming, saving, and deleting files! Whatever programs you use to manage and stream your media library, set up the preferences in that program to allow your devices to find and access your digital files. The whole point of organizing your media library is to be able to sync and stream it to whatever device you choose. Always name your files yourself and never let programs choose the name. There is nothing worse than searching for a media file without any identifying information in its file name, just a string of letters and numbers. Keeping your digital media well organized and backed up will also prepare you for easy transitions in the future. As new technologies, programs, and devices come out, your already organized media library will ensure that upgrading will never cause a headache. The better organized your media, the easier it will be to find on whatever device you use to enjoy it. Someone will need to alert the media: "Man Finds Media!"

> ### O.C.D. EXTREME
>
> I once lost my entire media library due to a corrupted hard drive. It will never happen again because now I back up my backups! That gives me three layers of data protection. I also rotate my backup drives, just to make sure every drive has all of my data. There is nothing wrong with being overprotective when it comes to your precious data. No technology is foolproof, so be prepared and plan ahead for the worst.

MEDICAL RECORDS of vital importance should be scanned and kept on file on your **COMPUTER** in DOCUMENTS → INSURANCE AND HEALTH → MEDICAL → NAME OF DOCTOR and backed up. They just might save your life in an emergency if Doogie Howser or Dr. House isn't available. These vital **DOCUMENTS** can range from major surgeries to **X-RAYS** to yearly physical exams. Items such as **RECEIPTS** for insurance reimbursements can be scanned, shredded, and filed to make sure you are getting back what you are owed. Keep a folder called "Outstanding Reimbursements" in your medical folder and file the document you submitted to your insurance agency here. Once the reimbursement comes in, move that document to the folder with your doctor's name. If you are keeping a physical **FILING CABINET**, create a folder labeled "Medical," and keep only the receipts and forms for reimbursements you are expecting to get back. Everything else must be scanned. If the government is requiring doctor's offices to start keeping their records digitally, it's probably a good idea for you to do so as well. If you haven't been keeping your records, you can always ask your doctor for a copy of your file. They are required by law to give it to you. Medical records can be kept for your entire life; having your complete medical history can aid in any future medical issues that may arise. Just don't try to Google-diagnose your-self or you might start to think you have the first case of smallpox in almost forty years.

MEDICINE can be prescription or over-the-counter. If it's prescription medi-cation, it should be kept in a private place, not in your **MEDICINE CABINET**. You'd be surprised how many people open medicine cabinets when they use someone else's bathroom. It is no one's business what prescriptions you use for yourself, unless you don't care, in which case, use your medicine cabinet and be an open book. If you do care, take your prescription medicines, grab an inexpensive storage container with a lid, and place your prescriptions in the **CONTAINER** in a **LINEN CLOSET** or a **DRAWER** in your bathroom. If the medicine is sealed in a container, people are far less likely to snoop. The one exception is birth control: keep that near your toothbrush and toothpaste so you always remember to take it at the same time each day. Always discard expired medication: it's probably still okay to use, but why risk it? This is your health we are talking about. If it's something you'd fear someone getting ahold of, flush it down the toilet. Otherwise, just toss it in the trash.

For over-the-counter medicine, first aid, and vitamins, keep them in a common area in the home accessible to anyone who might need it. Make sure everyone knows this location in case of an emergency. If someone uses an over-the-counter medicine, such as allergy medicine, or vitamins on a daily basis, they should keep it in their bathroom so they are reminded to take it. If you don't have space in your **BATHROOM** because you take a lot of vitamins, keep them in a **KITCHEN** cabinet, organized alphabetically. A note on vitamins: they are expensive! Find a great place online to buy your vitamins and **BOOKMARK** your sources. That way, when it's time to restock, you'll know where you ordered them.

If you are ill and need to take a lot of medication, or you are traveling,

M

consider using a weekly pill organizer with sections for each day. Take your time and load it carefully at the beginning of every week. You don't want any double or missed doses.

The pill organizer is also useful if you are taking part in a medical trial. Take your pills as directed, but stop if you experience any fever or blindness or if you start speaking in tongues.

Always make sure any and all medicine is out of the reach of children.

MEDICINE CABINET has the best real estate in Bathroomville, but you don't get a lot of space for the money. It's easy to access but small, so the medicine cabinet should be reserved for daily-use items only. Discard or relocate anything you don't use on a daily basis. If you are using a product temporarily, keep it in your medicine cabinet only as long as you are using it daily and then get it out of there. As with any **CABINET**, divide and designate the **SHELVES** for different purposes: oral hygiene, hair care, shaving, **MEDICINE** (if you keep it in here), and so on. Most shelves are adjustable, so move them to accommodate what it is you have. Use organization products like small boxes for tweezers and nail clippers or hair bands. If you use a product daily but it just doesn't fit, put it in smaller bottles or jars so each one fits and label them. Only put things in your medicine cabinet that you'll be comfortable having **GUESTS** see if they get sneaky when they use your **BATHROOM**. Or stick a note in there during parties that says, "Mind your business. Now please wash your hands." Wipe down your medicine cabinet at least once a month. Completely clear out and reorganize your medicine cabinet at least every six months.

routine is your first step to having a great day. I give my clients the energizing experience of opening a tranquil and well-organized medicine cabinet every time they get ready for their day.

■ ■ ■ ■

MEETING LOGS are not only where lumberjacks hold their meetings, but also a document that is useful for any professionals moving forward in their careers. Having a list of everyone you've met with can come in handy when trying to think of references, making connections, networking, and creating opportunities. Keep a running meeting log in the notes section of your phone and make sure it syncs to your **COMPUTER**. Every time you take a meeting, add the names of the people you met with, the date, and any **MEETING NOTES** you may have taken. This is also a good time to add their addresses and phone numbers to your **ADDRESS BOOK**. Update this list every time you take a meeting. This will be a vital growing tool for you as your career progresses and as your experience builds. It will be your personal guide to the **RELATIONSHIPS** you are cultivating and allow you to be more prepared when walking into a room with previous knowledge to remind yourself that you've been there and what it was like. You never know how your career is going to evolve and how people you met in one context might be useful in another.

■ ■ ■

AN O.C.D. SUCCESS STORY

When I was acting on a regular basis and going out on auditions, I kept a journal of everyone I met. When I transitioned from actor to professional organizer and brand builder, it was amazing how many opportunities grew from the people I had met as an actor. It was incredible to have this organized tool that was a history, log, and journal of my relationship building. Naturally it was in digital format, so it was easy to find and search when I needed it. This story can apply to everyone. Take note of the meetings in your life and keep those notes organized in a digital journal. It will be fun to look back on your journal one day and it will be an incredibly useful tool for networking, future meetings, job interviews, and opportunities, even if your profession changes.

MEETING NOTES are a good way to review what was discussed at a meeting, any follow-up tasks, and anything you want to remember about the people you met with. They should be organized the moment your rear end hits your desk chair after the meeting. The notes will only be of real value to you if you create them during or soon after your meeting, when the information is fresh. No matter what you will be using your notes for, it is important that they are clear and concise. The best way to take and keep meeting notes is to create an e-mail with the meeting title and date in the subject line. Take notes as the meeting goes on and then e-mail it to yourself and anyone else who wants it. You can address any action items in the e-mail, and then file it in the appropriate **E-MAIL FOLDER** once complete. If you took notes in shorthand, rewrite the e-mail, send it to yourself again, and then file it. Sometimes it's not appropriate to pull out a device and take notes during a meeting. Ask the people you are meeting with if they mind if you take notes. If they do mind, jot down your notes as soon as you can after the meeting while you still remember everything. Include a note that they mind your taking notes during the meeting so that when you review your meeting notes before the next meeting, you don't have to ask about taking meeting notes again.

AN O.C.D. SUCCESS STORY

I've trained assistants who were missing important information and action items because they weren't properly taking and filing meeting notes. Anyone who has worked in the entertainment industry knows you rarely get a second chance as an assistant, so they were very thankful to have my system. Once they started using it, they never missed important points or tasks again, and they got to keep their jobs! Eventually they were promoted, and suddenly I found that I had powerful industry connections. Now I get tickets to Medieval Times whenever I want.

MEMBERSHIPS are anything and everything you belong to, from supermarket customer loyalty programs to automobile associations and pasta-of-the-month clubs. All of your memberships, including any pertinent information to manage the membership or use online features, should be kept in your **ACCOUNTS** document. Memberships tend to come with materials like cards or mini-cards for **KEY CHAINS**. Rather than take up space in your **WALLET**,

PURSE, or on your key chain, keep the card as a photo on your phone. The bar code will still scan and you won't have to carry anything extra around. To accomplish this, scan the card, both sides if necessary, on your home scanner or use a scanning app on your **SMARTPHONE** and then e-mail it to yourself. Save it as a jpeg on your **COMPUTER** titled by the membership name to PIC-TURES → SMARTPHONE → MEMBERSHIP CARDS. Then create an album on your phone titled "MEMBERSHIPS" and sync these photos by making sure your synching software has your memberships folder selected to upload. You'll never be searching for a card and your wallet will never be fat again. Stay disciplined to keep the wallet weight off. Anytime you cancel a membership, remove it from your phone, but keep it on your computer in PICTURES → OLD MEMBERSHIPS in case you ever need to refer back to it.

O.C.D. APPROVED TECHNOLOGY

Smartphone scanning apps are powerful time-saving tools that produce results almost as good as a desktop scanner. They let you take a picture of your document, then they automatically identify the edges, fix the perspective, correct the color and contrast, and then let you save the file in a variety of formats. From there, you can e-mail or share your files. Some great scanning apps to check out are Cam Scanner+ and Genius Scan.

MEMORABILIA consists of anything you want to keep for sentimental or valuable reasons. We all have that ribbon from the science fair, photo-booth photo strip, stuffed animal you won in an epic game of skee ball, baby blanket, concert ticket stubs, or essay you got that A++ on. These are important memories of different times in our lives and worth the space they take up to keep. Feel free to display some of your memorabilia in your home, but pick only a few of your most cherished items. Think of creative ways to display your memorabilia, like turning old **T-SHIRTS** into a framed quilt or scanning **TICKET STUBS** to make a collage. The rest should be handled carefully, organized effectively, and stored in a way that protects them from time and weather. Each person in your family should have a labeled airtight and waterproof memorabilia **BIN** kept in your **BASEMENT** or **GARAGE**, or an office if you are continually accessing it. This bin will house any **PAPERS, ACADEMIC PAPERWORK**, special photos, cards, trinkets, **COLLECTIBLES**, anything that may not have a proper spot to be displayed in a home but will be valuable and exciting to look at and pass down in the future. You don't need to save everything. If you have multiples of a type of item, such as baseball trophies, for example, pick one or two favorites and get rid of the rest. If a photo of an item is enough to preserve the memory, snap it and trash it. Even if you are putting special items in your memorabilia bin, you should still scan or take pictures of them and save them on your computer in DOCUMENTS → MEMORABILIA. You'll be glad to have the backup in case anything ever happens to the original. Don't plan on saving a lot: start off with a small bin and, as your memorabilia collection grows, expand to a bigger bin if necessary. Keep an itemized list on your computer in your memorabilia folder of everything in your bin so you are never searching for anything. If it is in the bin, it should be on the list, and if it is out of the bin, take it off the list. Go through your bins every year to remind yourself of what you are keeping. It's fun to look back and you might also discover that something you kept is no longer significant and you can get rid of it—maybe you broke your old skee-ball record and that stuffed frog doesn't mean as much as it used to.

AN O.C.D. SUCCESS STORY

As a parent, it's hard not to think everything is important as your child grows up, but your child will go through a huge amount of work, clothing, trophies, and other memorable items. It's difficult to decide what will stand the test of time. I helped a client create a system to make those tough choices. I told her that she could save everything her instincts told her was important, but she had to limit herself to keeping it all in one bin. If the bin was full, she'd have to go through it and get rid of anything that wasn't significant anymore. She of course completely filled up the bin immediately. But when it came time to add something new, she had to get rid of something else. This sounds like a tough exercise, but it worked well. When it was time to add something new, something else in the box seemed less important than it did when it first came home. She started to learn the value of her items in relation to her space and kept her child's most precious memorabilia without it growing out of control. When it comes to memories, you'll use up as much space as you have. While your child is in second grade, every paper seems important, but once they are in tenth grade, you realize that maybe only one or two assignments from second grade are worth keeping.

MEMORY CARDS are tiny removable **HARD DRIVES** for portable devices like cameras, video recorders, phones, music players, and your secret robot child. Memory card contents should be uploaded to a temporary folder on your desktop, the files renamed and put in the appropriate folders, and then the card wiped clean after every trip or event for which it was used. Don't use them as storage for long periods of time because they are very delicate and can be damaged easily or have their data corrupted. Additionally, memory cards are very small, and there is a greater chance of losing them. Once they are emptied, store them properly inside the appropriate device so they are ready for use the next time you grab it. If you purchase extra memory cards, possibly because you are going on a long trip or take a lot of video, keep them in the carrying bags along with the device they are used for or with your **ELECTRONIC ACCESSORIES**. Memory cards come in many different sizes, so make sure that you buy an appropriate-size memory card for the device you are using. Cheaper isn't always better when it comes to memory cards. Sometimes you get what you pay for, which could turn out to be data loss or incompatibility. Reliability and speed are factors, so make sure you read reviews and get something you can trust with your data.

MONEY (see FINANCES)

MONTHLY BILLS (see BILLS)

MOVIES should be organized by those that contain Jeff Bridges and those that don't. But they can also be organized in three other simple and effective ways. You can organize your **DVD COLLECTION** and Blu-rays on **SHELVES** in one area of your home in alphabetical order for people to see. This is a very functional and simple way, but if you are limited for space, you can buy DVD books. On the inside cover, create a master alphabetical list and file your movies in the DVD book. Get rid of the cases. You won't need the cases again unless you plan on keeping a DVD as a collector's item or you plan on reselling the DVD one day. The most advanced method of movie organization is to digitize your entire movie library and stream your movies through a home media server. For any movies you keep digitally, save them in MOVIES → GENRE and name them by title and date. Whenever you add a movie to your collection, make sure to add it to your organized system. If you still have movies or home movies on VHS, see **VIDEO TAPES**

to get them digitized in a lasting format. There is no place to stick a VHS tape into your **iPAD** without voiding the warranty.

MOVING can be one of the most exhausting and stressful things you'll ever do in your life. In fact, moving is ranked third in terms of stress, after the death of a spouse and divorce. On top of that, the average person moves 11.7 times in their life. Do the math, don't forget to carry the .7, and it equals *a lot of stress*! Moving in the O.C.D. Way will relieve tremendous and unnecessary stress so you can focus on your new beginning! In the course of my life I have moved about ten times, four of which were across country, and I have streamlined the perfect move.

Moving is an incredible chance for growth in our lives. But how is that possible when we crowd our future with too much stuff from our past? Before you start to pack up your old place, carefully go through everything you own and ask yourself this one question over and over again, "Do I want this item to be included in my new beginning?" When you move, you are giving yourself the opportunity to start new and fresh. Why would you want to bring old memories or old things you will never use and not know what to do with into your new home? Leave things behind that you know won't be of any substantial service or value to you in your new beginning.

You must also know how much space you have in your new beginning. Are you **DOWNSIZING**? Do you have less closet space? Will your current **FURNITURE** fit in your new spaces? The point of these questions is to determine what you can actually bring with you. Sometimes you want to keep something, but it just doesn't make sense in your new space. If you are considering amputating part of your couch to make it fit, it's probably best just to let it go and find a new couch. Know your new space before you pack up your old one. You do not want to be unpacking in your new space with too much stuff. In fact, I refuse to take on a client for a move who will not let me predetermine how much stuff they can bring. Do the same for yourself.

Now that you know what you want to bring and what you have room for, estimate how many **BOXES** you will need to pack it all. It is simple because it is just an estimation. This will help you get more accurate quotes from moving companies because now is the time to find your guys. Before you call any company, know the date you want to move, a rough estimate of the number of boxes, and the big pieces of furniture you are for sure keeping. Get at least three bids. Don't necessarily go with the lowest bid: read reviews. These are your possessions and you want reliable and trustworthy movers handling them. You should also ask them if they sell recycled boxes or if they would be willing to buy back your boxes after the move because this can change your overall cost and help you pick your mover.

Now is also the time to find out if your insurance policy covers moving and damage and what your coverage is. If the policy doesn't cover moving, or coverage isn't enough, purchase additional moving insurance from your movers. Not only will this cover your possessions, but it will also encourage your movers to handle your items more carefully, since they are on the hook financially. Trust me, they don't want to pay for your plasma TV. If you are taking any lighting or plumbing fixtures, schedule an electrician or plumber to remove them the week of the move. Schedule your utilities and service providers to set up or transfer your services to your new home prior to your even moving in. If you can't take possession of the property before move-in day, have them come the day of the move. Now is also a good time to update your address at every place that may have it on file. Contact the post office, your bank, credit card companies, the Department of Motor Vehicle, insurance companies, and any subscription-based services you have and tell them your new address and move date. Most of this can be done online. Your **ACCOUNTS** document will come in very handy to make sure you've changed your address for all your accounts.

Ask your moving company to drop off boxes and tape for you to pack. Don't be afraid to overestimate because most moving companies will refund you for any boxes you don't use, but make sure you ask this question. If you buy your own boxes, most supply centers will refund you for any unused boxes with your **RECEIPT**. It is better to have extra boxes than have to wait for the movers to drop off more or have to run back to the store in the middle of your packing process. Running around will take up more time and energy and means more stress and more money spent.

Time to start packing. Start with the least used rooms and spaces in your home so you can continue to function normally up until moving day. If your cooking, eating, relaxing, working, and bathing never get interrupted, the moving process will affect your life much less. You'll be fed, rested, and continue to smell delightful. As you pack, take a second opportunity to question every item. Ask yourself why you need it. If you don't have a good answer, don't bring it. Create a master list of all of your items, divided by room and box number, as you pack. Instead of writing contents on the boxes, which can be a waste of markers and time, just put numbers on your boxes. Simple: 1, 2, 3, 4, and so on. The numbers should correlate to the room and contents for each box on your master list. For example, you just packed a box in your **FAMILY ROOM** with **BOOKS**, your universal remote control, **DVD COLLECTION**, and blankets. Your master list would read:

Box 4—Family Room

Blankets
Books
DVDs
Universal Remote

If you have someone to help you with your move while you pack, which you should, have that person type the list as you put things in boxes. The more detailed, the better. Try to pack like items together, but this isn't critical because you will have a map to where everything is and where it should be placed in your new space. It's better to use box space efficiently. Take the time to bubble- and tissue-wrap valuable items. At the end of each day, e-mail yourself this list and add the boxes and contents to the master list on your **COMPUTER**. As you work on your master list, alphabetize the contents of each box for easy searching later on. You now know exactly where that universal remote is. You will also know exactly how many boxes you have, which will guarantee that nothing is lost. It's also a good idea to keep an **INVENTORY** at the end of your master list of all of your furniture, since those won't be in boxes. While it's hard to misplace furniture, it can take a while for you to realize that an end table or guest room **NIGHTSTAND** isn't around.

Continue this process, going area by area and room by room, until the rest of your home is packed up. There will be some items that you won't be able to pack until the morning of your actual move. These also tend to be the items that you need immediately after moving, like **CLOTHES**, routers, modems, **CLEANING SUPPLIES**, toiletries, chargers, computers, and Sour Patch watermelon gummies. Make a box for these items, number it, and add it to your master list with the contents "Day-of Items." Valuable and delicate items, such as **ANTIQUES**, mirrors, TVs, artwork, and chandeliers, should be professionally wrapped and packed by your movers also on the day of the move. However, you can handle your own china and dishware just by bubble-wrapping them. If at all possible, start unpacking the day of your move, but if you absolutely can't, you'll want to pack an overnight bag with clothes and toiletries so you're not rummaging through your boxes to change and shower.

The big day has come. Grab that master list and get ready to conduct a flawless move. When your movers arrive, introduce yourself, offer them water, and then show them through your home. Give the foreman a copy of the master list, show him how all the boxes correspond to the list, what they need to disassemble, and what they need to wrap. Your master list will serve as the moving list for your movers and help you keep your sanity when looking for boxes and items in the chaos later. Remember that the movers' job is to move your stuff; they couldn't care less about the structure and organization of your move. You need to be in control of your move. The more prepared and organized you are, the easier it will be to instruct your movers.

Everything that gets loaded on the truck will come out in reverse order. Tell your movers the order you want to unpack so they can load the truck appropriately. Before they start unloading, make sure they know where each group of boxes and piece of furniture are supposed to go by walking them through the new space with your master list and pointing it out. This will save you time and energy later because you won't have to move anything again once the movers leave. Have them unwrap and assemble anything they packed and took apart, and test out the bed to make sure it doesn't collapse after they leave. Your movers will thank you for being organized because they will be able to finish the job more quickly and not have to move things twice in your new home. After everything is unloaded, thank each mover individually for the hard work and tip him or her twenty to fifty dollars, depending on the difficulty of the move. Don't hand all the tip money to the foreman; it doesn't always trickle down.

Get organized before your move so when you are finally in your new space, you can unpack your belongings and put them where they truly belong without even thinking about it. What a great time to organize your new **CLOSETS, KITCHEN, HOME OFFICE, FAMILY ROOM, BED-ROOMS, BATHROOMS,** and other spaces the O.C.D. Way. You'll be settled into your wonderfully organized home in no time and disciplining yourself to keep it that way. Congratulations on your flawless move and your new beginning!

■ ■ ■

AN O.C.D. SUMMARY

Organize: Go through all of your belongings. Decide what you'll be taking with you to your new space. Measure your new space and ask yourself if your things will fit. Select your mover and schedule appointments to set up your utilities and services.

Create: Make a master list as you pack with the contents of each box. Start packing the least used rooms and spaces first so you can remain functional in your home up until the move. Have your master list completed and ready for the day of the move.

Discipline: Give the list to your movers and make sure you are in control of the move, telling them the order in which you want things packed and unpacked and where. Once in your new home, be disciplined in your unpacking. Set a goal for a number of boxes to unpack each day. Unpack everything in an organized way, putting it where it belongs according to the O.C.D. Way.

■ ■ ■

O.C.D. EXTREME

I won't stop unpacking until every box is broken down. I cannot relax in an incomplete environment. The moment the movers leave, I try to take everything out of the boxes so the movers can come back the very next day to retrieve them. It ends up being a twenty-four-hour day for me, but by the twenty-fifth hour, 95 percent of my place is unpacked, functional, and free of packing materials and any other memory of the move.

MUDROOM was a scary word for me before I knew what one was. To me, it sounded like a place to send a misbehaving O.C.D. boy as a punishment. "Go to the mudroom!" Now older and wiser, I know a mudroom can be neat and organized, even though it's designed to get dirty. It is much easier to clean up a room where everything has a place and has purpose than a room that is a complete disaster. Your mudroom should be laid out so that when anyone enters the space, they know where to wipe their feet, where to put their wet clothes, where to hang their umbrellas, **SCARVES**, and **HATS**, where to take their **SHOES** off, and how it all cleans up. Use your mudroom closet to house the more outdoor and rugged articles of clothing and accessories. Most people have their mudroom off of their back door or **GARAGE**, but if yours is combined with your **ENTRYWAY**, have a mat inside your **ENTRYWAY CLOSET** to lay out during those rainy days prior to your leaving the house. Hang, hang, hang . . . find wall space that isn't being utilized and set up areas and hardware to hang all kinds of accessories. The hanging of the articles will allow for faster drying. No one likes putting on wet gloves or boots, and you don't want to step out of the house with a damp-induced cringe. If you have the space and cash and a dedicated mudroom off of your garage, create custom cabinetry, cubbyholes, and storage-bench seating for effective and simple organization options. Don't clutter the room, but give yourself plenty of specific functionality so no one is confused about what articles go where.

O.C.D. EXTREME

Stick a space heater in your mudroom to brush off that chill from outside and to dry your items faster. It feels great to put on warm boots and gloves.

MUSIC is rapidly becoming entirely **DIGITAL MUSIC**. If you still keep music in physical formats, see **CASSETTE TAPES**, **CDs**, and **RECORDS** for organizing and converting them. Remember, the O.C.D. Way is to get as much digitized as possible.

N

NAILS, screws, nuts, and bolts definitely come in handy for that odd repair job, so I condone keeping a reasonable amount of shapes and sizes. Reasonable. Don't act like a nut with a screw loose. When I see that people have kept every piece of hardware that's ever entered their homes, it's like nails on a chalkboard to me and makes me want to bolt. You can let go of left-over hardware from that cabinet knob, TV mount, or self-assembled piece of Swedish **FURNITURE**. You can always run to the hardware store. A good way to control yourself is to have a toolbox with compartments on the top for these small pieces of hardware. If the only place you allow yourself to store these items is in this section of your toolbox, divided by type, you won't end up keeping too much. Resist the urge to toss everything into a hardware **JUNK DRAWER**. The purpose of keeping things is to be able to find them when you need them, and a junk drawer is a black hole. No matter the size, every home should have a toolbox with a basic set of **TOOLS**. Keeping all of your tools and hardware in one portable place is effective and efficient.

If you are very handy and have a dedicated tool area and workstation in your **GARAGE**, **BASEMENT**, or elsewhere on your property, you can have a larger collection. Use different size labeled mason jars to store your hardware. Be sure to keep like hardware together and never start to mix them even when you are in a hurry. Use a label maker to label the outside of the mason jars so you know what type and size hardware is housed in each jar. Grabbing your hardware will only be hard if you don't know where it is. Whatever system you are using, make sure it's uniform.

NEEDS are vital to your mental health and the health of any **RELATION-SHIPS** in your life. You need to know what your needs are! How can you succeed in your life without knowing your own needs? Before you can have a healthy love, work, family, or friendship relationship with anyone, you have to know what fuels you and what makes you the individual that you are. Then you can communicate honestly and candidly with everyone in your life. Organizing your own needs is as simple as creating a list of the things that are truly important to you. Don't stress about this list because no one has to see it but you. It's just a tool to get you to be honest with yourself about the things you truly need. Brainstorm your needs list and then arrange your needs in the order you think they are a priority to you. Don't worry about getting it "right" because this is a constantly evolving process. Everyone's needs are different and needs will continually change or change priority as you change in your life. Update, review, and reprioritize your needs list any time you feel disconnected, lost, confused, or out of balance in your life. Your needs list will help you diagnose what's wrong and allow you to refocus and get back on track. Anyone you are in a relationship with should do the same, and you should always be aware of their needs in addition to your own. Even better, write your needs out together as a couple-building exercise and keep the list somewhere where you can both review it from time to time. Know your needs and know your partner's needs so you never have to live a life where you feel unsatisfied. Be clear with yourself so you can be clear with others.

AN O.C.D. SUCCESS STORY

Sometimes with clients, I'm half organizer, half life coach. The way people relate to their possessions is oftentimes indicative of how they live their lives. I remember a time when I came to organize a home with a client and instead ended up talking about her needs. She couldn't tell me what any of her needs were. I left her with the homework to create her needs list. When I came back for a follow-up, my next organizing job had already been done: she organized her entire office. Once my client realized that a peaceful space was a need of hers, she was honest enough with herself to take charge of her space. I love succeeding to the point where I put myself out of a job because it means I'm doing something right!

NEWS comes from so many sources, it can be overwhelming: print, TV, social media, Web sites, blogs, newsfeeds, **APPS**, oh my! It seems like everything is headline news these days, from puppy rescues to Kim and Kanye officially becoming "Kimye." Know where you want to get your news from so you don't let it distract you. Pick your preferred format and set a time to read the news. I like to get my news online or through the Pulse app on my

SMARTPHONE because I can customize newsfeeds based on my interests as well as eliminate newsfeeds I have no interest in. If you are a breaking-news junkie, subscribe to your favorite news companies on Twitter. It's the fastest news delivery system available. If you still get the newspaper delivered to your home, read it and recycle it. Don't keep that bulky stack! If you are a print purist, know that now you can get your favorite newspapers delivered digitally to your devices, but still with the traditional look of a print newspaper. Getting news digitally makes it much easier to read your news on the go and to save any ARTICLES you may want to keep. You can just e-mail yourself the link instead of having to clip and scan. I don't believe that no news is good news, but I do think that paper news is bad news.

O.C.D. EXTREME

I believe that all news sources tend to be biased. To get a clearer picture of any situation, I read at least three articles about it from different sources to get a balanced perspective. This is another reason I like online news: it offers you multiple sources for every headline.

NIGHTSTANDS are part of the bed space, which should be used for the three Rs: resting, recharging, and romance. If you clutter the top, or use the storage space for anything not related to these purposes, it will be distracting and you won't get the best of the three Ss: strength, sleep, and sex. Nightstands usually have some organizational elements like DRAWERS or a CABINET with shelves, which often become places we just tend to throw the stuff left on us at the end of each day. In a perfect world, these spaces should contain only items relevant to anything you do in bed: sleep clothes like nighties or pajamas, sleep accessories like masks, or romance-related items like lubrication, condoms, and SEX TOYS. Each spot in your nightstand should have a specific purpose. Use drawer dividers if necessary. On the top of your nightstand, you can keep the book you are currently reading, a small JEWELRY holder for your everyday rings and necklaces, a phone charger, a lamp, and a picture. Try not to keep much more than this. If you are trying to reclaim your disorganized nightstand, which probably is a bunch of JUNK DRAWERS, pull everything out and find a better home for anything not bed-related. Designate spaces in and on your nightstand and maintain the discipline to only put items where they are supposed to go. Doing so will help you keep your bed space to the Rs, so you can get your Ss and catch your Zzzzz.

NURSERY organization needs to service the parents and the child, not the teddy bears. For you, the parent, having a baby is stressful. Don't add to your stress by having a disorganized or overstuffed nursery. Setting up a nursery requires proper planning, preferably a few months in advance of baby's actual arrival, because the closer you get, the more hectic things get. Most effective nurseries need only a crib, a **DRESSER** for **BABY CLOTHES** and blankets, a rocking chair and ottoman, a trash can, and my favorite . . . a changing table with a tricked-out organizational system for diapers, wipes, powders, ointments, and burp cloths. If you are on a tight budget or short on space, use the top of your dresser as a changing table and keep everything you need in the dresser, in designated spaces, of course. Keep your **DIAPER BAG** nearby for easy restocking. You can also use baskets around the room for simple organization, but designate each basket for a specific item. Label what is supposed to go in all of your spaces, especially if you have help, so you and your support team can maintain the organization you set up. You want to spend your time raising your baby, not reorganizing. You want your nursery to be both functional and warm, which is not always an easy task. Paint murals or find colors to paint the walls that are calm and relaxing. Hang pictures in the nursery that promote serenity and creative stimulation. Remember, you are going to get tons of gifts, so don't overbuy before your child arrives. Buy only what you think you'll need. Don't feel like you have to put everything that people give you in your nursery. This is a sure path to chaos and to a nursery that feels like an FAO Schwarz. Your baby will grow quickly, so reevaluate your spaces often based on baby's new needs.

You must also realize that the nursery is the starting point for your new-born's mental growth, comfort, and understanding of what a healthy environment should be. Make it just that: healthy! The more things that are surrounding them, the more chaotic the environment you are putting your child into. Teaching our kids at such a developmental age that an overabundance of stuff is necessary and comforting is heading down a dangerous path. Show them they can function without chaos so that when they grow up, they can make healthy choices as to how much stuff and chaos they want in their lives. If you have the space, keep children's **TOYS** and **GAMES** in a **CHILD'S PLAYROOM**. If you don't and your nursery serves as both, store toys in a designated area, leaving plenty of clear space for your child to explore. Bring toys out when you want to stimulate your child so you are in control of when your child is being stimulated. Return toys to this area after playtime. Let's all work together to raise an O.C.D. generation: be the rubber nipple on the bottle of organization and discipline!

AN O.C.D. SUCCESS STORY

Two weeks before their due date, a pair of first-time expectant parents called me in need of my help. They explained that they had way too much stuff as a result of gifts from excited friends and family. And the chaos was continuing to grow. They knew they had a disaster on their hands and time was running out. Neither Mom nor Dad felt peaceful in the nursery as it was, and that would of course spill over into their energy in raising their child. I came in and simplified the nursery to the bare essentials, returned a ton of gifts for store credit to be used later on, and transformed the space into a soothing and functional environment for the parents and their incoming baby. We added a few cherished photos, painted a wall to add some color to the room, and made sure everything was organized and functional. This put Mom and Dad in a much better state of mind, and Mom could focus on the insanely difficult task of giving birth. Dad could focus on the insanely difficult task of watching Mom give birth.

NUTS AND BOLTS (see NAILS)

O

OFFICE should be your home away from home; just don't forget to actually go home. Most people spend a significant amount of time in their office, which is why it is so vital to have a space that is catered, comfortable, and organized for you. How many of us get assigned an office, throw our laptop on the **DESK**, and don't make the space ours? Create your own sense of life and style so you actually want to be there.

Just like your **HOME OFFICE**, take the time to move anything and everything you want to create an environment that feels free and accessible. Whether it is the placement of your phone, **CABINETS, DRAWERS**, pencil/pen holder, or even desk, move it to a place that feels right and helps you accomplish your work. If wires are too short or outlets aren't available in the desired location, ask the office manager to help you or put in a request for the changes. You are not being a pain in the butt; most employers would rather have their employees comfortable, happy, and at ease than miserable and complaining about their work environment. Don't be afraid to ask for things that will make you more productive and functional in your office. Order the necessary things you need for your office, but don't overbuy or overstock on **OFFICE SUPPLIES** until you know exactly how your work will flow and what supplies you will actually use and need. Remember: you don't need to have all of your equipment in your office. Make use of the equipment in the common areas of your workplace, like printers, faxes, and scanners to keep your office uncluttered. Don't forget to add those personal and fun touches, such as a bowl of candy, candles (if allowed), pictures, rugs, throw pillows, tchotchkes, stress balls, USB foam missile cannons, whatever makes it *your* space. But keep your work space minimalist and organized to function at your most efficient. This includes your **DESK**, drawers, **CUBICLE**, office supplies, **FILING CABINET**, and **BOOKSHELVES**, as well as digital spaces like your **COMPUTER**. Make sure you create systems to process your daily work, your **MAIL**, and your e-mail. Don't let work pile up or go unfiled. Undistracted by a chaotic office, you can now set your sights on getting that promotion and that corner office with the view of the park or yoga studio across the street. People will notice the space you keep.

To keep your options open when your workday ends, or in case of accidents, it's a good idea to always keep a change of clothes in your office. If you like to commute in casual clothes and then change once you arrive at work, designate an area for your nice clothes or uniform. If you walk to work, and need to wear comfortable shoes, consider having a shoe organizer hidden under your desk or in your closet with your most versatile pairs of work shoes. You can still look your best at the office without having to sacrifice your comfort to and from the office.

If you own your own business, or the responsibility falls on you to design and organize the entire office, think about how people work and use their space. Do people need quiet and private space to focus on their work? Will having **GAMES** and social areas promote creativity and social engagement among employees? Might an open floor plan among departments create synergies or will it just cause distraction? It really depends on the nature of your business, but whatever you think will make your company perform at its best, promote that in your use of space. Make sure everyone has easy access to anything and everything that will make them more efficient, such as the coffeepot. The goal for any business is to grow and thrive, and spatial organization is a valuable tool to achieve that goal.

◼ ◼ ◼
O.C.D. APPROVED TECHNOLOGY

To do your best work, you need to be comfortable. You don't want to be distracted by the little aches and pains that come from sitting long periods of time on a less-than-adequate office chair. This is why I recommend the Aeron chair by Herman Miller. You can buy a chair and adjust all the supports to accommodate your body size and type, making it the most ergonomic chair on the market. I have three in my home office and it really is like sitting on air. They are more expensive than run-of-the-mill office supply megastore chairs, but your back and butt will thank you, and you'll produce better work without your body being a distraction.

OFFICE CUBICLE (see CUBICLE).

OFFICE DESK (see DESK)

OFFICE FILES, like all of your **DOCUMENTS**, should be digital and kept in a well-organized folder system on your **COMPUTER** or office's network. If you are beginning a new job, get familiar with the scanner. Introduce your-self. "Hi scanner. I'm new here. I hear you can help me get organized!" If the **OFFICE** doesn't have one, ask the supply manager to purchase one. If the supply manager asks why, tell him or her that it will make it easier for you to find and file work, which will make you a more efficient and effective employee. Scanners are so inexpensive these days, you can even buy one for yourself and keep it in your office. If you file digitally, make sure you down-load attachments from any e-mails that arrive and file them in the appropri-ate folder. If you are receiving a lot of attachments for a specific project, make sure you create a folder for that project.

If you must keep paper, the filing process is the same. Create main folders for your files based upon the project you need files for and keep them in your **FILING CABINET**. Within the main file folders, have manila folders for the little subprojects that fall within that project. Don't create excessive fold-ers that are too specific because all you will be doing is creating more folders to search through when looking for files. Save and file only what you will need. Let me repeat . . . save and file only what you will need. So many of us think we need to save everything that comes through our office to cover our ass. You know what you will need. You also know what files can be found on your computer or on a company server, so there is no need for a paper double. Once a year, go through your office files and purge the **PAPERS** you no longer need or haven't accessed since you stuck them in that folder. If you inherit a filing cabinet by taking over someone's job, ask a coworker if that work needs to be kept. If no one knows what those documents are, it's likely that no one actually needs them, so go ahead and toss them.

In the short term, as office files are still being reviewed, edited, and passed around, you can keep them in a file organizer on your **DESK**, but once you complete a project, scan and file them. Remember, you don't want any unnecessary paper on your desk. The goal is to have a completely clear desk so you can have a clear mind. Don't create piles on your brain!

- - -

AN O.C.D. SUCCESS STORY

Space in an office is a precious commodity. Why waste space using a method that is obsolete when that space can be used to add function-ality to your office? I worked with a small company that had a filing room. I took the time to digitize all of their files and set up a system for them to digitize future documents. Now the file room is a recreation room, giving their employees a space to recharge and socialize, leading to synergies among departments. It's amazing what you can use free space for when you embrace digitization!

■ ■ ■ ■

OFFICE SUPPLIES should be purchased only when you know what supplies you will actually need and use for your work and **OFFICE**. Until then, buy only a short-term amount of the essentials. Don't buy supplies just to make your office feel "professional." You aren't a set dresser. Just because the company is paying doesn't mean it's okay to go hog wild on staples and highlighters. So many people purchase too many office supplies, which is one of the biggest contributors to overspending and disorganization within companies.

Keep all of your office supplies in a single designated area. Choose and label a space for each type of supply. Keep like items together: paper with paper, inks with toners, paper clips with binder clips, pens and pencils, and so on. You want people to know exactly where to find a particular supply, so create self-explanatory zones with the more frequently used items in the easiest-to-see and -reach places.

Don't get crazy stocking office supplies for the apocalypse. You aren't a Staples. Office supply delivery is usually quick—a one- or two-day turn-around after placing the order. You can always get more. Have enough supplies so you never run out. This can be as simple as marking a line on a **SHELF**, and whenever your supplies dip below that line, you reorder. Know the **QUANTITY** of each item that fits in your designated space. For example, you should know how many reams of paper you can fit on your designated paper shelf in your supply closet. That way you'll always know exactly how many reams of paper to reorder when you run low. Know the model numbers of any equipment for which you need to order specific supplies, such as ink cartridges for printers, toner for copiers, or tape for postage meters. Always have a replacement ready to go for your office machines. As soon as you replace one, order another one. If you discover you have never reordered a particular supply, no one is using it. Get rid of extra jumbo binder clips and use that space for something better.

Don't let packaging dictate your organization! You can pull office supplies out of their packaging and keep them in labeled **BINS** or cups that best fit your space. This works particularly well for pens, highlighters, or any other supplies where the packaging can create a mess or hide the remaining quantity of a particular item. Employees will take the last and leave an empty box, but you won't know it's empty. It's easy to see an empty cup.

Order and store only the supplies that enhance your workflow, not what looks interesting. Keep them organized, easily accessible, and restocked, and you'll never have to worry about your business being inefficient or unprofitable due to your office supplies. Instead, you'll know it's because no one wants your product, so think of something else!

0

215

ONLINE ACCOUNTS (see ACCOUNTS)

ONLINE BANKING these days pretty much makes it so you never have to leave your home to do your banking. Banks want you online: it makes them more profitable. Online banking is an organizational win-win. Have you ever deposited a check from your **LIVING ROOM** in your bathrobe with a terrible case of bed head? Now you can! In fact, you can do almost anything online or through your bank's smartphone app that you'd need to visit a branch for, including looking up account information, transferring money, and making **DEPOSITS**. It also makes your life simpler with features like automatic bill pay, digital payroll, the ability to download your statements and summaries directly into your financial planning software, and ordering gifts and rewards just for banking there. Get your statements delivered online and you'll also reduce the amount of paper consumption you have in your life and be able to access previous statements with the click of a button and without hassle down the line. If you don't save or download your online statements and you want a statement from too far in the past, sometimes you still have to call or visit in person. My bank keeps info online for 540 days. Keep all of your online banking account information in your password-protected **ACCOUNTS** file. Make sure you include all of your usernames and **PASSWORDS**. When you set your passwords, make sure they are strong and secure. You don't want anyone figuring out your password and wreaking havoc with your money. Online banking is a convenience that will help you be smarter with your **FINANCES**, allow you to keep a weekly watchful eye on your money, and save you time (while even earning a free gift). The only reason I visit the bank is to get two-dollar bills to give out as tips because, after all, every encounter is an opportunity to make an impression!

AN O.C.D. SUCCESS STORY

I worked with a client who was trying to buy a house. In order to secure his loan, he needed to send his loan company copies of all the checks he had written in the last year. He tried to do it in person at a branch, but tellers don't always know the procedure and passed him around from person to person. Once he finally found the right person, the banker told him that it would cost five dollars per check copy and would take six weeks to receive them by mail. That would have delayed his securing the loan and thus closing on the house, putting the deal in jeopardy. What a pain in the ass! When he recounted his troubles to me, I suggested that he set up and access his account online. He was able to download PDFs of all the checks in about ten minutes, and he printed them on his own for just the cost of paper and ink.

P

PACKING for a trip reveals four types of people when it comes to organization: those who bring too much, those who bring *way* too much, those who don't bring enough, and those who actually understand their **NEEDS**. We want you to be the last type. If you are organized before you pack and understand the nature of your trip, you are already a step ahead of the game. Do yourself a favor: pack at least a day or two ahead of your trip. Packing the day of your trip is beyond stressful and you'll end up missing items or bringing too much or, worse, missing your flight.

Prepare for a trip by making a list of your daily activities. The more specific you can be, the more specific you can plan and pack, which is why organizing your **TRAVEL** schedule is incredibly helpful. If you aren't sure exactly what you'll be doing, make a sample itinerary. Will you be attending nice dinners? Will you be going zip-lining or doing other outdoor activities? Will you be exercising? Do you need business attire for meetings? Look up the weather for your destination and consider that as well. Once you've broken down your trip by activities and weather, envision what you could wear for each particular day and night. Lay these clothes out on a clean surface, such as your bed. You don't need a completely different outfit for each day, night, and photograph of your trip. Instead, make every piece of clothing count and pick items that can do double duty. Bring a few pairs of pants that all work with a few tops and mix and match throughout your trip. Pick like and complementary colors so you don't end up with a massive piece of **LUGGAGE**. Ladies, this means no extra luggage for your **SHOES**.

While what you bring really depends on what you are doing, where you are going, and for how long, there are some simple guidelines you can follow: Pack one or two tops per day depending on your activity. Pack one bottom for every three tops. Pack one bra for every two or three days. Always have one pair of **SOCKS** and **UNDERWEAR** for each day and bring one or two extra pairs of socks and underwear depending on your trip duration and your body type. If you have the room, pack a few extra shirts as well. Then pack specific outfits you know you'll need for your activities and weather. This could be a dress, a suit, **BATHING SUITS**, workout gear, a winter coat, and so on. You don't need three winter coats for your weeklong ski trip, or a bathing suit for each day of a tropical trip. Reuse a few bathing suits and save space in your luggage. You also don't need a new pool shirt or wrap for each day. Using this packing formula, a five-day trip shouldn't require more than seven tops, two pairs of pants (including the one you'll wear on the plane), one pair of shorts, one dress, and three **BRAS** if you are a lady, or a guy who needs some extra support up top. It should all be able to fit in your carry-on luggage if you don't want to check anything. In fact, if you pack like this, and have access to a washing machine, you never really have to check your luggage, no matter how long your trip.

P

Most people bring way too many shoes for a trip, and shoes take up the most space in your luggage. You don't need a different pair for every day and night. Just as with your clothes, pick a few shoes that work with the outfits you selected and based on your activities, and shoo the rest away. Wear your bulkiest shoes on the airplane to save space in your bag.

Your toiletries should be in their own self-contained **TOILETRY BAG**. You should always have this toiletry bag packed and ready to go, so buy doubles of the daily items you use. That way, you can always have a set in your toiletry bag ready to go. This will expedite your packing process: just grab your toiletry bag and toss in any prescription **MEDICINES**. Another timesaving tip: keep an extra phone charger in your luggage, ready to go when you grab it.

The biggest pitfall of packing is asking "what if?" This is a sure way to bring too much. If you know your potential activities and the weather, you'll know what you need to bring. Chances are you won't need that evening gown unless you've already planned to go to a ball or got invited to George Clooney's house. Another danger is feeling like you'll need "options." I understand that fashion is important, but you are traveling and some sacrifices have to be made. If you've picked clothing wisely that can be worn with multiple outfits, you'll still come off fashionable.

If you check your luggage and choose to bring an additional carry-on, think of it as your in-case-of-emergency, in-flight entertainment, valuables, and work bag. Use it for a full change of clothes and underwear, your **COMPUTER** and phone charger, a book, magazine, or tablet, and a short supply of any prescription medications, just in case your luggage is lost.

When you get to your destination, if there is space, unpack everything and iron or steam whatever you need to. You want to feel settled and be able to grab anything you want to wear without rummaging through your suitcase. The longer your clothes sit in your luggage, the more wrinkled they will get and look like they were used to practice origami. Unpacking in one specific area instead of all over the room will help you make sure nothing gets left behind when it's time to go. Bringing a garbage bag for your dirty laundry will make repacking your dirty clothing easier—you can squeeze the heck out of it and tie it off. If you simply refuse to unpack when you arrive, pack your luggage with the things you'll need least at the bottom and work your way up to socks and underwear at the top. If you can, keep your socks and underwear in the mesh compartment some luggage provides. You don't want to have to pull everything out to reach an essential item. Keep wrinkle-prone items on top, take them out immediately, and get them hung up.

If you're traveling to a foreign country or going on vacation where you know you will be shopping and bringing back some new clothes or souvenirs, don't forget to leave room for those extra items or pack a small duffel bag. If you are packing for a trip with some scheduling leeway, pack a few extra pieces in case you decide to stay an extra night or two.

Emergency scenario—you've packed your luggage and just can't get it closed, even with your spouse sitting on it. Here are some space-saving tips: Wear your bulkiest clothes and shoes on the plane. If you are bringing any equipment, like snowboards or golf clubs, keep clothes and accessories for that activity in your equipment bag instead of in your luggage, wrapped around your equipment. Getting that ski jacket and pants out of your luggage will save a ton of space, and it will also protect your equipment when in transit. Pack **BELTS** and accessories in your shoes. For bags without form, such as duffel bags, roll clothing. Fold it halfway and roll as tight as you can. Squeeze the air out of bulky jackets, roll them, and wrap them with a cord to keep them small and compact. If you still can't get your luggage closed, think about using something bigger or just bring less.

As soon as you get home from your trip, or within twenty-four hours, unpack, do **LAUNDRY**, and get your clothes, shoes, and accessories back in their homes. Refill your toiletry bag and put it away as well. Return your luggage to your designated luggage storage area and lament that your trip went by so quickly. Start planning the next one!

■ ■ ■ ■
AN O.C.D. SUMMARY

Organize: Think about how long you'll be going away on your trip. Check the weather reports for your dates and locations so you'll be prepared with what you are bringing. Make a list of all of your planned activities or create sample itineraries so you know what you'll need to pack.

Create: Select clothing, shoes, and accessories that can be worn with many different outfits. Everything you pack that can serve double duty means one less item you have to bring. Grab your prepacked

toiletry bag to take with you on any trips or overnights so you don't
even have to think about toiletries. If you plan on doing a lot of shopping, bring a small duffel bag in which to bring back your purchases.
If you are traveling with a carry-on bag, use it for in-flight entertainment, for valuables, and as a work bag. Keep a change of clothes and
underwear, your computer and phone charger, a book, magazine, or
tablet, and a short supply of prescription medications in it, in case
your luggage is lost.

Discipline: Don't play the "what if" or "options" game when packing. Pack only what you know you'll need for your activities and
weather. Unpack as soon as you get to your destination. Separate your
clean clothes and dirty clothes as you travel, and, if you can, do laundry before returning home. Unpack as soon as you get home.

PACKING FOR A MOVE (see MOVING)

PANTRY (see FOOD PANTRY)

PANTYHOSE (see UNDERWEAR)

PAPERS can be any documents that make their way into your home, **ARTI-
CLES** you want to keep, **MEMORABILIA** if it's something emotionally significant or valuable to you, or an accessory kept with your **MARIJUANA**. For
all papers other than rolling, the most effective way to organize your papers
is to scan them, save them in your **DOCUMENTS** folder on your **COM-
PUTER**, and back them up. You'll be able to search through your papers with
ease and create less clutter in your home. If you must keep actual paper,
keep it in a **FILING CABINET**, a memorabilia bin, an accordion folder in your
OFFICE, or a **SAFE** if it's sensitive information. If you carry paper with you
because it contains information you need to refer to, like paper **MEMBER-
SHIP** cards or insurance cards, keep a photo of it on your phone instead. It's
easy to e-mail if anyone needs a copy.

PASSWORDS should be organized and kept in your password-protected digital **ACCOUNTS** document. You can also use one of the many password-storing **APPS** on your smartphone. The only password you actually need to remember is the one to your accounts document or password-storing app, which makes it your passwords' password. I know we can all keep one password in our head, but make sure the one you choose is easy for you to remember. Any time you create or change an account or password, update your list. You don't want to write down passwords all over the place, making them less secure and easier to lose. Don't be cocky and think you can remember them all. You aren't Rain Man and you'll end up having to reset passwords frequently because you forgot. Most resets don't allow you to use a previous password, so you'll get into a pattern of creating more obscure and harder-to-remember passwords.

To create a strong password, you want to use a combination of letters, numbers, and characters. Know if the passwords are case-sensitive or not. The complexity of the password should depend on the sensitivity of the information it protects. You might wonder why not just use the same password for everything. If someone cracks it, they'll have access to your entire life. Mix it up but keep it easy to remember: have a base password and then complicate it as necessary. Use the simplest version for low-threat Web sites and social media, and the most complicated version for anything financial. For example, my password for Twitter could be OCDWAY712. My password for Amazon could be OCDWAY712$. My password for **ONLINE BANKING** could be OCDWAY712$$!!. Those aren't my actual passwords, by the way, so don't even try it! There are many ways you can set up your passwords, but the point is, don't make every password the same, but keep them easy enough for you to remember, and have a more secure password for the sites that need it.

Many Web sites will ask you to answer security questions to recover your password if you forget it. Choose the questions for which you know your answer will never change and add those answers to your accounts file. The name of your first pet will always be the same, but your favorite color may change. My dog will always be Taxi, but my color is only forest green for now. However, if you properly organize your passwords, you should never have to reset them. If you've picked strong passwords to begin with, you shouldn't need to change them, but if you do for peace of mind, change them every six months and update your accounts document.

■ ■ ■
O.C.D. APPROVED TECHNOLOGY

There are many options when it comes to password-storing apps on your computer or smartphone. I like the Keeper app, available for phones, tablets, and computers. It keeps your data secure with military-grade encryption, lets you backup your data to the cloud, and will self-destruct if anyone steals your phone and tries to access your information.

PET SUPPLIES and toys should be kept in a specific area in your home, on a **SHELF** or in a **BIN**. I know how much some of you like to pamper your pooch or puss, but try to keep pet supplies to just the necessities and only a few toys. Pets have basic needs—they don't care about brands and styles, except for maybe that Beverly Hills Chihuahua. Buy for your pets, not yourself. Pet supplies can emit an odor, so keep them in an area where the odor doesn't bother anyone, like the **GARAGE, LAUNDRY ROOM**, or **MUDROOM**, or just make sure you keep the bin sealed. It's also a good idea to wash your supplies often.

All food that comes in large bags should be poured out of the bag and housed in airtight **CONTAINERS** for easy access and to preserve freshness. Make sure you find a container that isn't too large, but big enough to house a bag and a half of your pet's favorite food. When you're running low, you can get to the store and buy a new bag but still have room to pour it into the container. Keep a measuring cup in the container to give your pet the proper amount of food every feeding. If you use canned food, make sure that you aren't overbuying. Cans can be kept in your **FOOD PANTRY,** or in your garage in a dry area if you buy in bulk. If you have numerous pets, then make sure to have separate food bins labeled to denote which food is for which pet.

Keep toys in their own bin labeled "Pet Toys" and make sure they stay separate from children's **TOYS**, because at a certain age, they all seem to squeak. You can leave one or two toys out for your pet to play with.

Tie a poop bag to your pet's leash or buy a leash with a built-in poop bag system. Replace it every time you get back from a walk, assuming your pet did its business. You never want to find yourself figuring out what to scoop up your pet's poop with. Also keep some baby wipes or a towel near the front door to wipe off your pet's feet before it enters the house. Paw prints are cute, but not on your carpet.

Being a pet owner requires the ability to discipline yourself as well as your pet. Always return toys and grooming products to your pet supplies area after using them. Pull hair from brushes so they are ready for next time. Clean litter boxes daily to prevent smells. Take **INVENTORY** of your supplies and restock as necessary so you never run out. Throw away destroyed toys and replace them if necessary. Stay on top of your pets' needs by being organized so you can focus on enjoying their company, tickling their bellies, and watching them chase a laser pointer around the **LIVING ROOM**.

■ ■ ■

O.C.D. EXTREME

I take my shoes off at the door because I don't want to track contaminants from the outside world into my clean home. Pets don't get a pass just because they are animals! Buy some pet booties and put them on your pets when you take them out. Take the booties off before they come back in.

PHOTO ALBUMS are slowly becoming obsolete as people begin to keep their photos digitally, but there is still something satisfying about creating a tangible album of photos from your trip to Rome or Wisconsin and thumbing through it on your lap. If you still like to create tangible photo albums, there are a few ways to get organized. At this point, you really never have to get any photos developed. Upload your photos to your favorite photo-hosting site and create digital albums that can be printed in high quality and mailed to you. This makes it easy to design great layouts and flow with your photos because you can simply drag and drop until you like what you have. The quality of a professionally printed book is incomparable to one of those plastic-sleeved photo albums. Not having to develop photos also takes a step out of the process, which is always O.C.D. approved.

If you can't get past that scrapbooking instinct and insist on developing your photos, do it as quickly as possible at your favorite store or through an online service. But think about your album first! Don't just print every photo on your **MEMORY CARD**. It's a waste of money. Import the photos from your memory card onto your **COMPUTER**. Then create a folder on your desktop called "To Develop" and only add copies of the photos you want to have in your album. Put a star next to photos you've printed on your photo program so you never accidentally print anything twice. You look great from that angle, but one print is enough. Now get your photos developed and all you have to decide is what order to put them in in the album.

Chances are that if you keep tangible photo albums, you have more than one. Keep them organized by date and event in a designated space or **SHELF**. Label the spine with a label maker, or fill out the card in the plastic sleeve. Try to always buy the same type of album for uniformity: your shelf will look much nicer. Avoid buying giant albums that become archives for multiple years or events: you want an album to bring you back to a certain memory or trip, not represent large periods of time.

Don't forget to look through your albums once in a while. That's the whole point! You can even keep one on your **COFFEE TABLE** for people to look at. You can rotate it as often as you choose, but keep only one out or it's not the O.C.D. Way and I'll have to confiscate your merit badge.

O.C.D. APPROVED TECHNOLOGY

Check out Mixbook online for an easy and affordable way to create custom photo albums. You can start with great templates or simply create your own vision with their easy-to-use interface that lets you import photos and save your works in progress. Once your vision is created online, you can purchase high-quality photo albums of all shapes, sizes, and finishes, as well as customized greeting cards, calendars, and more.

PICTURES (see DIGITAL PICTURES, PHOTO ALBUMS)

PLANNERS should be used as toilet paper in case of an emergency or as kindling in the event of a worldwide blackout. All joking aside, taking the time to update a handwritten planner every year is far from the O.C.D. Way. It's time-consuming and draining. Go digital! Why would you want to re-add everyone's **BIRTHDAYS** and anniversaries into your planner every year? Get them into your digital **CALENDAR** and it's done forever, and synced among all of your devices. If you are sentimental about your old planners, scan them and trash them. It might take a while, but it's better than keeping a bloated book for every year of your life. If you don't want to take the time to scan them, they can't be that important to you. The O.C.D. Way is a digital one: taking the leap now will be less painful than waiting another year and having another bloated book to scan.

AN O.C.D. SUCCESS STORY

A client boasted that she always bought the same exact planner every year, kept every single one, and could look back at any day in her life in the last thirty years and know exactly where she was. She was proud of her system and her discipline, even though it took up an entire shelf in her office. But she started to feel silly when I asked her how long it took her to transfer all of her important annual dates into her new planner at the beginning of each year. She felt even sillier when I asked her what would happen if she lost her planners to fire or water damage. She finally saw the O.C.D. light and moved to a digital system. We took the time to scan all of her past planners and backed everything up. She is now even more proud of her new digital system, especially because she only had to set it up once.

PLASTIC BAGS should be recycled when you get home. Even better, get reusable **BAGS** and save a plastic tree. If you keep plastic bags from a grocery shop or mall visit for other uses in the home, fold them and store them in a designated location or put smaller bags inside larger bags and hang them in a **CLOSET**. But don't be the person that has three hundred plastic bags under your sink. You'll never use that many bags before your next trip to the grocery store or mall. Keep an assortment of different shapes and sizes within your main storage bag, but consider going green and ditching plastic bags all together. Some supermarkets will even give you a discount to encourage B.Y.O.B.: Bring Your Own Bag.

PLAYLISTS (see DIGITAL MUSIC)

PLAYROOM (see CHILD'S PLAYROOM)

POTS AND PANS can be a good investment for the avid home chef or amateur child percussionist, but you don't need every shape, size, and material. You don't need sizes at the very large and small end unless you are hosting regular crab boils or want to cook a single Brussels sprout. You also don't need a nonstick, cast-iron, and stainless-steel version of every size. Buying that huge set might seem like a good way to save money, but in truth it's a waste because you don't need all that cookware. Think about how you really cook and buy single pieces or small sets as you need them. This will be cheaper and also save you space. You'd be surprised how many things you can prepare in a single, high-quality, medium-sized pot or pan.

As you add to your collection, make sure you don't keep old pots and pans because you're afraid to purge. Keep only what you use! You know what pot you haven't used in years. Donate the old pots to Goodwill or any donation center and make room for yourself to be able to put your cookware away more easily. Stacking pots and pans under a counter is an effective way to use your space. Stack them by size to maximize the space you have, largest pot on the bottom going up. Deep **KITCHEN** drawers can also be a great place for pots and pans. As for the pot lids, they can be tricky—to keep them with their parent or not? The pot/lid combination is much harder to store efficiently, so this is the one time I condone breaking up a family. Kids need to grow up sometimes. Keep the lids together in a designated **DRAWER** or in a **CABINET** with lid dividers and stack the pots and pans. The drawer under some ovens is also a good place to keep your lids.

If you are in desperate need of space, consider hanging some of the larger pots and pans on the wall or from the ceiling. This will also make grabbing them easier while you're cooking. Wherever you keep your pots and pans, make sure they are in close proximity to your range and oven. You don't want to waste time and energy grabbing supplies that should be close to where you actually use them. Don't get panned by the critics for where your keep your pots.

■ ■ ■
O.C.D. APPROVED TECHNOLOGY

Add functionality to your kitchen by mounting Magic Wall panels by Felix Muhrhofer. They are magnetic panels available in many sizes and finishes to match the design of your kitchen, even butcher block. You can stick pots, pans, knives, or anything made of metal to them and purchase magnetic accessories to add shelves or even a wall-mountable cutting board. Wall space will be dead space no longer!

POWER CORDS (see CORDS)

PURSES should be used for carrying around the things you need on a daily basis, not an annual basis, or never basis. To keep an orderly purse, handbag, or clutch, you should get in the habit of emptying it out after each day. I know, ladies—this seems daunting. But do you really like lugging around an unnecessarily heavy purse? Or holding up a checkout line searching for your **WALLET**? The nightly sort also provides you with a seamless opportunity to choose another purse for the next day. Fashionable and functional! As for those items collected on a daily basis, file or scan important **RECEIPTS** and throw away anything that you will not use or need again. Take all that loose **CHANGE** and put it in your change jar. **BUSINESS CARDS** should be immediately inputted into a digital system. Depending on how many compartments are in the purse, make sure that each compartment has a purpose (i.e., **MAKEUP**) and that you don't get them confused. Keep your favorite lip balm, a stack of your own business cards, and some gum and mints in each of your purses because these are items that can remain without having to be removed each night. Make sure the purse isn't stored in a warm place; otherwise the balms will melt and ruin your purse, making it forever smell of artificial cherry.

Your collection of purses, handbags, and clutches should be organized and properly maintained. All of your bags should be kept in one area so you always know where to find them. Ideally, your bags should be kept on a designated **SHELF**, organized by color, size, and occasion, in a dark, dry, cool area of your home with good air circulation. Leave enough space for each bag to breath (which prevents irreparable dye transfer), be seen, and grabbed without anything else falling down. This is the best way to preserve those expensive purchases. I don't recommend keeping your purses, handbags, and clutches in the protective felt bags they came with because you won't be able to see them, which means you'll forget them and will be less likely to select them. Instead, make sure you dust them on a regular basis. If you handle them gently, give them space, and keep them out of direct sunlight, you won't need the protective bag. If space is tight, an empty wall with hooks is also a great way to store your bags in a way that makes them easy to see and fun to choose. Hang each bag on a separate hook. If your bags don't have handles, like some clutches, keep them in a drawer, **BIN**, or on a shelf near your hanging bags, organized by color, height, and occasion. Be sure to put your bags back after each use and, once again, don't forget to empty them out on a regular basis.

Do a thorough clean of your purses every few months by emptying everything out and wiping the purse down with a moist cloth inside and out to get dust and dirt off, or by following the manufacturer's directions for care. Take any purse that needs repair to your local shoe and purse repair. This is also a good time to do a purse purge. Donate any purses you no longer use so the less fortunate can get a chance to know Marc Jacobs.

AN O.C.D. SUMMARY

Organize: Dump everything out of your purse and decide what it is you really need to be carrying on a daily basis. Find a better place for everything else. If you are organizing your purse collection, get rid of any purses you no longer use and get any repaired that are damaged but worth keeping.

Create: Designate each compartment of your purse for a specific item, such as cell phone, makeup, and wallet. This way you'll always know where to find them. Keep a duplicate set of lip balm, business cards, gum, and mints in each purse you own. Arrange your purse collection by color, size, and occasion, on a designated shelf in a cool, dry area that isn't in direct sunlight.

Discipline: Empty your purse out each night. Take the appropriate actions for the important items you collected that day—scan them or file them. Return your purses to their designated homes after use. Every few months, do a thorough cleaning of your purses, ensuring that they remain in good condition, and purge any you no longer use.

O.C.D. APPROVED TECHNOLOGY

Leaving your purses on floors, tables, or counters is a sure way to damage them. They'll get stained or stepped on. A designer label means nothing next to a boot print, unless that's the trend this season! Buy a purse hook, which is a small hook that comes in a velvet carrying case, and keep it in every expensive bag. Using gravity and the weight of your purse, they hang easily and securely off of any flat surface, giving you a safe place to keep your purse wherever you are.

Q

QUANTITY is the characteristic of an item that describes magnitude or multitude . . . or we can be less confusing and just say how much and how many. A multitude of any item in your home or **OFFICE** can become chaotic if not properly maintained or organized. The best example: bulk purchasing at a warehouse store like Costco. Most people head out to the store without thinking where they are going to put all the items they are bringing home. They are blinded by the good deal. Know your space and your **NEEDS**, so you know what quantity of an item you need and how much of it you can actually store. Do you have room for forty-eight rolls of toilet paper? If you don't, consider going in with a friend and each taking half of the pack. Bottom line: know your space and your needs so you can decide the quantity you keep of any item. Never let it work the other way around or let a good deal bully you into a toilet paper dilemma.

QUESTS (see TRAVELS, ROAD TRIP)

QUICKIES (see TIME MANAGEMENT)

QUOTES can motivate, inspire, and cheer you up, or make you jealous you didn't think of them. If you organize your favorite quotes from artists, politicians, leaders, celebrities, or the average person with a profound moment of wisdom, you can actually look back at them when you need to. Create a document called "Quotes" on your **COMPUTER** and save it in DOCUMENTS → INSPIRATION. Every time you read or see a quote that is significant to you, add it to the document. Include who said each particular quote. You may want to alphabetize the quote list by the first or last name of the person, or by subject matter. If you have a lengthy list, consider making a quote book of all of your favorite quotes, with some inspirational pictures or portraits of the people whose quotes you admire. It will make a great **COFFEE TABLE** book and keep you on track in difficult moments. "A journey of a thousand miles begins with a single step."—Lao-tzu

Q

R

RECEIPTS are among the usual suspects that hang out in **DRAWERS, DESKS, WALLETS, PURSES,** and **AUTOMOBILES**. Don't fall in with a bad crowd. It may seem like just a small slip of paper, but when you have dozens of them, they still create overwhelming chaos and a paper infestation. Create a great system for receipts and eliminate the pile from your life. Or use that junk paper to make beds for puppies. Your choice.

The biggest mistake people make is that they save every receipt. "Better safe than sorry" sometimes leads to sorry as well. When it comes to receipts, you really need to keep very few: receipts for larger purchases, anything with a warranty, items still within the return policy, and anything you paid for in cash that can be a tax deduction. But for anything you buy with a credit card or debit card, or online, you'll have a record of the transaction online and don't need to save the paper, unless the store requires it for a return or exchange. Using a credit card is smart: you can potentially earn things for your purchases, like airline miles. Less paper *and* you get to see London: it's a no-brainer! You can even designate **CREDIT CARDS** for different purposes: one for personal and one for business. This is the easiest way to stay organized because you'll know at the end of the year that all of your purchases can be found in your transaction histories and anything on your business card is deductible.

The best way to deal with incoming paper receipts is to either keep an envelope on your desk and mail them to your accountant twice a month, or, if you do your own accounting, keep a receipts box or a restaurant receipt spike on your desk and reconcile your **ACCOUNTS** weekly. If you go with the spike, try not to put it through your hand when you add a receipt. Shred whatever you don't need to save. Keep the rest, as outlined above, in a small and sturdy accordion folder. You can find them with the appropriate labels for receipts preprinted. If you can't, make your own: entertainment, donations, meals, purchases, and so on. For substantial purchases, you may want to keep the actual bill of sale, but also scan the receipt for backup purposes. This would include **JEWELRY, FURNITURE,** cars, and any and all major electronic purchases.

If you keep receipts for deductions, write on the back of the receipt what it was for so you or your accountant knows how to properly process them. If you keep your receipts for tax purposes—that is, in case of an audit—keep them in a clear plastic shoe box, seal it up at the end of the year, and label it. Keep the **BIN** anywhere you have storage space: it does not need to be easily accessible, but it should be with the bins from other years. If you do get audited, crack your bin open and dump your receipts over your auditor's head.

If you have a business whose **FINANCES** you maintain yourself, have two separate files for your personal and business receipts. You don't want to have to sort at the end of the year. If you need to submit receipts for reimbursement from clients, scan them and keep them in a folder specific to the project, unless the client requests the original.

If you'd like to take organization of your receipts to the next level, the O.C.D. Extreme level, go fully digital and scan your receipts, but only the ones you don't have a record of elsewhere. Many stores will also offer to e-mail you a receipt. Take them up on their offer. Hopefully, the receipts that you can't get online will be an insignificant amount, and scanning them won't take too much time. Save them in DOCUMENTS → MONEY → RECEIPTS, or if they are tax deductible, in DOCUMENTS → MONEY → TAXES → YEAR.

Make sure that you're constantly keeping up on your receipt filing so your receipts do not pile up all over your home or office. The more overwhelming the pile, the less likely you are to deal with it, and it will grow more and more out of control. Eventually, you'll have to deal with it one way or another; it's better to manage it in smaller, organized doses than swallow a gigantic pill. Keep up with your receipts and you'll never be hunting for a receipt ever again or live in a house filled with confetti from all your purchases. Keep it in the parades where it belongs!

■ ■ ■ ■
AN O.C.D. SUMMARY

Organize: Gather all of your receipts. Trash anything that can be found online or that you don't need for tax purposes, returns, or warranties. Write a note on the back of the receipts you keep to help you remember what they were for.

> **Create:** Put all incoming receipts in a receipts box or restaurant receipt spike on your desk, or send them to your accountant. At the end of each week, file or scan receipts that need to be kept and shred the rest.
>
> **Discipline:** Make sure your desk is clear of receipts at the end of every week. Stick to the system and never let receipts pile up. Use a credit card wherever possible to ensure there is an online record of the transaction so you don't even have to deal with a receipt.

RECIPES for those dishes that blow everyone's mind are precious and invaluable. I know I'd be lost without my grandmother's noodle kugel recipe, which only existed in her head until I added it to my organized recipe portfolio. It could have been lost forever! If you organize your recipes properly, not only will they be safe, but you'll be able to find them more easily and plan tastier **MEALS**. You can also ditch the stacks of cooking **MAGAZINES** you keep to find that one recipe you liked. But if you think a folder or **BINDER** full of loose clippings and handwritten notes is organized, you are wrong.

The goal is to have a recipe book, either kept in a binder or digitally, that organizes your recipes alphabetically by sections: appetizers, entrées, side dishes, and desserts. You can go one step further and divide each section by food type: chicken, beef, vegetarian, or pasta.

If you keep your recipes in a binder, use three-holed plastic sheet protectors and store the recipes in the protectors in the appropriate section. This will shield them from spills and drips while cooking. Anything that is handwritten or in your head should be typed and printed out. Create a table of contents on your **COMPUTER**, print it out, and keep it in the front of the binder. Update the file anytime you add a new recipe to the book so you will be able to find that triple chocolate brownie recipe quickly and easily.

You will discover that true power as a chef comes from keeping your recipes digitally. You can keep a searchable PDF of every recipe you have and keep it on your mobile device, organized just like the binder. Then you'll be ready to cook anytime, anyplace.

Scan ripped-out **ARTICLES** using OCR (text recognition) and save them as a PDF so the text is searchable. **BOOKMARK** recipes you find online and save them as a PDF. If you are on a mobile device, e-mail the link to yourself to create the PDF when you get home. If it's your own recipe, or passed down from Grandma orally, type it out as a Word document and save it as a PDF. All of your recipes should be saved on your computer in DOCUMENTS → RECIPES → DISH TYPE. Once on your computer, you can combine all of your PDFs to create a single, ultimate, digital recipe book that would show Wolfgang Puck a thing or two, or break them down into different PDFs, again by food or dish type. You can even create a table of contents that has "anchors." These are links that you can click on and they will take you directly to the page you are looking for.

Sync these PDFs to all of your mobile devices and you'll have your recipes backed up and with you wherever you go. An easy way to do this is to e-mail the PDF to yourself, open it, and save it on your mobile device. When you find a new recipe, maintain the discipline to add it to your PDF portfolio and sync to your devices. You always want the most updated version of your PDF with you so you can be ready for any **KITCHEN** throwdown or bake-off that comes your way.

Bon appétit!

■ ■ ■
AN O.C.D. SUCCESS STORY

One of my friends is a prominent chef. She had hundreds of recipes from various sources and kept them all in a single binder. She tried to organize it, but it was overwhelming. There were just too many different kinds of paper, some handwritten, some clipped, some printed, and some passed down through generations, wrinkled and browned. It was chaos in a binder. She could never find the recipe she was looking for and instead settled for the recipes she could actually find. We scanned, retyped, and reorganized her recipe bible, which now exists digitally on a tablet in a searchable format with a table of contents. As a result, she is able to make exactly what she wants instead of what she can find.

RECORDS, unlike **CASSETTE TAPES**, actually have a reason to be kept. Records hold their value, and nine out of ten purists agree that Pink Floyd's *Dark Side of the Moon* sounds better on vinyl. Records can also be viewed as art. Try hanging a cassette tape on your wall: it's just silly.

If the record has no value to you beyond the audio recording, digitize it using one of the cheap devices available for purchase online. Or just download the album online. But if you collect vinyl, it must be organized.

Get rid of anything you don't care about or that is damaged beyond playability. Organize the rest by artist, alphabetically, or by genre and then artist if you have a very large collection. Records are deep, so you may need to build custom **SHELVES** or buy shelves made specifically to hold your vinyl. Shelves may force you to section your collection, so do so smartly and make sure you put a label under each section, for example: "HIP-HOP: A-F." Make sure you leave some space to add to your collection.

If it's an especially valuable or signed record, keep it in a polyethylene sleeve. If you don't use the record, consider having it professionally framed and displaying it on your wall.

Now that you are organized, put on a record, throw on your bell-bottoms, sit back in your egg chair, and groove out. Just remember to put your record back in the proper place when you are done!

RECYCLING should be a constant and convenient habit in your home or business. We all love Mother Nature, at least as much as Mother Goose or Superior, and recycling is an easy way to help her out, but only if you have a good system. Depending on where you live, some states require you to separate your recyclables whereas others let you throw them all into one big bin. Know your local recycling program. If you don't need to separate your recycling, do not waste your time doing so. Either way, set up your recycling bin or bins in a common area of your home or **OFFICE**, such as the **KITCHEN**. Have signs on the specific bins if you need to separate paper, plastic, and metal. Constantly take out the bin, or give this **CHORE** to someone accountable, and empty it into your city's provided recycling receptacle or bring it to a recycling facility. Some will even give you a shiny nickel or dime for every can! Stick this in your **CHANGE** jar. The biggest reason people stop recycling in their home is because the **BINS** become too full and people don't take the time to empty it out. Keep on it, and remember: recycling doesn't just cover trash. Donating is also recycling. You can have a bin just for donations in your **GARAGE**: bring old **TOYS**, **GAMES**, **FURNITURE**, dishware, or anything else that can have a second life with someone else to charities when you're thinking about throwing it away. You'll get a tax deduction and someone will get that rice cooker you never use at a steal.

REFRIGERATORS should be cleaned out and organized every month. Otherwise you end up with science projects hidden in the back. Who hasn't pulled out a fuzzy jar of mystery sauce to absolute horror? It is important to take everything out so you know exactly what is in your refrigerator. Otherwise, you end up overbuying things or coming home without a key ingredient. Once everything is out, check the expiration dates. If anything is expired, toss it. If something's borderline, better safe than sorry. Food poisoning is a terrible experience. If there are items in the refrigerator that aren't expired, but you haven't used them in a while and don't plan on using them, toss them.

Once you have the items that you'll be keeping, separate them into piles: beverages, fruit, vegetables, meats, leftovers, condiments, and so on. Designate an appropriate place in your refrigerator for these goods. Don't be afraid to adjust your shelves to suit your habits. Some of the designating work is already done for you because many refrigerators have drawers specifically labeled for vegetables, dairy, and so on. That doesn't mean they are always right! Don't let your fridge boss you around. Many people are tempted to put condiments in the narrow section in the door, but if you keep them in a clear small **BIN**, you can remove the entire bin each time you need it instead of trying to grab and juggle six different bottles and jars. You'll drop one and cleaning relish off your **KITCHEN** floor is a pain. Using these bins makes cleaning out your refrigerator easier as well. Just pull out the bins, wipe down the shelves, and put them back. Once in a while, wipe down the inside of your bins too. Always keep items in the same place and discipline yourself to put them back every time. You'll know you're doing it right if you can go to your refrigerator in the middle of the night, grab something out of it half asleep, and then wake up in the morning to find everything in its place.

Make sure you have an extra **LIGHTBULB** that fits your refrigerator, as

R

well as a replacement water filter. Don't fool yourself into thinking you are drinking filtered water if you haven't replaced the filter in three years.

Having an organized refrigerator will help you create an accurate **GROCERY LIST** and will make cooking, eating, and refrigerating more fun.

■ ■ ■

AN O.C.D. SUMMARY

Organize: Pull everything out of the fridge. Toss what's expired or is questionable. Group similar items together.

Create: Designate spaces for your groups. Adjust your shelves to fit your needs. Put smaller items, such as condiments, into clear plastic bins so you can grab them all at once.

Discipline: Each time you use something, make sure it goes back into its designated space. Every month, pull everything out and clean your refrigerator.

■ ■ ■

O.C.D. APPROVED TECHNOLOGY

Recently, refrigerator manufactures have begun making what is known as "counter-depth" refrigerators, which are refrigerators designed to fit flush with standard cabinets instead of jutting out. Not only do these take up less depth in your kitchen, but they prevent you from forgetting about items that get pushed to the back and blocked by other things in a standard-depth fridge. French door units allow you to fit wider items, like trays of hors d'oeuvres or whole turkeys, whereas side-by-side refrigerators would not.

RELATIONSHIPS can be organized just like anything else in your life: some you should have, some need some thought, and some belong in the **GARBAGE**. Understand why you have certain people in your life and if those people add or take away from your life. Nurturing relationships is time-consuming, so before you spend any more time, make sure that relationship is a positive one. Prioritize the relationships in your life, practice good communication, and set boundaries with those people. Control your level of contact by using your phone and e-mail as a convenience to you and not as a habitual distraction: you do not always have to answer every call that comes through to you. Responding to e-mail in a timely manner has become standard in this day and age, but be aware of who you respond to and how quickly. People will develop expectations based upon your actions. Stay consistent with your behavior; it will force people to stay consistent with theirs. It is completely up to you whom you give your energy and attention to, but make sure people understand your priorities and **NEEDS**. Be clear, concise, and direct with anyone you have a relationship with, no matter how closely you are acquainted: it will only earn you respect, help you grow closer, or help you identify unhealthy relationships. Cultivate any new relationship from a place of honesty to create a strong foundation that yields positive and rewarding results. Be clear what your intentions are so that you never mislead people you care about or end up in an awkward situation saying no to a proposal on the Jumbotron at a Miami Heat game. Relationships are complicated, so there is no need to complicate them even more.

RELIGIOUS ITEMS can be stored with **HOLIDAY DECORATIONS** if they are specific to a certain holiday. Otherwise, designate a space in your home to keep your menorahs, statuaries, candles, challah covers, prayer rugs, drums, incense, or whatever else you need to practice your chosen religion, spiritual journey, or ascension to the astral plane. Ideally, this area should be close to where you use your religious items. As with anything in the O.C.D. Way, have what you need but don't be excessive: it will only take away from your focus. Make your most used religious items the most accessible. Keep your items cleaned and polished: the better you maintain them, the nicer it will be to pass them down from generation to generation. My menorah was handed down to me and it's a precious possession.

REMOTES should be a singular noun in each room: one room, one remote. Don't get plural! I know every device comes with its own remote, but having six remotes on your **COFFEE TABLE** looks ridiculous. No one without expert knowledge will be able to watch TV in your home! They'll pick up every remote, press buttons, change inputs, and then you'll have to forensically determine what they did wrong to get back to your **DVR**. Invest in an easily programmable universal remote. You plug them into your **COMPUTER**, identify which devices you have, and then the remote is programmed for you. You can store all those extra remotes with your **ELECTRONIC ACCESSORIES**. If you can't afford one, or can't figure out how to use it, only keep the remotes out for devices you use frequently. Put the rest away in a nearby and easily accessible **DRAWER**. If they are out, they will confuse someone. Also, know what **BATTERIES** your remotes take and always have extras on hand with your **OFFICE SUPPLIES** or electronic accessories so you never have to actually walk over to your television. It's like six feet away, there *and* back!

O.C.D. APPROVED TECHNOLOGY

Most smartphones can double as a universal remote these days. By buying some hardware and downloading the appropriate app, you can eliminate another piece of equipment from your life and have your phone serve as your remote. You can also repurpose an old smartphone or tablet. Logitech makes a device and corresponding app called Harmony Link, which works great. Buy the device for under one hundred dollars, plug in your model numbers on Logitech's Web site, and your phone will be the most powerful remote you've ever owned.

RESEARCH is tedious, whatever it's for. Don't add to the tedium by being disorganized and having to re-search for your research. Perhaps you're working on a term paper or just trying to find that perfect new car; you want your research to be easily accessible and searchable so you can reference it effectively to make your points or decisions.

If you are doing research on the Internet, create a folder within your favorites or **BOOKMARKS** for the subject you are researching, and save all of your sources to this folder. Title the bookmark in a way that reminds you of the relevant information that is on the page. If you pull research from **MAGAZINES**, scan the articles according to the guidelines in **ARTICLES**.

When doing academic research in a library, check out the book, take it home, use sticky tabs to mark pages with relevant information, and scan them. Also scan the publishing info for making a bibliography later on. Save these scans to DOCUMENTS → SCHOOL → NAME OF CLASS → NAME OF PROJECT. You can now return the book without worrying that you'll need it again, thereby giving that late-to-the-game student a chance to check it out. You can also start to reclaim your **DESK** from the tower of books you checked out in order to complete your **ASSIGNMENT**.

If you cannot check out the book, use your favorite scanning app on your **SMARTPHONE** to take scans of the relevant pages and publication info and e-mail them to yourself to add to the project folder at home. Once your project is complete, you'll be able to pull all of your bibliography info easily from your scans and bookmarks. Now you just need to figure out how to properly format a bibliography according to MLA style!

AN O.C.D. SUCCESS STORY

When I was in college, my roommate had a major research paper he was working on. He had what seemed like hundreds of books, marked with sticky tabs, all over his desk, the floor, and the windowsill. For me it was a nightmare! I scanned all of his articles for him, along with the publishing info page, so he could return the books to the university library, we could reclaim the space, and I could breathe again. His articles were now easy to find and search for on his computer, without having to move around books and thumb through thousands of pages.

RESPONSIBILITIES are any tasks you are accountable for, either to yourself or to others: **CHORES, ASSIGNMENTS, APPOINTMENTS,** feeding pets, picking up little Mikey, and so on. In the pace of today's life, chances are you could create an infinitely long list of responsibilities, so the key to organizing your responsibilities is to *prioritize*. What are absolute necessities for the day and what can be done at your discretion? If something has a set time, put it into your **CALENDAR** as an appointment. Otherwise, add it to your digital to-do **LIST** according to priority. If you find that you have a responsibility on your list that you keep missing or ignoring, try changing it up. For example, if you continually see "workout" from 9 a.m. to 10 a.m., and you never get it done, move it to a different time slot. If you *still* ignore your responsibility, it's time to have a frank conversation with yourself about discipline. The way you view your responsibilities has a direct impact on how you complete them, so you must see them as necessities. Start knocking off your responsibilities as quickly as possible, but don't forget to give yourself some time to relax! I firmly believe this is a responsibility to yourself. Seeing friends, maintaining **RELATIONSHIPS,** or just kicking back and watching a movie is a responsibility for mental health. All work and no play makes Jack a dull boy. But keep it in balance! If you find yourself killing a few too many hours in front of the TV, schedule your leisure time in your calendar with a set beginning and end time so you can stay disciplined and get back to your responsibilities. Little Mikey can't drive himself home from soccer practice! He can't even see over the steering wheel!

RIBBON adds the finishing touch to your wrapped gifts, baskets, and bouquets. Without ribbon, gifts just seem a little naked, so keep it as a staple in your **CRAFT ROOM** or with your **GIFT WRAP** so your gifts don't catch a draft. But there's nothing worse than opening a **DRAWER** or **CONTAINER** to find ribbon all over the place, as if a clown exploded. There are many options to organizing your ribbon, but what's most important is that you keep it with the rest of your craft or wrapping supplies in a way where it is never overflowing, creased, or damaged. You can buy ribbon organizers online or in stores to suit your ribbon collection needs, but at home DIY solutions are cheap and easy. If you have a craft room and use ribbon regularly, consider hanging a rod on the wall and keeping spools of ribbon on it for an effective and visual way to select your ribbon. Organize your ribbon on the rod by color, from light to dark. If you don't have a craft room, you can also mount rods in a shoe box, cut holes in the side, and pull your ribbon through. You can also just store your spools of ribbon in labeled clear, plastic **BINS.** For loose pieces of scrap ribbon that are still usable, store like-colored ribbon together in **PLASTIC BAGS** with the rest of your craft supplies. Don't be a ribbon pack rat—it's not worth keeping scraps so short you'd have to tie them with a pair of tweezers. Keep your ribbon collection organized and you'll blow people's minds with your fanciful wrappings!

O.C.D. EXTREME

Most people like to give gifts wrapped specifically for the occasion they are giving it for. This means having a lot of different gift wrap and matching ribbon in your home. If I can save space by having things serve multiple functions, I will. I only keep one roll of plain gift wrap and one spool of matching ribbon. It works for all occasions and I don't have to devote much space to it. Sometimes a simple wrapping can be just as beautiful as an ornately wrapped gift. It's understated elegance.

ROAD TRIPS are one of the best ways to experience a country. You'll see off-the-beaten-track places and jaw-dropping rest stops you'd never see traveling by plane as you bond with friends or family in the cozy space of your car while listening to great **MUSIC**. Half the adventure is being spontaneous, but that doesn't mean you get to be disorganized! Road trip organization begins with a plan.

Where are you going? How long do you have to get there? Where would you like to stop? How much are you willing to drive each day? Make a map of your road trip route and mark any stops you'll be making. Don't worry—this is just a framework. You can deviate from it, but it will help you decide what to bring. I like to use Google Maps to make my route because it allows you to set markers and breaks down your directions between stops. You can then upload your route to your phone, and now even your car. Designate some markers as guaranteed stops so you can book some lodging in advance, but allow yourself the freedom to deviate between guaranteed markers. Make your reservations at these guaranteed stops so you'll know you have a bed to recharge in.

Once you know your destinations and activities, you can decide what to bring. Will you be swimming? Camping? Hiking? Pack appropriately, but remember—you have limited space in your car, so see **PACKING** for the most effective ways to decide what to bring. If you are going on a long road trip, car chargers for any electronics you bring are a must. If you don't have GPS, bring a road atlas in case your phone isn't getting reception and you get lost. We've all seen those horror movies where people get lost in the woods with no reception and encounter a gang of inbred cannibals. Inbred cannibals are entertaining on-screen but will ruin a road trip by dismembering you, so stay clear by being prepared!

Clean your car thoroughly before leaving. The feeling of getting into a clean car where everything has its place will be comforting and soothing. To make sure you have a trash solution while on the road, keep a grocery bag for trash and empty it at every stop. You'll be spending a lengthy amount of time in your car, so keep it a sanctuary. Packing and using baby wipes is an easy way to stay clean on the road. You can wipe down the car, as well as other areas in emergencies, as necessary. Accidents happen.

The week before you leave, check out your car and make sure that all of your fluids are topped off, that your tires are inflated, including your spare, and that everything is working properly. Eat, drink, shower, fuel up, and use the restroom before you leave. Don't be like my friend Burl who has to pee ten minutes into the trip and kills the momentum before we even get going. Pack some snacks and drinks for the road, but don't go crazy because you can always restock along the way.

Carefully plan some entertainment to help everyone stay energized on those long stretches of road. Make playlists, bring a small DVD case or pre-loaded **iPAD** with **MOVIES** for your kids or impatient friends, and look up a few road games to play along the way. I'm a Punch Buggy master. Staying entertained will keep up morale. That being said, be smart about whom you invite: nothing reveals how you really feel about a person like a road trip.

When packing up the car, it's all about accessibility. The things you'll need frequently, such as snacks, drinks, entertainment, diapers, cameras, and jack-ets, should be easy to grab. Everything else should be packed according to how often and how soon you'll need it. Don't keep anything in the car that isn't a necessity for the time spent in the car while driving.

Preparing for a road trip is all about thinking ahead and making sure you are ready for anything that comes your way. Don't overpack, and leave room for the spontaneity that makes a road trip so memorable. How else would you have ever ended up with that photo of you and Ewan McGregor at that chinchilla farm?

O.C.D. EXTREME

On a road trip, the inside of my car looks as if it just came from the car wash. I maintain this appearance throughout the entire trip by requiring everyone to be on his or her best behavior when eating or drinking in the car. I do a mini-clean at every rest stop and gas station, where I make everyone get out, dispose of their trash, and shake out their floor mats. I wipe down all of the cup holders and side-door compartments. Then I clean the front and back windshields. Gentlemen, start your engines!

RUGS are usually on your floor and don't require organization other than putting the right size rug in the right size room. Done. Move on to the next entry. But if you have more rugs than rooms and need to store them, I suggest taking pictures of the rugs, rolling them up, wrapping them in clear polyurethane bags, and taping the pictures to the outside of the bagged rugs along with the dimensions so you don't have to unroll the rug to know what it is. Keep a master list of the rugs you have. When you wrap the rug, make it as sealed and airtight as possible to prevent damage. Keep the rugs in an area that's protected from the elements. If they are extremely valuable, you may want to keep them in a climate-controlled storage facility. When you decide to use the rugs again, think about having them professionally cleaned before putting them back in your home. The O.C.D. household is a shoeless household, but if people wear shoes on your rugs, it's a good idea to have the rugs professionally cleaned/repaired every few years to keep them looking their best. Don't just sweep them under the rug.

RV organization is a combination of **APARTMENT** and **AUTOMOBILE** organization with the mind-set of a **ROAD TRIP** and worse gas mileage than a 1960s Cadillac. You'll need a basic set of everything you'd need in a small apartment: **LINENS**, plates, cups, cookware, silverware, **CLEANING SUPPLIES**, toiletries, food, and drink. You'll also need the items you'd keep in an automobile for emergencies, such as important documents and jumper cables. But you'll also need the Zen mind-set of a road trip: take only what you need, for the people you are bringing, and keep your RV clean! Wipe down surfaces often and take out the trash regularly so you don't pick up infestations along the way.

As with any small space, utilize your wall space. Magnets and hooks will be invaluable to add storage for those smaller but frequently used items. Use Velcro to keep **REMOTES** and other small accessories attached to the wall or table where you can always find them. Designate spaces for **LAUNDRY** and **GARBAGE** and make sure everyone respects the rules. RVs tend to have a lot of hidden storage areas. Make sure you utilize these spaces, but define them for a specific purpose and have it make sense for the location of the space. For example, the hidden storage under the bed can be used for extra linens and towels. The space under the dining bench can be used for board **GAMES**.

Most RVs have great storage space underneath. After checking for stowaways, use this area for large items you don't need while driving. Stock it with all of the equipment you'd use for activities once you've set up camp, such as **GRILLS**, propane, fishing poles, badminton sets, or whatever else you are planning on doing. You can also keep extra supplies and paper goods in labeled clear plastic **BINS**. But again, bring only what you need. Just because you have the space doesn't mean you need to cram it full of anything and everything.

If you are making the move from a brick-and-mortar home to a mobile unit, think about how **DOWNSIZING** is going to affect your lifestyle. If you are buying an RV in addition to your home, or renting it for a road trip, stock it with only the things you need. Remember, you are in a mobile home: you can drive up to any Big Mart, Bargain Barn, or Buy-N-Eat in any city and purchase anything you need.

AN O.C.D. SUCCESS STORY

One of my O.C.D. Experience team members moved her parents into an RV while they were between homes using principals from the O.C.D. Way. This was obviously a major downsize for them. While it was uncomfortable at first, her parents quickly realized that with their possessions properly organized, they had everything they needed in their small but cozy space. Once they returned to their brick-and-mortar lifestyle, they realized that they didn't even need most of the stuff they had put into storage. Sometimes living more simply is living more fully!

S

SAFES are meant to keep your most precious items secure from thieves, snoops, bandits, burglars, robbers, crooks, criminals, little brothers, and disasters. The name "safe" says it all. So use it for things that need to be kept safe and don't store things in there just because you don't know where else to keep them. Your safe should be used for important **DOCUMENTS** or copies of documents, such as your passport, driver's license, **CREDIT CARDS**, deeds, wills, and titles. It should also be used for expensive

JEWELRY and extra pieces of jewelry, such as watch links, high-value COL-LECTIBLES, a set amount of cash in case of emergency, and precious met-als. It's also smart to keep a spare set of all of your KEYS in your safe, as well as a HARD DRIVE backed up with all of your important data. If you keep a weapon for home defense, it also belongs in a safe, along with some ammo. You can keep it in your regular safe, or buy a separate gun safe, ideally with a fingerprint scanner in case anyone ever figures out the password.

Safes aren't generally built for organization, but try to designate shelf space for specific purposes and keep like items together. Believe it or not, companies do make organizational tools for safes, so check those out. It's a good idea to figure out what you'll be keeping in your safe before you buy it so you can buy the right size. Whatever safe you purchase, make sure it's fireproof. If your home burns down, your fireproof safe will be like a treasure chest of your valuables and give you a jump-start on rebuilding your life. Drill your safe into your floor. Don't assume a thief won't take the whole thing to crack later on just because it's heavy. Thieves work out too, you know. When you are desperate and on a breaking-and-entering adrenaline rush, a little heavy lifting is a minor deterrent.

Keep your combination in your password-protected accounts file on your computer or in your smartphone PASSWORD app in case you ever have a brain fart and can't remember it.

If your safe has a key, MAIL the spare set of the keys to a relative or trusted friend and hide the others in separate set locations in your house. Do *not* keep them on your key ring. If you worry about forgetting where they are hidden, you can keep this information in your ACCOUNTS file as well, or draw yourself an old-fashioned treasure map so you know the keys are forty paces north and six skips to the right of your DISHWASHER. There is no reason to take your safe keys out of your home and risk losing them or having them stolen.

Keep your safe in an infrequently accessed part of your home, such as the back of your CLOSET or your BASEMENT. Don't keep it in any guest areas. If you have the money, consider building a safe into your wall. With some proper planning, your most precious possessions will be kept safe in your safe, so you can feel safe knowing they are safely secured in such a safe place: in your safe.

SCARVES are fashionable and functional—a fun accessory that keeps your neck warm and also hides that hickey. Scandalous! Depending on the size of your scarf collection and available space, you have a few options. First, seperate your fashion scarves from your winter scarves. Your winter scarves should be kept near your other winter accessories, such as your coats.

Hang your scarves in your **CLOSET**, color-coordinated. If you have only a few, you can use hooks or even mount a towel bar on the back of your closet door to hang them. If you have many scarves, hang them on **HANGERS**, three or four to a hanger, tied so they don't slip off, or buy scarf hangers. There are many O.C.D.-approved scarf hangers that are functional, orga- nized, nonslip, and effective. But before you buy anything, make sure you know how many scarves you have and how exactly you'll use this accessory.

Alternatively, you can designate a **DRAWER** for your scarves and *roll* them. Don't fold scarves because it makes taking them out of your drawer very difficult without making a mess.

Like all the **CLOTHES** in your closet, go through your scarves once a year and get rid of any scarves that you no longer wear or that are in poor shape. Keep your collection organized and your neck will make all other necks jealous.

and over again. I told her to roll her scarves instead of folding them, and place them side by side. She did, and her drawer stayed clean and organized. The end result: she wore more of her scarves, making her more fashionable and more excited about fashion. Sometimes simple changes have big effects. Trusting in the O.C.D. Way, even when it seems like a sidestep or a silly change, will surprise you.

■ ■ ■ ■

SCREWS (see NAILS)

SEX TOYS should always be clean and ready to use. Make sure you store them in a place that is protected enough so kids won't find them: either high up, out of reach, or locked. Explaining the birds and the bees is hard enough without having to explain why Mommy and Daddy have a purple silicone penis under the bed. If you have a large supply of sex toys that can't be kept in a bedside **DRAWER**, get a box that can be locked and kept under your bed. Pick out a box together. You can even personalize it. Discipline yourself to clean (follow the manufacturer's instructions) and put away your toys right after they are done being used. Also, organize them neatly, as you would your **TOOLS**, arranged in the same direction with some space between. There is nothing sexy about a mixed-up pile of sex toys. Like anything exciting in life, there comes a time when it gets boring. Go through your toys and get rid of any that no longer do it for you. Don't *ever* keep a toy that you've used with an ex. Make sure you have extra **BATTERIES** somewhere close by. Nothing kills the mood like frantically searching for a triple-A battery in the heat of the moment.

■ ■ ■

AN O.C.D. SUCCESS STORY

It's happened many times on the job that I stumble across "the box" in an odd place. Guest closets, kitchen cabinets, I've seen it all. Usually the client isn't around, but every so often, I'll be standing right next to them. They are embarrassed, but I quickly relieve their embarrassment by telling them that everyone has a box like this. What they *should* be embarrassed about is that the box is out of reach, dusty, and underused. Organization knows no shame, only that everything has a function and should be placed to maximize that function. I encourage them to choose a more readily accessible location for their toys. I get a lot of referrals, so I must be doing something right.

SHEET MUSIC is a musician's bible, and even the bible is organized! If you are a singer or an accompanist, this entry will be especially helpful to you. Create a master **BINDER** with a table of contents. The table of contents should list each song in the binder, the artist who made the song popular, and who wrote the music and lyrics. Alphabetize by song title or artist name. Keep your music in clear sheet protectors, with a page of music showing on each side, but don't print on both sides of the paper: you want to be able to pull out each sheet individually. Keep the table of contents up to date as you add or remove music from the book. If you have a collection of music songbooks, organize them alphabetically by artist or name of group or show. Keep them in a designated space on your **BOOKSHELF**. But if you only use one or two songs from a songbook, scan the songs you want and sell the book on **eBAY** or donate it to a library to save space. Take the songs you scanned from the book, print them out, stick them in sheet protectors, add them to your binder, and update your table of contents. Also, before you buy an entire songbook for a few songs, check online: there are now many sites that let you download sheet music for individual songs, even letting you transpose the key. Print them out and add them to your binder. If you find yourself running out of space in your sheet music binder, you can always start another one and split the alphabet between the binders: A–M and N–Z. Make sure you are always updating the table of contents and that you are taking songs out of the book you won't be playing, singing, or needing in the future. You'll always be ready to play or sing at any impromptu jamboree, hootenanny, jam session, festival, performance, jubilee, or department store lobby.

O.C.D. APPROVED TECHNOLOGY

Pretty much everything is available digitally these days, and sheet music is no exception. Musicnotes.com offers downloadable sheet music for almost every instrument, will let you change the key, and will even let you play the music online to decide if you like it. You can redownload any previously purchased music, so you'll always have a digital backup of your purchases.

SHELVES are either my favorite space or most-hated horizontal nightmare. Because they are so visible, and usually high up, a well-organized shelf makes me feel like everything is going to be okay, but a mess of a shelf is distracting and oppressive. Shelves should be organized with a "less is more" mentality. The less you have on a shelf, the easier it will be for you to find what you are looking for on that shelf. Additionally, shelf space should be designated, specific, labeled, and maintained that way. For **BOOK-SHELVES**, have your books and perhaps a picture or two on the shelf. For supply shelves, it is crucial that supplies are neatly arranged so they don't get out of hand. You should be able to locate a specific supply without being distracted by clutter and disorganization. Labeled **BINS** and jars will be essential for small and loose items. For display shelves, give your decorative or meaningful items room to breathe and to be featured and seen. Nothing detracts from the emotional value of an item like burying it in clutter. Keep your shelves clean by dusting them once a week and continue to purge items you no longer need or don't have space for. Every three months, take everything off the shelf, do a thorough cleaning, and take the opportunity to really question what you are keeping. Don't let shelves become multipurpose storage spaces for stuff you don't know where to put. Stay disciplined so you don't have a distracting, oppressive shelf hanging over your head! The more you overload your shelf, the greater the risk something can fall on you, and that decreases *your* shelf life!

S

249

AN O.C.D. SUCCESS STORY

Most busy households have a lot of shelves that become dumping grounds for anything and everything. It's too easy to allow shelving space to become vague storage space. I worked with a family full of repeat shelf offenders and bought them a label maker. I made them label every shelf for a specific purpose! It may seem like a nuisance to label your shelves or strange to have labels on display in your home, but think of them as training wheels to develop discipline. You can always remove them later, after you've developed good habits to maintain the integrity of each shelf, which is exactly what happened with my clients. Their kids would fight over who got to label the next shelf. Kids love to play with label makers, making them a great tool to teach children organizational skills. When I introduce label makers to families, it always helps them to maintain organization.

■ ■ ■ ■

SHOES. Shoes, shoes, shoes. You've heard the phrase, "Walk a mile in their shoes," but that doesn't mean your shoe collection should stretch for miles. Shoes can and will take over any closet or floor area, especially when you buy shoes without considering your available space or without getting rid of old shoes to make room for the new.

To organize your shoe collection, you must know your space so you know how many pairs of shoes you can fit. Measure the linear **SHELF** space of your dedicated shoe-storage area. Shoes come in all different widths, but in general, sneakers will be your widest shoe and take up eight inches of space, so you can fit about seven pairs of sneakers in five feet. Heels will be your narrowest and should be placed with one toe facing out toward you and one toe facing the wall, toe to heel, to save space. Placed like this, heels should only take up five to six inches. This will also allow you to see the front and back of a pair of heels when dressing.

If you have more shoes than space, you'll need a solution: get rid of shoes, build yourself a new shoe-storage area, create a new system, or amputate one foot so you can throw out half your collection. Luckily, I've never had to resort to that last one with a client. Go through your shoes and donate any you no longer wear or need. You should be doing this at least once a year. This is a good time to take any shoes that need repair to the cobbler. If you still need more space, add shelves to your **CLOSET**, buy wood or metal shoe racks to keep on the floor (the plastic ones break), or find other places in your home for shoe storage, such as purchasing a small **WARDROBE** specifically for your shoe collection. I hate those door-hanging shoe solutions because they swing around every time you open the door and they rarely fit a pair of normal shoes, so if you have to use this solution, try to keep only flats and sandals in it. If you build shelves, design them in multiples of eight inches wide so you can always fit a complete pair of shoes instead of getting left with space for only a single shoe. Never leave a foot soldier behind! Also consider the height of your shoes and design your shelves accordingly. Measure your tallest pair of heels and boots to make sure you have enough space between shelves for your collection. People always forget to consider their boots, leaving no space to adequately store them. The last thing you want to do after spending hundreds of dollars on a pair of Louboutin boots is to shove them into a space where they don't fit. If you buy a lot of shoes, think about redirecting your spending and invest that money to build yourself a great shoe organization solution. This doesn't have to be expensive. Your local handyman or carpenter can build shelves much more cheaply than specialty closet companies can. Going the professional route can be a good solution if you have the cash, but have a few experts come in to give you their thoughts and bids before you select one. The O.C.D. Way is to have enough space for all of your shoes in your closet, visible and accessible, plus some room for a few new pairs.

Now that you have the right number of shoes for your space, it's time to organize them. Unless you are extremely lucky to have a closet with a large dedicated shoe wall, or you are Jennifer Lopez with a giant in-wall rotating shoe jukebox with a digital selection system, chances are you won't be able to keep all of your shoes together. You may have to keep some or most in a less accessible location, such as on your top shelf, on the floor, or even in another room or closet. If this is you, divide your collection by how often you wear your shoes. The shoes you wear the most should be given the prime real estate, which will be the most accessible location in your closet. These will probably be your work shoes, exercise shoes, casual shoes, and your other favorite pairs. If you wear a pair of shoes at least once every two weeks, they belong in this category. Organize them by type and then by color. Arrange the types of shoes from lightest to bulkiest—that is, from heels to sneakers—to create an organic flow for your shoe collection.

The rest of your shoe collection should be kept in the area designated for your less frequently worn shoes. Again, organize them by type and then color, ideally from lightest to bulkiest. Most important, *ditch the shoe boxes*. This goes for all your shoes. They take up too much space and don't let you see your shoes. I can't tell you how many times I've been on the job, opened up a shoe box, and had my client proclaim, "Whoa! I forgot I even had those!" Shoe boxes are a shoe coffin. Don't let your shoes rest in peace before they've had a chance to live! The same goes for shoe bags. You need to keep only enough bags for the most shoes you'd pack for your longest trip. Keep your shoe bags inside another shoe bag along with any other shoe accessories in a **BIN** in your closet. If you have a lot of those "special" high heels and value them like you would value a priceless antique, keep them in a place that is safe from water and dust collection or make sure they are being dusted once a week. If you absolutely can't stand the idea of your expensive shoes being exposed, keep them in clear plastic bins. If you really want to go O.C.D. extreme, take a picture of the shoes and stick it on the front of the bin. If you have very large shoes that don't fit in your shoe area, such as tall boots, keep them wherever you can, but all together. If it bothers you that they won't stand upright, stuff the boot with tissue paper or spare bags so they hold their shape.

You should also have a shoe rack in your **ENTRYWAY CLOSET** or shoe storage in your **ENTRYWAY** to keep a few pairs of everyday shoes used by you and your family and to provide people a place to put their shoes when they take them off at the door. If you live in a home with four people or more, limit the amount of pairs per person to two pairs each. You may also want to keep two pairs of flip-flops in the front for people to kick on and off as they grab the **MAIL** or take out the **GARBAGE**. If you take off a pair of shoes at your door that belongs in your bedroom closet, make sure you return it to its proper home immediately and don't leave it in the entryway closet or entryway.

Organize your shoes the O.C.D. Way and you'll have a closet worthy of a *GQ* pictorial or a *Sex and the City* close-up. How did Carrie Bradshaw afford all those shoes, anyway?

AN O.C.D. SUMMARY

Organize: Pull out all of your shoes and get rid of the ones you no longer wear. Repair what needs repairing. If you don't have room for all of the shoes you've decided to keep, which can be determined by measuring your space and then your shoe collection, it's time to make tough decisions and only keep your favorites. Donate the rest.

Create: Build shelves, buy shoe racks, or find other areas in your home to designate for shoe storage. If you can't keep all of your shoes in a single area, divide your collection by frequency of use and keep the most frequently worn shoes in the most accessible location. Arrange your collection by shoe type and then by color.

Discipline: Return shoes to their proper place when they come off your feet. Don't leave them at the front door or around the house. Ditch the shoe boxes and bags and dust your shoes regularly. Every year, or every time you run out of shoe space, go through your collection and get rid of what you no longer wear.

■ ■ ■

O.C.D. EXTREME

Create a digital master list of your entire shoe collection with photos of each pair, brand name, heel height, and date of purchase. This will make it easy for you or your styling team to pick shoes without having to go in your closet. Keep your list updated any time you add or remove pairs from your collection. Save your list as a PDF to bring with you on your smartphone or tablet when out shopping so you can make informed purchases based on what you already own.

■ ■ ■

SHOPPING LISTS remind you what you need buy when you are out so you don't forget to pick up a baseball glove for your child yet again. Don't make him start the season with a loaner! A shopping list should be kept simple and on your **SMARTPHONE**, just as you keep all of your **LISTS** in the O.C.D. Way. The real trouble people have with a shopping list isn't its organization, it's having the discipline to keep a running list and routinely knock items off that list. Similar to a **GROCERY LIST**, a shopping list will help you make sure you get what you need. Keep the list active: as you go about your day and things occur to you, add them to your list. Don't include unnecessary information about the items on your list: if you already know where to buy your **SOCKS**, you don't need to write "buy socks at Sock Mart." Just simply put "Socks." If you are buying for members of your household, include their name and any size info on your list. If you are buying a lot of items from a single place, like a trip to the hardware store, create a separate list for Hardware Store. Only add items to your shopping list that you *must* buy. It's not the place for that pretty little dress. That should be on a separate list for discretionary purchases, along with that video game system, fancy watch, and trampoline. If you are having trouble checking items off your list, set **APPOINTMENTS** in your **CALENDAR** to go shopping and get it done.

O.C.D. EXTREME

Keep a list of measurements on your phone for all members of your household. Update it as they grow, gain, or lose weight. You'll always know what size to buy when you go shopping, which will save you from having to go back to the store to return items that don't fit.

SMARTPHONES aren't yet smart enough to organize themselves without your help. Smartphone organization encompasses a lot of areas like **PASS-WORDS**, font preferences, **CALENDAR** view options, alarm reminders, app organization, **ADDRESS BOOK**, tasks, and memos. These all require attention and familiarity, so experiment with settings to figure out what works best for you. Don't be afraid to change things up—it's always easy to restore the default settings if you somehow put your phone in Chinese.

Phone organization is specific to each person, but there are four things to keep in mind: uniformity, discipline, functionality, and simplicity. The more uniform the entries are in your phone, the more easily searchable they will be. The more disciplined you are in keeping everything uniform, the more functional your phone will be. The simpler you keep your phone, by not downloading too many **APPS**, for example, the calmer you will be using it. If you have numerous cell phones in your life that you know you will never use again, donate them to one of the numerous organizations that accept cell phones, but make sure you wipe them prior or someone else may end up with some intimate pictures that were only intended for you! That's not the kind of goodwill you meant to give to Goodwill!

O.C.D. EXTREME

I keep a backup smartphone charged and ready to go just in case I break or lose my current phone. All I have to do is stick in my SIM card or get a replacement SIM card and I'm back in action. You'd be surprised how handy an extra phone can be in case of emergency.

SMARTPHONE APPLICATIONS (see APPS)

SOCIAL NETWORKING is becoming so prevalent in our everyday lives that it now requires organization. These days people are expected to belong to Twitter, Facebook, Pinterest, Instagram, the dating Web site of their choice (I like OCDlovers), and, of course, whatever the next big thing is. Even MySpace is making a comeback. All of those sites then have friends, **APPS**, followers, matches, feeds, messaging, streams, pictures, privacy settings . . . OH MY!

It's easy to get overwhelmed quickly by information overload. Obviously, the first place to start is to ask yourself which sites you really need to belong to. If you can eliminate any sites from your life, it will be that much easier to keep them organized. Also, you don't always have to sign up for that new site: many sites will let you join by logging in with your credentials from another social networking site.

Once you've boiled down your social networking sites to the essentials, create a social networking folder in your **BOOKMARKS** and bookmark them. On your phone, create a folder for social networking apps. This is an easy way to keep track of the sites you belong to. Keep the usernames and **PASSWORDS** for those sites in your **ACCOUNTS** file. Visit them at least once a month to make sure your profile information is current and so that you can respond to any messages sent to you. You may have given up on that dating site, but the "one" may have sent you a message and you are letting him or her get away! Then you'll have to look for the other "one."

Depending on how important your social networking is to your life, consider creating a new e-mail address specifically for social networking so that you don't clutter your **E-MAIL IN-BOX** with unnecessary notifications and updates. Add that to your accounts list as well. Alternatively, you can change the notification settings on your accounts to receive only the information you want.

Twice a year, go through your friends/followers' list and delete anyone you no longer have an interest in. This will keep unwanted information out of your feeds. You don't really need to know what your childhood acquaintance cooked for dinner, even if it was really delicious-looking veggie tacos. Resist the urge to add everyone and every company your social networking site suggests.

Remember, once you put something out on the Internet, you might not be able to take it back. So always consider the repercussions on your work and social life from anything you post. Never assume those worlds won't collide, because they will, and then everyone at work will know you are lousy at doing keg stands.

SOCKS are the unsung heroes of the clothing world. They spend all day in the dark getting walked over and trampled on, never complaining. Show your gratitude by reorganizing them every three months. Take everything out and see what is being worn, what has been hiding in the back and never touched, and what has holes or stains and needs to go right into the trash. Ball up your remaining socks by folding one matching sock around the other. Place them in rows in your sock drawer, organized by type and color. They should all be in a single layer to keep them all visible. Try to buy the same brand and type of socks over and over again to keep your sock drawer looking as uniform as possible. This also makes it easier to find matching pairs after doing **LAUNDRY**, so find a brand of socks you like and stick with it. You can even buy your socks online and have them shipped to your home. When a sock loses its mate, you can hold on to it with the hope that the other half will show up, but only until the next time you do laundry. If it doesn't turn up after that, look for a pair that is more worn out and replace one of the socks with the newer one. Instant upgrade. Throw away the worn-out sock or turn it into a dust rag or a puppet. Most people have too many socks at any given time, which makes sock drawers scarier than they have to be. Think about it: you probably do laundry at least every two weeks. Even if you wore two pairs of socks a day, that'd be twenty-eight pairs of socks. You certainly don't need more than this, so if you are a sock hoarder, it's time to sack some socks and save some space.

O.C.D. EXTREME

Every year, I throw away almost all of my socks and start fresh by buying all new socks. I love the feeling of putting on a brand-new pair of cushy socks. New socks can help preserve the life of your shoes and also keep your feet and shoes smelling fresh. Who doesn't appreciate odor-free toes? If someone doesn't, they are no friend of mine!

SPICES are the secret to transcendent flavor, but they have a way of hiding in your **KITCHEN** so you can never find the one you are looking for. Don't set yourself up for a freak-out searching for the coriander while something is boiling over on the stove. Cumin is a lousy substitute! Get your spices organized and be a better chef!

Every kitchen is different: some offer built-in spice storage and others will require that you purchase a spice solution. Whatever your setup, the goal is to keep all of your spices together and to be able to find and grab any spice without having to move any other spice out of the way. If your kitchen has a built-in solution that works for you, use it! Try to buy the same brand of spice to make your spices easier to organize and more uniform in appearance. If you need to create your own solution, designate a **DRAWER** near your stove for your spices and lay them out with the labels facing up. This makes it easy to grab what you need and put it right back without knocking anything over. You can also purchase tiered spice shelves that go in your **CABINET**, or racks to keep on your counter or to mount on your wall. These are inexpensive solutions and can be found at any kitchen supply store. Always keep your labels facing out so you can identify your spices. Another solution is to keep your spices in a basket or **BIN** in your **FOOD PANTRY** or dry foods area. Label the top of each spice with a black permanent marker so that when you are looking from above, you know exactly what's what. You can simply grab the basket when it's time to cook. If you want to be really tech-forward, buy magnetic spice jars and keep the spices on the side of your **REFRIGERATOR** or on the wall-mountable magnetic panel that comes with some magnetic spice sets.

However you choose to keep your spices, return them immediately after cooking. If you are low on a certain spice, add it to your **GROCERY LIST** so you are never without an ingredient for that next **MEAL**. Pretty soon, you'll be cooking like an Iron Chef.

■ ■ ■

O.C.D. EXTREME

I always buy the same brand and size when it comes to spices so my jars look uniform. I also keep my collection alphabetized. As soon as I'm done using a spice, I wipe down the jar to remove any food residue gathered during cooking and place it back into its proper home in the alphabet. There's nothing worse than grabbing a spice bottle coated in grease and spice, touching your eye, and going temporarily blind while sautéing vegetables.

SPORTING GOODS can become sporting bads if you keep them in chaos. They should be kept organized in your **GARAGE**, if you have one. Equipment can be stored in labeled **BINS**, placed on labeled **SHELF** space, or mounted on the wall on pegboards or hooks, whatever works best for the equipment. For example, hang baseball bats, skis, lacrosse sticks, and your golf bag from the walls to save floor space for other things. Loose items such as balls, Frisbees, helmets, and baseball mitts can be stored in plastic bins, separated by type. Balls can also be kept in mesh laundry bags hung from the wall, next to a mounted pump. This will keep them from rolling away and will make cleaning up easier. All you or your child has to do is throw the ball into the bag. Keep the pump attachments nearby in a **CONTAINER**. Bikes can be hung from walls or the ceiling to keep your parking spots open. If you have the space and want to keep your bikes on the ground, make sure that they have a designated parking spot just like your car.

Camping supplies need to be maintained in the same way you maintain your car. When they are done being used, rinse them off, clean them out, and get them ready for their next outing. Keep all of your camping supplies, such as tents, sleeping bags, lanterns, first-aid kits, cookware, and your cooler, together. Depending on the size of your cooler, you can even use it as storage for your other camping gear, like that gorilla suit you wear to prank your friends at night in Yosemite.

If you have more than two tennis rackets, make sure you have a tennis bag to transport them in. You should keep extra balls and replacement grip tape in your tennis bag as well. That way, you can just grab your bag and be ready for the next Wimbledon. The same goes for your golf bag. Everything you need for golfing should be in your golf bag. Make sure you have an adequate supply of balls, your glove is in good condition, you've trashed all those broken tees and replaced them, and your golf shoes are clean. Clean your clubs after each outing on the course. You don't need to save every scorecard you've ever filled out. If you had a particularly great game, take a picture of the card or scan it and save it in DOCUMENTS → MEMORABILIA.

If you don't have a garage, designate a space in your home for sporting goods, such as a **CLOSET** or a section of shelf in your **MUDROOM**. Use the wall space in your closets to hang rackets, helmets, and other equipment. If you have a small **APARTMENT**, you'll probably have to make some harder choices or get creative by wall-mounting your bike or turning your golf clubs into a decorative focal point. But chances are you can't be equipped for every sport and activity. You'll know you don't have the space if you're trip-ping over your sporting goods or having to walk around them. Sell, donate, or get rid of any equipment for activities you no longer take part in. Just because you used to scuba dive eight years ago doesn't mean you need to keep two tanks in a closet in your cramped apartment.

Whatever equipment you keep, make sure it's maintained and that you have enough for your family and your guests to play. Nothing ruins a Sunday like being short a croquet mallet and telling Auntie Gertrude she has to watch from the sidelines. Poor Gertrude.

AN O.C.D. SUCCESS STORY

I helped a client organize his garage. He had all of his sporting goods spread across the garage with no rhyme or reason and without easy accessibility. As part of his garage makeover, we added an industrial shelf and designated a section of his wall to store, hang, and mount sporting goods. Months later, I ran into him at an event. He was fif-teen pounds lighter. He told me it was because he was actually using his now accessible sporting goods. Every time he pulled into his garage, he'd see his sporting goods on the wall and get inspired to be active.

SPORTS CARDS should be kept organized by sport in labeled **BINDERS** filled with card sleeves, organized by set, card number, and year. No need to save the chewing gum. It's probably crunchy by now anyway. If you idolize a certain player, you can devote a section of your binder to that player and keep his or her cards in that section organized by year. As your collection grows, you can easily add new card sleeves because you are organizing by date. If you are trying to complete a set from a previous year, leave spaces for those missing cards so you don't have to move all of your cards over when you finally obtain them. If you know a card is extremely valuable, keep it separate in a hard plastic case in your **SAFE**. Store loose cards that have yet to be organized in an airtight **BIN**. This will protect them from the elements until you get them in a better place.

If you are a serious collector with a very large collection, catalog your col-lection and use card boxes instead of binders. After you get organized, cre-ate a document that lets you know what sets, players, and card numbers you have. You can also note the **QUANTITY** you have of each card. This will make it easier to buy, sell, or trade cards as you can reference your catalog instead of flipping through your massive card collection. You can even keep your list with you on your **SMARTPHONE** as a PDF in case you come across any buying or selling opportunities while out and about. If you keep your cards in card boxes, stick index cards in between sets so you can locate a specific set or card quickly. Label the boxes with their contents—that is, year and set—with a label maker.

Let's be honest: for most of us, when we were collecting sports cards, what was our intent? We collected them either because we idolized the player or thought the cards would be worth a lot of money. Now that we are older, we can make some decisions. If you no longer idolize that player, you don't need to keep the cards. And most cards didn't grow in value like we'd hoped. Let's come to terms with that reality. Set yourself a price threshold, let's say ten dollars, and look up your card values on the Internet. Whatever is worth less than ten dollars, donate, use in an art project, or give to that kid down the street who never seems to blink. I gave away a card of some guy named Mickey Mantle I didn't care about, but my neighbor's son seemed really happy to have it. Kids are so cute, aren't they? A smaller collection takes up less space, is easier to organize, and leaves you only with high value or sentimental cards.

STORAGE UNITS can be the basis of an exciting reality show, or a dangerous tool for organizational procrastination. People take whatever they don't want to deal with, shove it in a storage unit, and put it out of their minds at the expense of their **WALLETS**. If you use a storage unit, it should be for a specific reason and for a predetermined amount of time: transition between homes or **APARTMENTS**, during a move, during **TRAVEL**, or for students going home over the summer. Some people also use storage units to house **INVENTORY** for their businesses.

Whatever you use your storage unit for, make sure to keep it organized. You will benefit down the line if you know exactly what contents are in your storage unit and you never have to search for anything. The trick to this is to keep a master list of anything that goes in and out of your storage unit, just as you'd do if you were **MOVING**. Keep like items together, or organized by room if it's the contents of your home. Wrap **FURNITURE**, **RUGS**, **ART**, **ANTIQUES**, and anything else you want protected in plastic. If you are storing a **REFRIGERATOR**, crack it open so as not to create a perfect environment for mold, unless you are trying to create your own antibiotics. Use heavy-duty clear plastic **BINS** to store smaller items and number each container on all four sides so you can spot it easily and can match it with its contents on your master list. This will make searching for things fast and simple. If you are stacking your bins, think ahead as much as you can and put the bins you'll have to access more frequently on the top of the stack so you won't have to move unnecessary items. If something is very heavy, keep it on the bottom for safety reasons: you don't want a heavy bin crushing your belongings below it, or worse, falling on your head. You killed enough brain cells in college. If you have a very large storage unit, make sure to leave yourself access paths between items so you can reach everything in your unit without traversing an obstacle course.

If you use a storage unit for business purposes, treat it like you would a storeroom in your own **OFFICE**: make sure you know where everything is, that everything is labeled and organized, and that you've set it up in a way that works for you, adding **SHELVES** and whatever other systems necessary to help you use the space efficiently and effectively.

Having an organized storage unit will make it much easier to access your belongings when you need them and simplify the process when it comes time to move out of it. There *should* come a time when you move out of it. Tell your storage unit it's been nice, but what you had is gone and now it's time to see some other spaces.

O.C.D. EXTREME

If I had a storage unit, which I don't, I'd keep a master list of everything in it. But that isn't O.C.D. extreme; it's just good practice. I'd also draw a map of the entire storage unit showing the exact location of all of my possessions. That way, I wouldn't have to look around to find that particular box. I'd just consult the map, which I scanned and filed, on my portable device and go right to it.

STUFFED ANIMALS can turn a room into an overcrowded fluffy zoo. Avoid the plush colorful stampede. Although stuffed animals can bring a child comfort, there is a limit to how many stuffed animals are appropriate. They shouldn't be covering the bed or lining every surface in the room. Every parent wants to give their child the best and make their child feel loved. Don't make the mistake of assuming this requires **QUANTITY**. Make a couple of stuffed animals special rather than showering your child with thirty unimportant sacks of cotton.

If you've already gotten yourself into a situation where your child's room is more animal than air, ask your child which animals they love and why, and which animals they may be willing to give to a friend or to someone who doesn't have any animal friends. Then keep only a select few animals on the bed, the ones they sleep with and have a special bond with, but no more than three. Keep another five on a shelf to rotate with and another three to five in a bin for playtime. There is no reason to have more stuffed animals than this. When your child is old enough to understand, teach him or her that each time they get a new stuffed animal, an old one needs to be given away. Limiting the amount of stuffed animals you give your child will teach them that their possessions are special and only increase their love for Benny the Snail and their stuffed bunny, Bunny.

■ ■ ■ ■
AN O.C.D. SUCCESS STORY

I walk into many homes in which children's toys and stuffed animals are overflowing all over the place. The kids have no idea what they even own. Once I get to know my clients and get them to trust me to discuss belongings with their children, things come into perspective. Children know what they want. It's incredible how they tell you straight to your face that they don't want half the stuff you are organizing for them. I'm always amazed when I give children a bag and tell them to put stuffed animals they no longer want in it. In three minutes, the bag is full. Within minutes of that bag being out the door, the child is playing with the stuffed animals they decided to keep. I'm training a brand-new army of tiny O.C.D. Team Members!

SWEATERS are usually a seasonal item, so they shouldn't be given a prominent location in your bedroom **CLOSET** unless it's the appropriate season, you live in the North Pole, or you have a very large closet. If you have a smaller closet, keep sweaters in clear **BINS** on your top shelf when not in season. When it is sweater season, stack your sweaters on **SHELVES**, in canvas bins, or in hanging sweater organizers. This will all depend on your space. Arrange them from light to heavy. Keeping sweaters in **DRAWERS** is a waste of drawer space because most drawers cannot house more than five or six sweaters. If you have no closet space, roll your sweaters and file them in your

DRESSER as you would your **T-SHIRTS**. Like any **CLOTHES**, make sure you go through your sweaters yearly, or any time you purchase new sweaters, to figure out what can be donated. A good time to do this is when you pull your sweaters out to clean for the upcoming season and reorganize your closet: take note of what you didn't wear last season. If you don't wear it this season, or it still doesn't win the ugliest Christmas sweater contest, get it out of your life.

■ ■ ■
O.C.D. APPROVED TECHNOLOGY

If you are tight on storage space for your winter clothing, consider buying a vacuum bag system for your puffy jackets and sweaters. Vacuum bags reduce your winter clothing to a fraction of the size for easy storage and keep them safe from dust and bugs. You may just need to iron or hang your sweater for a bit when it's time to break the seal.

T

TASKS (see RESPONSIBILITIES)

TAXES can be done the right way, the wrong way, or the *really* wrong way. The really wrong way is not saving any records and just guessing when it comes time to do your taxes. This robs you of valuable deductions or, worse, puts you at risk of an audit, penalties, or even jail time. You are way too pretty for jail.

You probably already know the wrong way to do your taxes: saving every scrap of paper that enters your life throughout the year and then spending days before taxes are due sorting them into what's relevant and what's not. It gets the job done, but what an organizational nightmare! Do your taxes the right way, the O.C.D. Way, which means being organized all year long, spending small amounts of time weekly versus a year-end Hail Mary. Wouldn't it be nice to send your taxes to your accountant on January 1?

In order to master tax organization, you *must use financial planning software*, especially if you don't have an accountant or business manager. Get yourself Quicken or QuickBooks, or use an online service like Mint. Like any new system, it may take some time to set up initially, but it will make your life so much easier and teach you more about your taxes. You simply input all of your **ACCOUNTS** information into the program. Every time you log on to the program, it will automatically download your transaction history from bank accounts, **CREDIT CARDS**, and investments, pulling every debit and credit you've made throughout the year. The only work you have to do is to add a description for each transaction and tell it what category to put it under. For example, if I went to Krispy Kreme to discuss the sequel to this book, I'd open up my financial planning software, see the credit card charge for Krispy Kreme, describe the transaction as "Book Sequel Discussion," and categorize my delicious doughnut as a "Business Meal." To keep transactions fresh in your mind, you should be logging on to your planning software every couple of days, but at least once a week. Otherwise, you might forget what a transaction was for. To combat forgetfulness, write descriptions on paper **RECEIPTS**, keep them in a receipts box on your **DESK**, and make sure you go through them weekly. This is also the time you'd manually enter in receipts from any cash transactions. Really try your best to make all of your purchases on credit or debit card so that you always have a digital record. Then you can shred the receipt. If you want to save receipts just to be safe, scan them and save them in DOCUMENTS → TAXES → YEAR, or toss them in a plastic shoe box that you seal up, label with the year, and store for seven years, which is the amount of time you can be audited for any specific tax year. Credit card statements are sufficient proof for the IRS for auditing purposes, so saving your receipts is really playing it safe.

If you stay on top of logging on to your planning software, at the end of the year your tax prep work is already done: you simply plug the totals into your tax return or send the file to your accountant. Trust me, your accountant will be elated to see how organized you are, and you might even see some tax prep savings if your accountant charges by the hour. If you don't, just feel good knowing you made an accountant's day a little easier.

As for all those tax documents you receive toward the end of the year, like W-2s, 1099s, earnings statements, and charitable deduction records, those should be scanned as you receive them and saved in DOCUMENTS → TAXES → YEAR and then sent to your accountant as well.

After you or your accountant completes your taxes, make sure you keep a digital copy of your tax return with all supplemental materials for seven years, and, of course, backed up on another drive. Ask your accountant to digitize your entire return and send you the file. Otherwise, scan it. Some-times, in order to rent an **APARTMENT** or acquire a loan, you'll have to provide copies of your tax returns. Having them on file will make sending them quick and easy so you can lock up that apartment with two tandem parking spots and a walk-in closet.

You have the power to change the nightmare that is doing your taxes. Stay organized throughout the year and you won't even care that it's tax time. While everyone else is scrambling to get their taxes in on time, you can be focusing on your business or your taxidermy hobby. Taxes don't have to be taxing.

AN O.C.D. SUMMARY

Organize: Go through all of your existing receipts and get rid of any that aren't relevant for your taxes or are documented elsewhere. This will pretty much just be cash receipts. From this point on, only keep receipts that fit these criteria. Process your receipts weekly instead of waiting until the end of the year to go through them all. Consolidate all of your account information for every account in your life. If you followed the instructions in the accounts entry, you already have this information ready to go!

Create: Choose a financial planning program. Store all of your account information in your program so it can download your trans-action histories when you log on. When it's time to deal with your cash receipts, enter your transactions into your program to keep your finances current and accurate.

Discipline: Log on to your program at least once a week to input transaction information. Scan other tax documents as they come in. At the end of the year, do your taxes or send it all to your accountant. Make sure to keep a digital record of your tax returns for seven years.

TENNIS RACKETS (see SPORTING GOODS)

THANKSGIVING is a time to be with family and friends, give thanks, and massacre turkey. If you will be a guest in someone's home, you are off the hook, so simply offer to bring a dish and a bottle of wine. If you are hosting your own Thanksgiving meal, you must be organized so you don't lose your mind. Start planning ahead! Invite people to your feast early and get confirmations so you know exactly how many people you'll be cooking for and how much food and drink you will need. In general, count on a pound and a half of turkey per person and half a pound of potatoes. These are generous amounts, but this is America and we are talking about Thanksgiving here! If you feel comfortable doing so, ask your **GUESTS** to bring side dishes to lighten your cooking load on the day of.

Like any holiday, the trick is to do your shopping early to avoid the last-minute in-store chaos and sold-out ingredients. Early means earlier than those who think they are doing their shopping early, at least two weeks early for nonperishables. Reserve your turkey so you get exactly the weight you need.

On Thanksgiving Day, success is really about **TIME MANAGEMENT**. Get your table set early! Have I said early yet? Do it first thing in the morning or even the night before. That way, you can focus on cooking. From here, it's really about knowing what time your guests are arriving so you can start cooking your dishes on the appropriate time schedule so everything comes out as hot as possible. Having your **RECIPES** organized and ready to go is a must. Consider creating a simple cooking schedule for the day: turkey in at twelve, casseroles in at four, potatoes at five, sleeping at nine. Whatever you can prepare the day before, like pies, do it! Unless you want a nightmare at the end of the night, clean as you go or assign someone the duty of cleaning. That's my personal favorite task because not only do I get to clean, but I get to start burning off the calories from my decadent **MEAL**.

The last twenty minutes before you actually serve the food are the most hectic. Know how you want to serve your food: buffet style, family style, or plating in the **KITCHEN**. Have a game plan for where each dish will go and preset any service utensils you'll need in those locations. When the turkey comes out of the oven, rest it for fifteen minutes in tinfoil and use this time to set out all of your side dishes and make your gravy. Present your turkey, get your oohs and aahs, and then carve the turkey as the very last task so it's as hot as possible.

After the main meal is done, clear the table, accepting any help offered, and start bringing out desserts, fresh plates, and clean silverware. While you prep for dessert, your assigned cleaning person can get a head start on the dishes until dessert is officially served.

Then . . . relax. Your work is done. Sit, have another glass of wine, eat some pumpkin pie or sweet potato pie (however you get your pie on), and enjoy the fruits of your labor: a successful, joyous feast with friends and family.

TICKET STUBS should only be saved for nostalgia or creative use. Otherwise, don't assume the paper cut risk. Scan them and save them in DOCUMENTS → MEMORABILIA → TICKET STUBS titled with the event and the year, or incorporate them into an art project to hang on your wall as a talking piece. Keep them in a small plastic **BIN** or **ZIPLOCK BAG** until you are ready to do your project. I create, frame, and hang colorful collages made from my ticket stubs. Each stub has its own unique story, which helps me reminisce about all the adventures I've had during certain periods of my life. I've got some stories to tell, but that's another book.

TIES prevent your head from floating off your neck during times of stress. If your job requires a tie so you don't lose your head, you probably have a decent collection. Tie organization is simple: they should be color-coordinated and kept that way. Take all of your ties and spread them across your bed. Get rid of any that are stained or worn out, give away any ties you don't wear, and then group the rest by color. Figure out how much space you will need for all of your ties with some room for your collection to grow. Buy a tie rack or two that can be drilled into the back of your **CLOSET** door or a wall in your closet. Place your ties on your tie racks from light to dark. You'll be astonished how good your tie collection looks and how much more fun it will be to pick out your tie for the day. If you want to get fancy, buy a motorized tie rack, but make sure you invest in a quality one—the cheap ones always break. Alternatively, you can roll your ties and keep them in a drawer. If you are designing your closet, closet companies make **DRAWERS** specifically for ties. However you keep your ties, make sure at the end of the day that you place the tie back where it goes in the color spectrum. Do yourself a sartorial favor: learn your Windsor knots!

TIME MANAGEMENT is vital for maintaining a healthy balance in your life. We can't control time, but we also can't let it control us. Between work, hobbies, **RESPONSIBILITIES, RELATIONSHIPS**, health, exercise, and relaxation, we've all got a lot to juggle! The only way to keep your job, stay healthy, and keep your spouse happy is to have a good system in place for managing your time.

The most important thing to keep in mind is to be realistic with yourself about how long it takes you to do things. You haven't gotten ready to go out in "ten minutes" since you were ten. You need to be able to predict your time requirements accurately, or no amount of scheduling will ever be helpful. This is different for everyone, so knowing yourself and being honest with yourself are critical. Having a watch, clock, or timer on your phone helps when you do a task. Take note of when you start and when you finish. As time goes on, you'll be able to more accurately allot the time you need to complete certain tasks. If you eliminate distractions prior to beginning a task, you'll be more efficient with the use of your time.

Now that you know how long it takes you to do things, you must schedule the things you want to accomplish in your **CALENDAR** by setting **APPOINTMENTS**. Take any travel time into account since we haven't figured out how to teleport people yet. A good rule of thumb is to try to leave an hour between appointments for breathing room in addition to travel time.

If you know how long it takes you to do things and keep it in your calendar, you'll clearly be able to see if you can take on more responsibility in your life. A huge problem people have with time management is that they simply bite off more than they can chew. You can only chew so much before you start to choke on that time burrito. Before you say yes to anything, look at your calendar. Do you really have time for it? There aren't unlimited hours in the day or days in the week, and you don't want to have to flake on things. If something is in your calendar, have the discipline to follow through on it. Though you can't see it or hold it, your time needs to be prioritized and organized just like any other limited space. You wouldn't buy more cans than you can fit in your **FOOD PANTRY**, so don't agree to more things than you can fit in your time.

If you are a parent or manager, you are probably responsible for managing other people's time as well. The same philosophy applies: know how long it takes your children or employees to accomplish a task. Create a calendar for them and teach them the discipline to stick to it. If they aren't accomplishing tasks as quickly as you think they should be, guide them by showing them a better method.

Most important, don't forget to make time for yourself! Even if something isn't serious, schedule it like it is. Hobbies, relaxation time, and quality time with loved ones are important to your mental health and just as important as your work and responsibilities. Discipline yourself to have fun by setting up appointments for those hobbies you've been missing in your life. This will help you stop squandering time as well. Think about how many hours you waste watching TV because you have nothing set to do in your schedule, unless you've scheduled "Watch TV." But if you add something to your calendar, even if it's silly, like "Make a Movie Starring the Dog," you are much more likely to do it! Use this philosophy to create a balance for yourself and bring a glow back into your life. Following through on those more arduous tasks will seem less daunting because you'll know you have scheduled time for yourself to do the things you enjoy.

The more organized you are in all areas of your life, the faster you'll accomplish tasks and the more time you'll have. At its core, the O.C.D. Way is all about saving you time so you can be more efficient, more effective, and live a simpler and healthier life! Isn't it about time for that?

AN O.C.D. SUCCESS STORY

One of my clients was using a wall calendar to manage the schedule for her husband, her six kids, and herself. I praised her for using a calendar but explained to her that it was inefficient to write down repeat events over and over again. It was also problematic because she couldn't bring the calendar with her when she went out. This forced her to keep the day's schedule in her head. I showed her how to take advantage of a smartphone calendar and created individual calendars for each member in her family. We taught her children how to add in events so everyone could always be aware of each other's schedules. She's happier, less stressed-out, and much more on top of her family's schedule than ever before. She uses the time saved to grab some much-needed personal moments of peace.

TO-DO LIST (see LISTS)

TOILETRY BAG should contain anything that you use on a regular basis in your normal life: toothbrush, toothpaste, floss, cotton swabs, tweezers, moisturizer, razor, shaving cream, anything else in your grooming routine, and hopefully deodorant. You should always have this toiletry bag packed and ready to go, so buy doubles of what you keep in your **BATHROOM** and

MEDICINE CABINET so you can always have a set in your toiletry bag. Purchase small three-ounce bottles and fill them with your favorite products to make your toiletry bag carry-on friendly. This will expedite your **PACKING** process for a trip: just grab your toiletry bag, toss in any prescription **MEDICINES**, and you are good to go. Don't keep **MAKEUP** in your toiletry bag; that should be in your daily makeup bag. Also, don't combine your toiletries and your **JEWELRY**: keep your jewelry and accessories in their own small felt bag or shoe bag. Once you create your toiletry bag, it should live in your home forever in your bathroom or **LINEN CLOSET**, restocked and refilled after each trip. You'll never toil over packing your toiletries again.

■ ■■■
O.C.D. EXTREME

Every few trips, I completely empty out my toiletry bag, shake it out, wipe it down, and vacuum it out. Little hairs and fingernail fragments tend to lodge themselves in there and build up. If left unchecked, you could end up with a full set of fingernails and an entire beard in there. Gross!

TOOLS are your way of proving to your spouse that you are handy, but you won't be giving anyone a hand if you can't even find your screwdriver. Tools have a way of being used and never finding their way back to a designated location. Choose a place to keep all your tools, no matter how small or large your arsenal!

For most of us, keeping a basic toolbox, and maybe a small battery-powered drill, in a designated location is all we need. Once you've designated a space, perhaps in your **UTILITY CLOSET**, **LAUNDRY ROOM**, or **GARAGE**, it's time to organize it. Keep your drill with all the accessories near your toolbox. Have two batteries and always keep one charging. Whenever you grab your drill, swap out the batteries. As for organizing the toolbox itself, collect all of the tools you have around your home so you can consolidate them into your toolbox. Most toolboxes have three sections: a top section with small compartments, a middle section with a removable tote, and a bottom section.

Use the top section for **NAILS**, screws, nuts, and bolts. Go to the hardware store and pick out a few standard sizes of nails, screws, nuts, and bolts that can handle most repairs around the home. You can designate one compartment for assorted hardware of all sizes, but just one. Don't get in the habit of saving every little random screw you find around the house.

The middle section, which is the removable tote, should store the most basic tools you'd use for home fix-it scenarios: a flat head and a Phillips head screwdriver, a box cutter, a hammer, superglue, an Allen wrench set, a regular wrench, pliers, electrical tape, and some Velcro. These are the tools you'll have to reach for most often. Just make sure that whatever you put in the tote, you can still close the lid properly. Unless someone is there to laugh at you, you don't want to reach for a toolbox, have it pop open, and spill your tools all over the floor.

The bottom of the toolbox should be used for bulky items, larger tools, and less frequently used tools, such as a staple gun and extra staples, a small saw, gloves, a tape measure, wood glue, a small amount of twine, and duct tape—you get the idea. Try to store your tools in such a way that you can access everything without having to rummage through the entire box or take everything out. If you have children, buy a toolbox with a lock and keep it locked.

For larger industrial toolboxes, use the same rules as above. Remember, just because you have more space in your toolbox doesn't mean you need to fill up every bit of that space. The space will still be there when you have a real need for it. If your toolbox offers organizational features beyond the basic three-section system, take advantage! Just organize your tools by how often you use them and make sure everything is accessible and has a designated home.

Be disciplined about what you put in your toolbox and where you put it. Don't just throw things in it because you don't know where they should go or don't have the patience to find them a home. Always return tools to their proper home in your toolbox and return your toolbox to its proper home in your house. You'll always be ready to leap to the rescue when a faucet is leaky, a cabinet door is loose, or something's in need of gluing.

If you are a person with skills beyond the basic tool owner, and thus own a large collection of tools and power tools, you are going to need to pick a place in your home to be your tool station with adequate space that is out of reach of children. This will probably be in your garage or a toolshed. Set up your station with an adjustable chair, a good work light, a power strip or surge protector, and an industrial fan.

For your regular tools, keep your basic set on a pegboard mounted on the wall. Outline each tool so you always know where it goes. For the rest of your tools, organize them by type in a tool chest with labeled sliding **DRAWERS**. If you buy a rolling tool chest, make sure it has wheel locks so you don't end up chasing it into your garage door. Nuts, bolts, screws, and nails should be organized by size and kept in labeled jars or in a screw organizer with the small **BINS** labeled by size and type. Make sure that when you notice a particular supply is getting low that you add it to your **SHOPPING LIST** and restock it.

For power tools, ideally have them set up and ready to use, but unplugged. Live tools can make someone cease to be alive. If you don't have the space, keep them in plastic bins or in their cases stored out of reach of children on designated **SHELVES**, labeled for each power tool.

For very large tools and accessories, like saw horses, chain saws, rakes, shovels, and ladders, hang them on the wall. If you can't, as is the case with a lawn mower, give it a parking spot that will serve as its permanent home and outline it with paint or tape.

If you organize your tools and maintain the discipline to always return them to their proper homes, you'll never be in a situation where you can't complete a task because you can't find the tool you need. You don't ever want to feel like a tool because you can't find your tool.

O.C.D. APPROVED TECHNOLOGY

I'm a sucker for simplicity and added functionality. That's why I fell in love with the Step 'N Store toolbox from Stack-On for a small portable toolbox. Not only is it a toolbox; it also doubles as a step stool. Complete those out-of-reach repairs by grabbing a single piece of equipment from your garage or utility closet.

TOYS seem to be reproducing when you aren't looking because you couldn't possibly have purchased that many for your child! But you did, or you allowed gifts from family and friends to clutter your child's life. Just as with **STUFFED ANIMALS,** you should teach your children to value their possessions. Show them how to keep their toys organized, and don't give them an overabundance.

Designate a place in your **CHILDREN'S BEDROOM** or **CHILD'S PLAY-ROOM** for toys. Each toy should have a specific spot. If your child is old enough to understand, do this with him or her or even let your child pick the specific places for the toys. Make sure your child knows where the toys should go and that your child must put their toys back in that spot after every use.

Go through your child's toys with him or her every few months, or whenever new toys are bought, and do a purge. Most kids play with specific toys and know what they want to keep. Ask them what their ten favorite toys are. Then ask them which ten toys their friends might want to play with when they come over (bonus lesson about sharing!). Then ask them to pick five toys that have some memory attached. Explain to them that someone needs the rest of the toys more than they do and donate those toys. Twenty-five toys is *more* than enough to keep your child entertained, especially with all of the other sources of entertainment, such as **iPADS**, and truthfully, you could easily have fewer than twenty-five and keep your child adequately entertained, especially if you don't have a lot of space.

Once you narrow down the toys, make sure your child knows where they go, why they go there, and why it's significant to put things away in the same place every time. Knowing where toys go makes cleanup easy and fun. For smaller toys, use labeled baskets or **BINS**. **BOOKS** can be kept in **CABINETS** along with puzzles and larger items. If you have more than one child, put your child's initials on the inside cover of his or her books to be able to separate them. Coloring supplies such as markers, pens, and pencils should be kept in harder-to-reach places just in case your child decides that he or she wants to color the couch purple one day. Disciplining your child to put away toys in the designated spaces will start him or her down the path of an organized life.

Don't forget, we adults have toys too! Just because they are fancier, such as **ELECTRONICS** and **COLLECTIBLES**, doesn't mean they aren't toys! Teach your child by example. Purge your unneeded toys, designate spaces for the rest, and always return your toys to their home after playing with them. Monkey see monkey do, so let's all strive to be organized monkeys.

O.C.D. EXTREME

When I was a child, I used to take apart my toys to clean the insides. My toys rarely broke and basically lasted until I no longer wanted them. Take apart, clean, and lubricate the insides of toys to keep them gunk-free and working smoothly.

TRASH (see GARBAGE)

TRAVEL provides us with some of our fondest memories. I'll never forget the time I was in France with my parents and my mom really wanted to try a particular restaurant. The menu had no prices. Not being very hungry and wanting to save some money, I ordered a cup of the lobster bisque and the house salad. When the bill came, it turns out my light meal was ninety dollars! Shocking at the time, but we always think back and laugh about it now. Worst of all, the lobster bisque was terrible! Make sure you make fond memories on your trip instead of dealing with the repercussions of not being organized and informed.

Travel organization can be broken down into the three Ps: planning, preparing, and preserving. Planning is figuring out the when, where, for how long, and with whom. It also includes booking flights, hotels, activities, and meal reservations. Preparing is gathering everything you need before traveling. Preserving is how to document and remember your trip.

The first step in planning is to set a budget. How much can you spend on this trip? Then decide what kind of trip you want to take. Beach? Snow? Cultural? Guilt? Maybe a **ROAD TRIP** in your new **RV**? Search the Internet for good places to travel for that time of year, then **RESEARCH** all the airlines that fly to that destination. As you research all your options, create a folder in your **BOOKMARKS** for your trip and save all the possibilities to that folder. This will make for easy retrieval and comparison and used for all aspects of your trip. Use travel sites to find the best airfare. Some sites, like Kayak, will show you a calendar of average airfares per day so you can see which days are the cheapest to fly.

Once you book your flights, you'll need a place to rest your head. Again, the Internet is invaluable. Whatever your hotel price point, read reviews from fellow travelers on sites like TripAdvisor. If you need transportation from the airport, get that booked as well. Many hotels will offer complimentary shuttles, so give them a call before you spend any cash. If at this point you seem to be going over your budget, perhaps you selected too expensive a trip. Consider changing your dates, picking a new location, or sacrificing the 300-square-foot marble bathroom with spa tub you selected. Planning a trip sometimes takes multiple rounds of investigation.

Now it's time to fill your days! Obviously, you'll want to leave plenty of time for spontaneous exploration, but it's also good to have some activities and meals planned in advance. As soon as you book anything, add it to your **CALENDAR** on your **SMARTPHONE**.

The trip is booked! That's half the battle. Now it's time to prepare. Before you leave for your trip, make sure you have every bit of information you will need organized and available to you at a moment's notice. You'll want to have your itineraries, airline boarding passes, ticket confirmation numbers, airline phone numbers, hotel confirmation numbers along with the address and phone number of the hotels you will be staying at, flight numbers, seat assignments, arrival and departure times, car rental confirmations, and current conversion rates. Basically, any and all relevant information for every planned moment of your trip should be typed up on a single master travel list, organized chronologically. Title the list by the name of the place or places you will be visiting. Under the trip name, have the date of your travel. Make sure everyone traveling has a copy of this list. Do not include personal information on the list in case someone loses it. Having all of this information for each person traveling will ensure that no one is confused about where they are going or where they need to be. If some in your party get lost, they will have every bit of important information and you won't have to worry that they'll end up in a country you can't pronounce.

If traveling to another country, you should also keep a copy of your passport tucked away somewhere with your travel items in case you lose it. Jot down the number for your country's embassy directly on the copy. If you are bringing a smartphone, make sure you have your password-protected **ACCOUNTS** file with your credit card numbers up to date in case you lose your **WALLET** or **PURSE**. Before you leave, call your credit card companies to notify them that you'll be traveling and to find out if they charge fees to use your card abroad.

Now it's time to pack. We all know that deserves its own entry, so see **PACKING** for detailed tips on bringing everything you need without bringing too much. While traveling, keep your dirty clothes in a **PLASTIC BAG** separate from your clean clothes. If you can, try to do **LAUNDRY** before returning so that all you will have to do is unpack when you come home.

Preserving your trip is a great way to look back on your vacations. Mementos picked up while shopping, **PICTURES**, maps, **RECEIPTS**, and **TICKET STUBS** will be worth their weight in gold when you want to revisit your experience down the line, unless the price of gold goes up significantly. Stay organized on your trip so that these precious articles make it home. If you plan on doing a lot of shopping, pack an extra duffel bag to carry your purchases home. Large purchases can either be shipped home or checked on your flight, so find out which is the cheaper, easier option, but always keep valuables on your person. Bring a small **ZIPLOCK BAG** with you to save any small paper documents from your trip and consider making a collage out of them when the trip is over. For photos, make sure you have fresh, empty **MEMORY CARDS** with enough capacity to take as many pictures as you want on your trip.

Once you are back home, unpack and download your photos to your **COMPUTER**. Make everyone jealous by posting some photos on your **SOCIAL NETWORKING** sites. Add any contact information from **BUSINESS CARDS** you collected from places that you'd want to revisit or buy things from in the future. Now you can start thinking about your next trip to keep you motivated when you have to go back to work on Monday.

AN O.C.D. SUCCESS STORY

I used to use a travel agent to book all of my travel. That will never happen again. I was in Amsterdam on Christmas Day one year when I discovered that my travel agent had booked me a train ticket for the following year! I couldn't wait around for twelve months to board the train, so I had to beg and plead with the conductor to let me on so I could get to my next destination. Be in charge of your own travel and make the master list. It will force you to double-check all of your travel information so you'll find any mistakes. Since then, I've handled my own travel and made a master list, and I've never found myself begging for a train ride.

TRAVEL BAGS should be easily accessible and stored together in the same place, if you have the space. Ideally, keep them with your **LUGGAGE**. Keep it to what you need: no one likes a person with excess baggage. Bigger bags should house the smaller bags to save space. Always keep the bag you use most frequently easily accessible because you don't want to waste time moving and searching through other bags to find the one you use often. Make sure that your bags are always unpacked and cleaned out as soon as you get back from a trip. This way, when you need that bag again, it's ready to go. You'll never be surprised by a pair of dirty underwear that didn't find its way to the washing machine. If you are looking for organization advice for your handbags, see **PURSES**.

TRUNK is not a long-term storage space. Let's take a bit of advice from the mighty elephants who use their trunks to transport things but never to store them. Don't put things in the trunk of your car just because you don't have room for them elsewhere. Get anything out of your trunk that's just being stored there without a good reason and find a better home for it. It should only hold the things you are dealing with that day and being transported among your home, **OFFICE**, and other destinations. If the Mafia can do it, so can you. Besides the items of the day, the trunk of the car should have an **EMERGENCY KIT**. This kit should contain, at the least, a full change of clothes including a pair of shoes, a twenty-dollar bill, a bottle of water, a flashlight, and a Swiss army knife. Use your discretion to choose what else you'd need in an emergency kit. Nothing besides emergency items should be left in your trunk longer than three days. Additionally, your trunk should contain a spare tire, **TOOLS** to change a flat, and a pair of jumper cables. On a long road trip you may want to have a small gasoline canister just in case you run out of gas. If you have children, keep a small **BIN** in your trunk with a few select **TOYS** to be able to keep them occupied on long car rides. Keep your trunk clean and vacuum it every time you get your car washed. Don't let it be your clean car's dirty little secret.

T

asked him when the last time he went rock-climbing was and he said six years ago. Whenever he'd buy anything, he never had enough space to put it in his trunk. He'd use his backseats, which meant if he had four passengers, someone was always sitting uncomfortably. I finally had a trunk intervention with him. We found a better home for his equipment in his garage. Now his trunk is empty and available for whatever he buys and I have never had to ride in the backseat with a box on my lap.

T-SHIRTS are like a clothing collection's greatest hits. We all have that sentimental T-shirt, worn so thin that it's really just the idea of a T-shirt at this point. We tend to buy too many T-shirts and hold on to old ones too long. Make sure your T-shirts aren't overwhelming your life and your **DRAWER**. Go through your T-shirt drawer, drawers, or **CABINETS**, take all of your T-shirts out, and lay them out on your bed. Make five piles for your shirts: casual, dress, lounge/gym, donate, and trash. Start with your casual and dress piles. Only put shirts in these piles that you've worn in the last month, or shirts you really want to wear but forgot about because of your disorganized drawer. All of your other shirts should go into the lounge/gym, donation, or trash pile. Based on the space you have to house your T-shirts, you know how many shirts are too many and how many shirts you can keep in each pile. But do you really need more than a three-week supply? The rest of your shirts need to go into the donation pile and get donated as soon as possible. Now put everything back in your designated T-shirt drawer or drawers in your **DRESSER** or **CLOSET**. Keep the casual and dress T-shirts in your top drawer and the rest lower. Color-coordinate your T-shirts, which will make picking out your clothing easier and your drawer more attractive. If your drawers are deep enough, use the filing system where you fold your shirts and load them vertically. This makes it easier to see every shirt and pull it out without messing everything up. To keep your drawer from overflowing, keep to the rule that whenever you buy two new T-shirts, you have to get rid of at least one old one. Two shirts enter, one shirt leaves.

TUPPERWARE (see CONTAINERS)

U

UNDERWEAR should be reorganized every six months or whenever your **DRAWER** is getting out of control. Take everything out and see what is being worn, what has been hiding in the back and never touched, and what has holes or stains and needs to go right in the trash. When you open your underwear drawer, you shouldn't have to search for a wearable pair. Every pair should be wearable, be comfortable, and fit you right! Return your wearable underwear to your underwear drawer, organized by type and color.

Make an attempt to buy the same brand and type of underwear over and over again to keep your drawer looking as uniform as possible, but try a few brands before you pick one. You can even buy your underwear online and have them shipped to your home. Most people have too many pairs of underwear at any given time, which makes underwear drawers scarier than they have to be. Think about it: you probably do **LAUNDRY** at least every two weeks. Even if you sweat profusely and wear two pairs of underwear a day, that'd be twenty-eight pairs of underwear. You certainly don't need more than this, so if you are an underwear hoarder, it's time to unload some underwear and unleash some space.

Underwear organization for women is slightly more involved. Between **LINGERIE, BRAS,** pantyhose, and all the different types of underwear, more organization is required but still easy. Organize your underwear by type, like briefs, bikinis, boy shorts, thongs, G-strings, and Spanx, and then sort by color. Get drawer dividers to keep each type separate to make picking out your underwear easier. You can also keep your pantyhose in your underwear drawer. You don't need many pairs. Once you've taken pantyhose out of the packaging, keep them in individual **ZIPLOCK BAGS** and write the brand and date opened on the bag so you know what's inside. Get rid of anything worn, frayed, or that has holes. At the end of every year, trash all your pantyhose and start with fresh hose.

Underwear is the first thing you put on your body every day. Picking it out should be pleasant, wearing it should be comfortable, and it should make you feel good. It won't matter how fashionable your outfit is—you won't feel your best dressed if your underwear doesn't feel right!

UNEMPLOYMENT works differently from state to state. Know your state's procedures so you can file your claim properly and in an organized manner. Look online or call the unemployment office in your city and state and have the enduring patience to wait on the phone until you actually reach a live human being. Know the right questions to ask. Are you eligible? How much are you eligible for? For how long? Make sure that you have all of your past employee information at your fingertips, including addresses, phone numbers, your work dates, and the amount of your last wages, which can be found on your last pay stub. It will expedite the filing process. Let them know you are eager to work, but unfortunately you are not finding work. You must be actively searching for a job to continue to receive unemployment. Don't lie about a thing! If you were let go for misconduct, they'll find out! Once your claim is filed, stay on top of filing your weekly or bimonthly claims. Take note of the due date on the forms and add it to your **CALENDAR**.

While you are unemployed, it's easy to fall into malaise, lethargy, and ice cream. When looking for a job, it's more important than ever to stay organized and maintain a routine. Make schedules for yourself and put them in your calendar. Make sure you are keeping your e-mail correspondence and contacts organized so that you can keep track of your job submissions and follow up on them. Shower and get dressed every day as if you were going to work because this will motivate you to *find* a job. Think outside the box—leverage all of your connections to identify job possibilities. This is where

looking through your organized contact and **MEETING NOTES** can lead
to opportunities you never recognized before. If you start to feel down
on yourself, start working on a project. Productivity is always productive.
There's always something around the house that needs to be done or some
creative project you can design. Instead of thinking of unemployment as a
negative, use this opportunity to reset, reevaluate, and create a new path
for yourself.

USER MANUALS sometimes seem to be written in Chinese. If that's the
case, put it down and look in the box for the English version. After your ini-
tial read, throw it away. Almost all **ELECTRONICS** and appliance user guides
can be found online. Search for the user manual online from the manufacturer's Web site, download it, and save to DOCUMENTS → USER MANUALS.
Every home I walk into has the manual **DRAWER**, loaded with every manual
dating back twenty years. People reference their user manuals maybe twice,
once, or never during the ownership of an item, so why let it take up any
space? A lot of companies are supplying their products with CDs that contain the manuals for cost-cutting effectiveness. Pop the CD in your drive,
grab the manual off the disc, and save it to your **COMPUTER**. Then get rid
of the CD. For manuals you can't get online, or for anything you plan on
reselling, keep them in a file folder labeled "Manuals" with the rest of your
files in your **OFFICE** or supply closet.

■ ■ ■

O.C.D. EXTREME

In the tech-support industry, there's an acronym that's an inside joke:
RTFM. It stands for "Read the F*cking Manual" and comes to mind
when people call asking questions whose answers can be found easily
in the manual. No matter how simple I think a device is, I always give

the manual a cover-to-cover glance when I first get it. People often overlook some simple functionality of their product because they didn't read the manual. Don't elicit an RTFM.

UTILITY CLOSETS should only store the necessary supplies for cleaning your home and for simple fixes around the house. If you've turned your utility closet into a jumbled multipurpose closet, reject the futility of saving your utility: get everything out of there that doesn't serve a cleaning or repair function and find a better home for it. When reorganizing the closet, use as much wall space as possible. Hang brooms and mops on the closet wall with hooks or clamps to keep them off the floor and save you space. Keep a small toolbox in your utility closet for quick access to screwdrivers, glue, tape, and other basic **TOOLS** for small repair jobs. Store your vacuum, along with an extension cord, in the utility closet and make sure that cords are wound neatly and hung up as well. If the attachments don't live on the vacuum itself, keep them close by but tucked away, since most attachments are used infrequently. When it comes down to it, they all suck. Keep a complete set of **CLEANING SUPPLIES** in a cleaning tote so you can grab it easily and move it from room to room. If you have a cleaning lady, she'll appreciate that you have a ready-to-go tote. If you have a bucket, make sure it is tucked away on the floor or on a shelf, and store supplies in it, such as floor cleaner, that are used in combination with the bucket. If you are tight on space, you can store sponges and extra dust rags/towels in the bucket as well, but you'll have to remove them every time you want to use the bucket, which is inefficient. Keep items that could be toxic on **SHELVES** out of the reach of children and make sure they are always secure when closing them. Better yet, put a lock on your utility closet. If you have the space, you may also keep a watering can for your plants and a small step stool.

When loading the utility closet, always put the largest items in first, such as vacuums or steamers, so that you don't put everything in and suddenly find you don't have space for that bulky item. Label where everything goes so anyone who helps clean your house can maintain the discipline of keeping your utility closet organized. Make sure that you reorder cleaning supplies and vacuum bags whenever they get low. You never want to run out and have to live in a dust bunny home until you can restock.

V

VACATION PLANNING (see TRAVEL)

VIDEO GAMES rival text messaging for creating the fastest thumbs on the planet. Use those fast thumbs to keep your video games on shelves in your **ENTERTAINMENT CENTER**, on **BOOKSHELVES** in your **FAMILY ROOM**, or to take them out of their cases and put them in a DVD book to save space. Keep the book in your **COFFEE TABLE** if it has built-in storage. You might have started to download your video games directly to your console. If this is you, make sure that you keep all **RECEIPTS** for the purchased games just in case your system crashes. However you keep your video games, they should be alphabetized. If you use a DVD book, keep a master list of its contents and update it whenever you buy or sell a game. If you plan to resell a game after you finish it, keep the game with the case and manual in good condition. If you have multiple gaming systems, keep your games organized by which system they work on, and alphabetized. If you are a serious gamer, you should also get into the habit of backing up your game data from your system onto a flash drive in case your system crashes. You don't want to have to play your way all the way back to the coin Buddha in Resident Evil 6 after spending forty hours to get there. When handling games, keep your fingers off the readable disc area to prevent disc error problems in the future. If you play computer games, create a games folder on your **HARD DRIVE** and always direct the game installer to that directory. After installing, keep the computer game discs along with your other video games as a backup so you can always revisit the island of Myst.

▪ ▪▪ ▪
O.C.D. APPROVED TECHNOLOGY

Stop taking a chance and buying games you don't end up liking or even playing. You can play demos of almost any game these days, or sign up for a GameFly account to rent games for a flat monthly fee. Just like Netflix, you receive a requested game in the mail, try it out for as long as you want with no late fees, and then return it in the postage-paid envelope. If you really like a game, they give you the option to buy it. The only downside is you will probably end up playing a lot more video games, so have the discipline to limit your game time!

■ ■ ■ ■

VIDEOTAPES aren't worth the ribbon they often spit out of your VCR. If you truly care about any of the footage on your videotapes, you should convert them to DVD or digitize them as soon as possible. Videotapes deteriorate rapidly and you are already racing the clock. Do you even have a VCR setup anymore? Has *The NeverEnding Story* been in it since it came out on videotape in 1992? Get your memories on a modern medium! Any tapes you have in your life should be converted: **CASSETTE TAPES**, 8mm tapes, DV tapes, DAT tapes, and beta tapes.

Gather your tapes and take them to your local digital conversion shop, which you can find easily by searching the Internet for "Convert Tapes to DVD" and then your zip code. If there isn't a place near you, there are many online services that let you **MAIL** in your tapes. Most will charge you per tape. Make sure before you send your tapes out that you know what is on them. Prepare a list for the place converting the tapes with start and stop times of the clips you want on each particular tape. If you do not have the means to watch the tapes because the teenager at Best Buy has never heard of a VCR, then just send them out and be surprised when you get your DVDs back, just like the old days when you found a roll of film that was sitting in a drawer for years. But if you can get your hands on a VCR, it may save you cash in the long run if you don't have to digitize two hours of tape with only five minutes of actual footage.

You can also take on the digitizing process yourself, but it's time-consuming and can be tricky. If you can afford it, I highly recommend using a professional service. If you do it yourself, make sure you do it in an organized way. Have all of your tapes in front of you, labeled, and spend some time each day converting. VHS to DVD converters are available online. Just pop in your VHS and two hours later, it will spit out a DVD. Some converters are stand-alone, ranging from $150 to $300, and some will interface with your **COMPUTER**, ranging from $20 to $150. If you are technically advanced and want to convert through your computer, purchase a VHS video converter that allows you to capture the footage to your computer. The advantage to this is that you can edit the footage, add flashy titles and transitions, make family clip shows, mix up a montage, and even break up the segments on the tapes into multiple chapters when you burn them to DVD. This way, each tape isn't one long file but easily navigable smaller files.

I've seen clients near tears when we go through their VHS tapes and find that they are no longer playable. Those precious memories are gone forever, swallowed in an unreliable rectangle of black plastic. Please save yourself the emotional pain of this experience and get your videotapes converted.

O.C.D. APPROVED TECHNOLOGY

I use FotoBridge to digitize all of my clients' tapes. They are reasonable, professional, reliable, and fast. In the five years I've worked with them, I've never had a problem with any of my clients' orders. They understand they are handling priceless memories and guarantee 100 percent satisfaction. Get your tapes and photos to them. They even offer trackable, free return shipping!

VINYL (see RECORDS)

VISION BOARD consists of the top optometrists in the country. It's also a tool that helps you develop your creative ideas. Since the optometrists' vision board meetings are confidential, I'll only talk about the latter. A vision board was harder to describe before the advent of Pinterest, which is just a digital vision board. A vision board is a **BULLETIN BOARD** that helps you dream up and define your creative vision. It can store images, **QUOTES**, clippings, anything that keeps you inspired when working on a project. Whatever you use it for, define the board for a single vision and only add things to the board that support the realization of that vision. As you add to your vision board, it will become clearer as to what your vision really is. Your vision board is also a great place to come back to whenever you become stuck or discouraged with your project. If you have multiple visions, have multiple vision boards. Just as is the case with everything else in your life, vision boards require organizational discipline. You may notice that your vision changes, expands, and progresses throughout the process. If it does, take down any postings that no longer apply. Pretty soon you'll see a seed that started as a single thought transform into a fully realized reality. The fruit it bears will taste all the sweeter, and also make a great jelly.

> ■ ■ ■ ■
> ### AN O.C.D. SUCCESS STORY
>
> People who use vision boards tend to be more focused on their vision and are more likely to see their vision come to fruition. I've personally grown the O.C.D. Experience using vision boards, and as my company has grown, so has my number of vision boards. Whenever I encounter creative clients who are full of ideas but never seem to ever act on them, I encourage them to use vision boards. Soon enough, I see them bringing their visions to life! Sometimes a constant visual reminder is all the motivation you need to get a project on its legs. You look at things in a whole new way, discover synergies, and link opportunities you never would have realized trying to keep it all in your head.

VITAMINS (see MEDICINE)

VOICE MAILS (see AUDIO FILES)

W

WALK-IN CLOSETS (see CLOSETS)

WALLET organization should be very simple. Keep only the things in your wallet that you use on a weekly basis. There was a very funny episode of *Seinfeld* where George reveals his wallet, and it's as thick as a brick. He's kept anything and everything in there for years and years. Finally, he tries to add one more slip of paper and the entire wallet explodes under the pressure. There's no need to have a Costanza wallet!

Your wallet should contain some cash, the **CREDIT CARDS** and ATM cards that you use regularly, your identification/license, and your insurance card, which you should also have as a photo on your phone. You can easily e-mail it to anyone who needs a copy. You should also keep no more than six **BUSINESS CARDS** in your wallet and remember to refill them as necessary. Designate spaces in your wallet for each item, so if one is ever missing, you know immediately. But that's all you need in your wallet! Everything else should find a new home or solution.

I'm sure you're saying, "But Justin! What about all those other cards I have in there? Don't I need my Circus Circus Player's Club rewards card?" Cards you might use once a month should be kept with other hardly used cards and grabbed only when you need them. You can keep these cards in an old wallet in your **OFFICE** or **NIGHTSTAND**. **RECEIPTS** that you collect from purchases can be kept in your wallet until you get home, but get into the habit of taking them out and dealing with them at the end of each day for **TAXES** if they are important enough to keep. If you travel a lot and want more business cards with you, don't keep them in your wallet. Keep them in a cardholder in your bag or in a stack with a rubber band. If you still use checks and want to keep a single blank check in your wallet, that's okay, but never bring your whole checkbook. You'll never write this many checks in one day without knowing about it in advance. For all those **MEMBERSHIP** cards, take a photo of them with your **SMARTPHONE**. Showing the photo at the register will work just as well as showing the actual card, and some stores only need you to enter your phone number or membership number to bring up your account. If you're living the O.C.D. Way, you can always find your membership number in your password-protected **ACCOUNTS** file. The only rewards cards you can keep in your wallet are the buy-ten-get—one-free punch or stamp cards because these must be physically presented at the store. But if you find that you have more than one or two such reward cards, admit that you have a yogurt problem, pick your favorite shop, and stay loyal.

Women's wallets tend to be larger than men's wallets. This isn't an invitation to stuff it with more unnecessary stuff. Just as is true with your **PURSE**, only keep the necessities; just distribute them evenly throughout the wallet. If your wallet has a change pouch, you don't need twenty dollars' worth of change in there. Empty it out each day into your **CHANGE** jar and only keep a few quarters, dimes, and nickels for parking and the always satisfying exact change purchase.

If you stay disciplined with your wallet, you should never have to reorganize it again. If you find that, like a cheesecake lover, it seems to fatten up over time, go through your wallet once a month, wipe it down, pull everything out, and get back to basics. Guys, a thinner wallet will make you look sharp and stop you from sitting lopsided. Ladies, it will lighten your purse. Keeping your wallet clean and organized not only makes purchasing things quicker and easier, but will also give off the impression that you are a well-organized and put-together individual.

■ ■ ■

AN O.C.D. SUMMARY

Organize: Pull everything out of your wallet. If it's not something you use regularly such as driver's license, credit cards, money, or key cards to your school or workplace, find a better home or solution for it. Membership cards can live on your smartphone as a photo, or simply as membership numbers in your Accounts file.

Create: Designate specific places in your wallet for all of your necessities. This way, you'll know immediately if something is missing. Keep everything else in an old wallet in your office or nightstand, for those rare occasions that you need to use it.

Discipline: Don't add things to your wallet that don't belong in there. Deal with receipts, change, and anything else that ends up in your wallet at the end of each day so you don't end up with a Costanza wallet.

■ ■ ■

O.C.D. APPROVED TECHNOLOGY

I searched throughout the world to find the best-made, most durable, and sleek O.C.D.-approved wallet on the market and branded it just for you. The O.C.D. Slimline Wallet comes with a tip card to help you rid yourself of receipts, membership cards, and business cards. Pick yours up at ocdexperience.com.

WARDROBE can mean your collection of clothing, in which case, see **CLOTHES**, or the piece of **FURNITURE**, which is like a freestanding **CLOSET** and portal to Narnia. A wardrobe is a great way to add storage space to your home, but use it responsibly. Don't buy one just because you are running out of space and want to house overflow. That only means it is time to go through your belongings. But if you need to create a new, specific space, perhaps in a room without a closet, a wardrobe can be a smart purchase. The most important thing to remember with a wardrobe is to define it for a specific purpose. Don't let it become a miscellaneous hanging and storage space. If it's meant for jackets, use it for jackets. If it's for linens, use it for linens. If you use it as an **ENTERTAINMENT CENTER** or for **OFFICE SUPPLIES**, keep it that way. Otherwise, you've just added another energy-sucking chaos space to maintain in your life. Don't get sucked into your wardrobe.

WATCHES keep us on schedule. Make sure that time is on your side by storing your watches in a **JEWELRY** box, a designated **DRAWER** with other accessories, a **SAFE** with other precious **ANTIQUES** or jewelry, or a special box meant just for watches. Finding the right storage option all depends on how many watches you have. If you are a serious collector, invest in a watch box or even have a custom piece built into your **CLOSET** with a lock. Organize your watches by occasion and color. Loose watch accessories, such as spare links, extra bands and straps, paperwork or warranty cards, should be kept in the box that came with your watch. Keep those boxes all together in your safe, the top of your closet, or another out-of-the-way location you won't forget. This will protect your investment if you ever need to service or sell it. However you store your watches, keep them in rotation, as a ticking watch is a happy watch. Clean your watches as necessary and get them tuned up if they are important to you. Rolex suggests getting your fine watch serviced every five to seven years so you don't have to watch your watch break down.

O.C.D. EXTREME

Every month, I make sure to set all the watches in my collection to the correct time instead of waiting to put them on my wrist. That way, I know I can always grab a watch and it'll be good to go, unless, of course, it's a winding or kinetic watch. It brings me peace to know that even my out-of-sight watches are keeping the correct time.

WEB SITE organization can mean two things: managing your favorite sites by bookmarking, in which case, see **BOOKMARKS**, or developing and managing your own Web site. Your Web site will be the digital face of you, your company, or your hilarious blog, so you want to make sure it's impressive and functional. A bad Web site will make visitors think less of your business by making you seem less professional.

The first moment it occurs to you to create a Web site, register your domain name! You thought it was hard to find an unused e-mail address? Just wait until you start seeing what domains are unavailable. Using a domain registration site like GoDaddy or Network Solutions, search your proposed domain names until you find the one that's available and speaks to you. If you find that your dream domain name is taken but nothing is actually hosted on that site, you may be able to contact the owner and buy the name from him or her, if you have the cash. Once you select your domain name, register it with the registration site and it will keep your domain names organized and easy to manage. Some can even host your site for you when it's finished. Registering the name for five or ten years is cheaper than renewing every year.

Now that you have your snazzy domain name that's catchy, unique, but easy to remember, know what kind of Web site you want before you take the leap in creating it. Search through the Web and take notes about Web sites you like. You can even print them out and add them to your **VISION BOARD**. Once you have an idea of what you want to create, it's time to design your basic wireframe and site map. A wireframe is just the layout skeleton for your site—breaking each page down into separate areas and defining purposes for those areas. You can find help on wireframe design sites like Balsamiq. Your site map provides an overall view of the hierarchy of pages on your Web site, complete with the Web address of each page. A site map will help you design how your audience will navigate your site.

Once you have your wireframe and site map completed, it's time to create and gather the content for your Web site because blank pages don't get the hits they used to. Organize and save everything you plan on adding to the site to DOCUMENTS → WEB SITES → WEB SITE NAME or DOCUMENTS → COMPANY NAME → WEB SITE. Create subfolders for each type of content: photos, videos, text, music, and so on. Having all of your content organized and ready to go will save you hours of work in the design process.

Now it's time to design your site or hand it over to a professional designer. Depending on your budget and how complex your Web site is, you can use Web design software, like Adobe Dreamweaver, or predesigned template-based Web hosting companies, like Wix, which allow you to plug in your content and launch your Web site as simply as possible. If you want to go a more custom route, hire a professional. A professional Web designer will give you a quote to complete the entire project or a quote per page, or will charge between $50 and $175 an hour depending on their experience. This is why it's important to know exactly what you want your site to look like and have your content ready to go before handing it over: it will save you time and money!

If you want people to be able to purchase products on your Web site, it's easy to integrate credit card payment functionality through payment Web sites like PayPal. They'll give you the code to paste onto your site to create payment links. You can then transfer received money into your bank account, withdraw one dollar, and frame it as the first dollar you ever earned from your billion-dollar e-business. Just make sure you have an organized system to process purchases and send out your products in a timely manner, or you'll never get there.

Your Web site is nearly ready to launch. Go through everything with your designer to check all the links and make sure everything is working and to your specifications before the site goes live. Congratulations, you now have a presence on the Internet! But your job is not done. Now you must maintain your site. Updating your content regularly will keep your Web site feeling fresh. It will also help search engines find your site more easily. But be cautious before uploading any new files to your site. Make sure it's exactly how you want it because once you put it up, anyone can see it, so it needs to be right. Like anything in the O.C.D. Way, maintenance and constant activity are the keys to prosperity.

If you design and operate multiple Web sites, the process is the same. Just keep them organized, with each site in its own specified folder on your **COMPUTER** so you don't accidentally upload an image to your toys and games site meant for your artistic photography site. Anytime you are editing a site, be sure to save files in their appropriate folders. It would be a shame to edit and update an entire site only to find you saved over the wrong files on your computer, overwriting another site. Being specific when naming your files for each site will help prevent this from happening. As always, make sure all of your data is backed up to another drive or the **CLOUD**.

The Internet is the new face of commerce and usually the first place anyone will be introduced to your business. Make sure your Web site is a polished diamond, representing your company and your message in the clearest and most concise way possible, and not a lump of digital coal.

Organize: As soon as you have the idea, decide what kind of Web site you want to create and register your domain name. Start searching the Internet for inspiration, taking notes about sites you like.

Create: Develop the layout of your site by creating a wireframe and a site map. Gather your Web site content and keep it organized in the appropriate files on your computer. Hand your materials over to a professional Web designer or take on the challenge and design it yourself. Once designed and troubleshooted for errors, take your Web site live!

Discipline: Update the site regularly with new content to keep your site feeling fresh and generating interest. Make sure anything you add to your site has to do with your business or message. If you are selling anything, aim for quick shipping and good customer service so that customers return to your site over and over again.

292

WIRES (see CORDS)

WINE collections can be a few bottles or take up an entire room. Whatever size the collection, the result is the same: a good time, especially with a fondue set. I've worked with clients with collections from five bottles to two thousand bottles. Small collections can be broken down into white, red, sparkling, and dessert wines. As your collection grows and you become more of an oenophile, you can organize your wine by adding the following attributes to your system in this order: country, region, grape variety, year, and then alphabetically. Some people will even organize their wine by what's drinkable any day, what's reserved for those special occasions or gifts, and what needs to be aged for many more years. However you choose to organize your wine, always store your bottles on their side in a cool, dark place; otherwise, the cork can dry out and your wine will be ruined. It's a shame to age a bottle for years and then find you now have a bottle of red wine vinegar. Buy a wine refrigerator, build a wine cellar, or just put a wine rack in a designated **CABINET**. If you have a wine cellar, put only wine in there and keep the floor area clear so you can always reach your wine. Make sure you drink your bottles during their optimal window. To keep track of those older bottles, use wine tags with a "Drink By" date on them. When people bring you gifts of wine, if it's a bottle you want, add it to your collection. Otherwise, keep it separate to give away or to regift. Anything that makes its way into your collection should be a bottle you want to drink. As with everything in the O.C.D. Way, know your space and don't buy more bottles than you have room for. Keeping your wine collection organized ensures that you do less whining and more wining and dining.

O.C.D. APPROVED TECHNOLOGY

A good red wine should be decanted before it's ready to drink. This means opening the bottle, pouring it into a decanter, which exposes a large surface area of the wine to the air, and letting it sit for upward of an hour. Exposure to the air oxygenates the wine, mellowing it out and bringing out the true flavors. Sometimes you just aren't that patient! Purchase a wine aerator to drink your wine as it's meant to be enjoyed without having to wait an hour for it to breathe. Pour the wine through the aerator, which mixes it with oxygen, into your glass, and then down your throat.

WIVES have an enormous responsibility to keep a home, family, job, and **HUSBAND** organized and maintained. Make this an easier task by helping her maintain the backbone of an organized home. Let her know she is appreciated with thoughtful words, gestures, and gifts. If you need help remembering to do these things, set **APPOINTMENTS** in your **CALENDAR** even if it's just to say something nice! In any marriage, your partner should be helpful on all levels. You should communicate and ask your wife her **NEEDS** when it comes to everything in your relationship, especially during that week when she needs extra sensitivity, help, and understanding. This includes organization! Just because you have a certain way of doing something doesn't mean it's easy for your wife to mimic or follow your lead. Design a system that works for her as well. In fact, design a system together! Be open to constructive criticism and trying new things to promote healthy organization and flow in your home that works for both of you. If there is something that you want organized or kept in a specific manner, just ask. If she has a problem maintaining a system, or vice versa, guide her or have her guide you through it. Patience and understanding go a long way in any relationship, especially when it comes to organization. A common example in any home is the lack of organization when it comes to **LAUNDRY**. It is all about communication and discipline. Know the rules behind laundry, where it goes when it is dirty, where it shouldn't go, and when laundry gets done. All laundry should have a home, a logical place to go when not on your body, and make it back into your **CLOSET** or **DRESSER** quickly. If you both stick to the rules you make together, clothing will never be lying around your home and insignificant arguments won't disrupt your relationship. This philosophy can be applied to every area of your relationship. If someone is slacking on any responsibility, don't be passive-aggressive. Just sit down and have a conversation that there has been a breakdown in something you are working on together and find the best solution to fix the problem together. *Together*. This will promote a healthy way of living as a couple and will ensure that organization never breaks down between spouses. You'll never have to divide a room down the middle with tape and declare the space "my side" and "your side."

AN O.C.D. SUCCESS STORY

In my experience as an organizer, I often find that couples have lived for years with organizational tension! Some spouses are afraid to communicate how they feel about "insignificant" issues in their relationship. Organizational issues often fall into this category: where your shoes go, how to put groceries away, leaving things in places they don't belong. These may seem like minor infractions not worth stirring the pot over, but anything small gets bottled up and becomes something big down the road. I encourage my clients to keep up an ongoing conversation about organization. If you don't communicate about the little things in your relationship, how will you ever be able to discuss the big things? Working together to create and maintain simple organizational systems helps my clients to solve bigger problems when they pop up.

WORKING OUT is a gift to your mind, body, and partner. Working out doesn't mean you need to build a lavish **EXERCISE ROOM**, have a costly gym **MEMBERSHIP**, a personal trainer, or a ton of equipment. It just means that you regularly maintain your mind and body by giving them the exercise they need, which can be done in your home, **OFFICE**, or outdoors. Some people are self-motivated enough to exercise regularly without any help. Judging by obesity statistics in America, this isn't most of us.

Everyone needs some discipline when it comes to exercise. The best way to help yourself stay fit is to create a schedule and keep to it! Set recurring exercise **APPOINTMENTS** in your **CALENDAR**. Not only will this help you leave time for exercise when scheduling everything else in your life, but it will remind and motivate you to stick to your routine beyond just thinking, "I should exercise at some point today." You can even write which exercise you want to do: bike ride, run, push-ups, sit-ups, Zumba, chase the dog around, and so on.

If you want to really get in shape, create a detailed regiment where you work out different areas of your body on certain days, like arms and chest on Monday and legs and butt on Tuesday. Tuesdays are grueling, but so necessary. You can even download a PEA, a personal exercise **APP**, on your **SMARTPHONE** that lets you input the exercises you do, at what weight, and how many reps. PEAs are a great ways to organize your workouts, track your progress, and even share your accomplishments with friends across **SOCIAL NETWORKING** platforms.

Stay disciplined! Never allow yourself to skip a scheduled exercise appointment. This is a surefire way to fall out of shape. Also, exercise doesn't have to be dull and boring. Get creative and snag exercise wherever you can. Take the stairs instead of elevators and escalators. Organize group activities with your friends. Mount a pull-up bar in your doorway and burn a few out every time you walk through. Even **VIDEO GAMES** can help you stay in shape now! Just get up, move, and break a sweat, whether it's five minutes or fifty. Your heart, brain, waistline, and mirror will thank you!

W

■ ■ ■

O.C.D. APPROVED TECHNOLOGY

Sometimes a personal trainer keeps you motivated simply by setting a goal, keeping track of that goal for you, and letting you know where you stand. You don't have to pay personal trainer prices to get the same effect if you embrace new technologies! Grab a Nike+ FuelBand and wear it on your wrist throughout the day. It tracks your activity and helps motivate you by setting goals. Also check out the iPump FitnessBuilder app for your smartphone. It lets you create workouts, shows you how to do certain exercises, and gives you exercise options based on your location. There are many other apps out there, so find one that works great for how you like to exercise! You can also download nutrition tracking apps and weight trackers to work in tandem with your workout apps to keep you further organized and motivated.

WRAPPING (see GIFT WRAP)

X-RAYS let doctors take a peek inside your body without making a mess. They should be kept as part of your **MEDICAL RECORDS** and saved and organized by doctor, date, and procedure. Ask your doctor or imaging center if they can provide you with digital copies of your X-rays. These days most X-rays are taken with a digital instrument and then printed, so ask them to e-mail your X-rays to you or to burn you a DVD. If you get a DVD, make sure to upload your X-rays to your **COMPUTER** when you get home. Save your X-rays to DOCUMENTS → MEDICAL → DOCTOR with the date and description in the file name. If it's too complicated to pull it off the DVD, file the actual DVD in your **FILING CABINET** in your Medical Records folder. If you can't get your X-rays digitally, get copies of the film and keep them in an area where they won't get damaged since they are nearly impossible to digitize at home without expensive equipment. Alternatively, bring them into an imaging specialist who can digitize them for you. Mark each X-ray on the top right with the relevant information using a grease pencil or by creating a label with a label maker. If you have many X-rays, get a portfolio book and keep your X-rays in the book organized by date. You can use dividers to separate X-rays from different procedures and doctors. You will never have a problem giving your insurance company or new doctors X-ray vision if you keep your records organized this way.

YARD SALE is a good option for getting rid of everything you no longer need after reading this book, while making a few bucks in the process. Just make sure to get any necessary permits if your county requires it so that you don't get shut down. I don't usually work with clients on yard sales because it just delays the process of purging belongings, but if they insist, I have only one requirement: after the yard sale, whatever is left over gets donated. We schedule a donation pickup for the end of that day.

Once you've identified everything in your home or **GARAGE** for the sale, figure out what you want to charge for everything. The easiest way to do this is the color code system. Purchase colored dot stickers and assign a value to each color. Don't use smaller increments than a quarter unless you want to be collecting dimes, nickels, and pennies! Rather than trying to give every item its own price, which will take you forever to write, just slap on the dot that is closest to what you want to sell it for. Make a poster board for your yard sale with the value assigned to each color and you'll never have to answer, "How much for the fishnet leg lamp?" Watch out for the sly yard sale con man that tries to switch stickers around while you aren't looking. He's literally got sticky fingers. You can always negotiate and say no to a sale.

Lay everything out on tarps or tables so you don't have your belongings sitting on wet grass. But don't use your grandmother's antique table to display items or people will think it's for sale and keep hassling you to buy it. Only put out what you are willing to sell. Organize your **INVENTORY** by putting like items together. Shoppers are less likely to make purchases if it looks like a bomb went off in your front yard. Keep the more valuable items closer to your pay station so that you can keep an eye on them. Make sure your sprinklers are off the night before so that your yard isn't muddy and you don't drench your inventory or your customers. Estimate how much change you'll need based on your inventory. Go to the bank the day before your yard sale and get a lot of small bills and coins. Don't use a cash box: it's an obvious target. Keep cash and **CHANGE** on your person.

As it gets close to the end of the yard sale, brush off the grass stains and start dropping the prices. Whatever doesn't sell gets donated! If you were able to put it out in the yard to sell, it no longer belongs in your home or garage.

YARN should be organized by material and color, from light to dark, so that you can darn with it instead of damn it. Pull out all your yarn, give away what you don't like or don't have enough of, and get the rest reorganized. When you are working on a project, you can keep the yarn being used for that project in a separate bin. Keep the rest of your yarn and yarn accessories in a clear plastic **CONTAINER**, or containers, labeled "Yarn" with your other craft supplies. Make sure you are buying a container that is large enough to house your entire yarn collection, with space to buy more. Keep the container organized by putting each skein (yarn bundle) back where it belongs and never let yarn get tangled because this can create chaos. Keep the container in a dry place. Moisture is the enemy of yarn and attracts bugs. If you find that your yarn has some insect squatters, dry it out in the sun for a couple of days or put it in the **FREEZER**. Nothing kills a bug like freezing temperatures! Worst-case scenario—toss the yarn.

Although it's tempting to go wild and crazy at the yarn store, try to buy yarn only for planned projects. Otherwise, you might find yourself with more yarn than you could ever possibly knit. Don't save little scraps of yarn. You can always buy more! When you buy a new yarn, take a snip of the yarn, place it on the label, take a photo, and save it in DOCUMENTS → CREATIVE → YARN. You'll be able to trash the label but still know what to buy again if you really like a particular yarn. If you are a serious knitter and have a huge yarn collection, create a knitting station with some cubbies to organize your yarn. If you're an on-the-go knitter, you can buy a yarn tote to take your projects with you. I'll keep an eye out for my thank-you sweater.

YOGA EQUIPMENT should be kept in a convenient area of your home but not visible. Be proud you do yoga regularly, but don't display your mat as a trophy to prove it. Let your flexibility do the talking. You want to be able to grab your mat easily when it's time for yoga, so keep it in your gym or **EXERCISE ROOM** if you have one. Otherwise, find a place in your coat **CLOSET**, **UTILITY CLOSET**, or guest room closet to keep your equipment. If you lack room in any of these places, keep it under your bed. If you do your yoga at a studio, get a yoga bag to transport your mat so it doesn't gather dirt and germs along the way. Your **TRUNK** isn't the cleanest place, so don't keep your yoga equipment in your car. Yoga equipment collects sweat and gets dirty; keeping it in your car will make your car or trunk smell as well. It will also make you forget to clean your equipment. Every month or so, you should clean your mat. Put it in your bathtub and rinse it down with water and a very small amount of gentle antibacterial soap. Make sure you rinse all of the soap off your mat or it might be slippery and you'll slide out of downward dog and kick your classmate in the head. After rinsing, let your mat air dry before its next use. Namaste.

O.C.D. EXTREME

It goes without saying that I never use "public" yoga mats. If I don't see how it gets cleaned, I don't trust it! I have my own mat and I rinse it after every use. I also put a clean towel on top of it. We often lie facedown on our yoga mats, and anywhere my face goes I want as clean as possible! I also keep an additional yoga mat solely for outdoor use.

Z

ZIPLOCK BAGS come in a lot of sizes, but you don't need every option. Amazingly, snacks can fit in the same size bag as a sandwich. Just have a box of small, freezer-safe bags for snacks and sandwiches and a box of large freezer-safe bags for leftovers and marinating. These two sizes will cover all of your bases. If you need another size in your life for a specific reason, buy it, but the average household can get by with these two sizes. Designate a **DRAWER** in your **KITCHEN** to house them. It can be the same drawer you keep your tinfoil and plastic wrap. If you buy ziplock bags in bulk, you can store them in a supply closet, in your **FOOD PANTRY**, or in your **LINEN CLOSET** if your linen closet is large enough. Again, the rule for buying in bulk is to buy only what you have room for. Don't try to reuse your ziplock bags. They should be disposed of in your **RECYCLING** bin. The seams will wear down in the washing and drying process and compromise the integrity of the bag, putting you at risk of a spill they said could only happen if you used the "other leading brand."

ACKNOWLEDGMENTS

Without these people this book never would have made it this far.

Alex Lorenz

Arthur Gradstein

Artist & Brand

BD Wong

Brooke Langton

Bryce Dallas Howard

Chad Fabrikant

Dan Roof

Donna Luskin (T)

Evan Lederman

Iris & Michael Smith

Jack Osbourne

Jason Low

Jean Kwolek

Joan Rosenberg

Joanna D'Elia

John Redmann

Jordan Roth

Julie Chen

Kaily Smith

Katherine Latshaw

Kristen Horn

Marc Anthony Nicholas

Meredith Wechter

Michael Lane

Phil Berman (PK)

Randy Zisk

Richie Jackson

Ross Barna

Ross Kohn

Seth Gabel

Sharon Osbourne

Shauna Bass

Suzanne Johnson

Tamara Rosario

Tara Smith

Thanh Tran

Tim Palazzola

And of course my family:

Abbie Klosky

Adam Saper

Alison Darling

Andrea Saper

Chad Klosky

Larry Klosky

Steven Darling

And my loving Misha, Fifi, Booty Bottom, Schmeather-Heather

In loving memory of Henry & Millie Rothstein